Bourdieu and Culture

BOURDIEU AND CULTURE

Derek Robbins

SAGE Publications

London · Thousand Oaks · New Delhi

SAGE Publications Ltd
6 Bonhill Street
London EC2A 4PU

SAGE Publications Inc
2455 Teller Road
Thousands Oaks, California 91320

SAGE Publications India Pvt Ltd
32, M-Block Market
Greater Kailash - I
New Delhi 110 048

British Library Cataloguing in Publication data

A catalogue record for this book is
available from the British Library

ISBN 0 7619 6043 0
ISBN 0 7619 6044 9 (pbk)

Library of Congress catalog card number available

Typeset by Dorwyn Ltd, Rowlands Castle, Hampshire
Printed in Great Britain by Athenaeum Press, Gateshead

For my wife, Diana,
and our sons, Oliver and Felix.

Contents

Acknowledgements

This book has been long delayed. This is not the place to describe the problems which arose with another publisher, but I am all the more grateful to Sage for moving so quickly to offer a contract for producing a revised text. In particular, I should like to thank Chris Rojek for his encouragement and support and I hope this publication will add to the reputation of Sage's list in relation to theory, culture and society in general and to its honourable record in advancing discussion of the work of Bourdieu by the publication of his texts and of constructive critical analysis such as that offered by Bridget Fowler in *Pierre Bourdieu and Cultural Theory. Critical Investigations* (1997).

Much of the research for this book has been undertaken 'on the ground' in Paris, but, in London, I am indebted to the librarians of the University of East London for their diligent pursuit of my inter-library loan requests. The services of the British Library have, as always, been essential. Occasional visits to Paris have been funded from the allocation to UEL's Sociology unit of assessment following the 1996 Research Assessment Exercise. In Paris, I am grateful to the librarians in the Sorbonne and the Maison des Sciences de l'Homme, and, in relation to my chapter on Manet, I benefited particularly from the help of Jacques Thuillier of the Collège de France and of the administration of the Musée d'Orsay. I have valued the intellectual support which has been provided by the team of researchers in the Centre de Sociologie de l'Education et de la Culture in the Maison des Sciences de l'Homme, now under the direction of Rémi Lenoir, and I have also appreciated the accommodation facilities which have been available through the good offices of Jean-Michel Ageron of the Paris American Academy.

Many of the thoughts in this book were tentatively articulated in sessions with students at UEL and I acknowledge the influence of discussions with students who have followed the third year Anthropology unit on Bourdieu that I have taught since 1995. Paramount, of course, is my indebtedness to Pierre Bourdieu himself and to staff associated with his work at the Collège de France – notably Marie-Christine Rivière, Rosine Christin and Gabrielle Balazs. As a team, they have been unreservedly open in their willingness to produce documents, papers, references or contacts in spite of the awesome workload that falls to a small workforce.

As for Pierre Bourdieu himself, I can only say that this work is offered with respect and deference. I have had the good fortune in my career to have had contact with three intellectuals who could be said to be 'charismatic' – Leavis, Williams and Bourdieu. Encounters with the first two were disappointing in that, in different ways, their 'charisma' had become routinised. Somewhat surprisingly, however, the words which Williams found, in an obituary of 1978, to commemorate the achievement of Leavis, succeed in expressing what all three have in common and what, for me, Bourdieu still represents. Wiliams blamed the academy for making something merely academic of Leavis's life work, and he continued:

> What this excludes and is meant to exclude, is what must, in Leavis's whole work, be seen as central: not a profession but a vocation; an overwhelming, often overwhelmed response to a sense of a major cultural crisis . . . But I could never forget, and do not now forget, the intransigence, the integrity, the fierce courage of the man.

Bourdieu rejects the notion of 'charisma', but his intellectual influence has been inspirational. He has not seen any part of this book in draft. In spite of his generalised encouragement and willingness to find time to meet with me at regular intervals, this book gives a wholly independent interpretation of his work. I believe that my attempt to treat Bourdieu's work with intellectual integrity cannot fail to do justice to the integrity of his endeavours.

Lewisham
November 1998

Journal of
Classical Sociology

ISSN 1468–795X

SAGE Publications

Journal of Classical Sociology

Edited by **Bryan S Turner** and **John O'Neill**

An Outstanding International Journal

There has been no dedicated journal that concentrates on the classical tradition, until now. Yet this tradition continues to be a vital, living resource in sociological debate and research.

The **Journal of Classical Sociology** is an essential new resource that focuses on international contributions to the classical tradition. The journal elucidates the origins of sociology and also demonstrates how the classical tradition renews the sociological imagination in the present day. The journal is a critical but constructive reflection on the roots and formation of sociology from the Enlightenment to the twenty first century. The **Journal of Classical Sociology** promotes discussions of early social theory, such as Hobbesian contract theory, through the 19th and early 20th century classics associated with the thought of Comte, Marx, Durkheim, Weber, Simmel, Veblen, Pareto and Mosca, through to contemporary work, such as network theory and transformations in social systems theory.

The **Journal of Classical Sociology** publishes papers that explore the intellectually contested nature of social theory. Although sociology is the primary focus of the journal, inter-disciplinary contributions from psychoanalysis, economics, political theory, anthropology and cultural studies are welcome. The **Journal of Classical Sociology** features special review articles on key thinkers and debates. In addition there are extended review articles to encourage critical discussion of newly published work.

Journal of Classical Sociology features articles on:

- concepts • theory • institutions • ideologies
- traditions • methods • values

Instructions for Authors

Journal of Classical Sociology encourages submission of papers from all and any of the relevant social and cultural disciplines, all papers should however, have a methodological focus, with reference to empirical research. Four copies of the manuscript should be submitted, typed in double-spacing on one side of A4 paper only. Authors will be asked to provide a diskette of the final version. Manuscript submissions address:

Jack M Barbalet, Professor and Head, Department of Sociology, University of Leicester, Leicester LE1 7RH, England, UK

Phone
+44 (0)116 252 5359 (Direct)
+44 (0)116 252 2738 (Secretary)

Email jmb34@le.ac.uk

Three Times a Year
March, July, November

ISSN 1468-795X

Volume 1, 2001 Contents Include:

Journal of
Classical Sociology

ISSN 1468-795X
SAGE Publications

Forthcoming 2002 Contents Include:

Subscription Order Form

 SAGE Publications,
6 Bonhill Street, London, EC2A 4PU, UK

Tel: +44 (0)20 7374 0645 • **Fax**: +44 (0)20 7330 1200
Email: subscription@sagepub.co.uk • **Website**: www.sagepub.co.uk

For credit card orders call our Subscription Hotline on
+44 (0)20 7330 1266 *and quote reference* 2073ABCDEFG

YES, I would like to subscribe to the Journal of Classical Sociology starting with Volume 2 (2002)

INTRODUCTORY INDIVIDUAL RATES*
☐ **1 Year** £28/US$44 (usually £35/US$55)
☐ **2 Years** £116/US$168 (usually £70/US$110)

INSTITUTIONAL RATE
☐ **1 Year** £170/US$267 ☐ **2 Years** £340/US$534

*Orders placed at the individual rate are intended for the personal use of the subscriber only and must be paid by personal cheque, personal giro or personal credit/debit card. All orders must be prepaid to the publisher. Orders from customers in UK, Europe, Middle-East and Africa should be in pounds sterling. Orders from all other customers should be in US dollars. Subscription prices include despatch by air-speeded delivery.

Name _____

Address _____

_____

Email: _____

Methods of Payment

☐ I enclose a cheque *(payable to*
   SAGE Publications) for _____ [ ]

☐ I have today paid by International Giro
   (to Giro A/c No. 548 0353) _____ [ ]

☐ Please charge to my credit/debit card:

☐ MasterCard ☐ VISA ☐ AMERICAN EXPRESS

☐ DELTA ☐ SWITCH * _____ [ ]

Card: [ ][ ][ ][ ][ ][ ][ ][ ][ ][ ][ ][ ][ ][ ][ ][ ][ ][ ]

Expiry Date: /   .   Issue number: /   .
                         *(*only applies if paying by Switch)*

Signature: _____ Date: /   /   .

Data Protection: your details will be added to or updated on the SAGE Publications Ltd mailing list for information about other products and services provided by the Sage Publications group of companies. Please tick here if you do not wish to receive such mailings: ☐ We do not rent or sell our mailing list to other companies. SAGE Publications Ltd, Registered in England No. 1017514

Introduction

Faust. And what are you that live with Lucifer?
Meph. Unhappy spirits that fell with Lucifer,
Conspir'd against our God with Lucifer,
And are for ever damn'd with Lucifer.
Faust. Where are you damn'd?
Meph. In hell.
Faust. How comes it, then, that thou art out of hell?
Meph. Why, this is hell, nor am I out of it.

(Christopher Marlowe: *The Tragical History of Doctor Faustus*, 1604)

Garcin: Estelle, we shall get out of hell
Garcin (to the two women): You disgust me, both of you. (*He goes towards the door.*)
Estelle: What are you up to?
Garcin: I'm going.
Inez (quickly): You won't get far. The door is locked.
Garcin: I'll *make* them open it. (*He presses the bell-push. The bell does not ring.*)
Estelle: Please! Please!
Inez (to Estelle): Don't worry; the bell doesn't work.

(J.-P. Sartre: *Huis Clos*, first performed 1944)

In the first chapter of *La Distinction*,[1] Bourdieu wrote: 'There is no way out of the game of culture . . .'[2] Just as Marlowe presents his Faustus as being mistaken in supposing that hell might be a place that could be objectively observed, so Bourdieu is arguing – without infernal associations – that it is one of the defining characteristics of the human condition for people to be situated within culture. Culture is enacted by everyone. It is a game in which there are no non-participating spectators. It is a *huis clos* from which no one is excluded and from which there is no escape. It is a self-contained phenomenological enclosure which has no point of reference beyond or outside itself.

Disconnecting Education and Culture

Why does Bourdieu make this point on the second page of his text? The book is a sociological analysis of 'taste'. In order to maintain the position of social dominance associated with the possession of 'superior' taste, those who possess such 'taste', Bourdieu argues at the outset, need to sustain a myth about their innate aesthetic sensitivies or gifts and to deny resolutely that these attributes can be learned. The objects of his sociological analysis, in other words, need to deny or negate its intentions. To counteract the self-sustaining, aestheticist ideology of the dominant classes, Bourdieu contends, however, that the sociologist has to do much more than demonstrate simply that 'taste' can be gained through education. Bourdieu implies that this is barely worth establishing precisely because the educational system itself is involved in endorsing pre-existent distinctions and in legitimating the notion that differences are the consequences of differing innate abilities rather than of differing social backgrounds. The sociologist may appear to have demonstrated that 'taste' is related to education but, for the dominant classes, this link already seemed self-evident precisely because education was not itself culturally neutral. Indeed, the degree of perceived self-evidence in the correlation between education and taste could be taken to be an indicator of the cultural partisanship of the educational experience. The research of the sociologist could be made to appear to state the obvious for as long as the sociologist failed to problematise the cultural function of schooling. Bourdieu proceeded to argue, therefore, that the sociologist must ' . . . unravel the paradox whereby the relationship with educational capital is just as strong in areas which the educational system does not teach'[3] – or, in other words, that the sociologist needs to recognise that schools as institutions function in maintaining class distinctions without reference to the cultural contents which they transmit. The collection of statistical data has traditionally sought to clarify the relationship between educational achievement and social origins, but, for Bourdieu, this very analytical process presupposes and imposes the notion of the cultural neutrality of the institutional means by which achievement is educationally secured. Unless this notion is challenged, unless we question the relation of education to culture which educational research 'tacitly privileges', we have no hope of puncturing the self-fulfilling complacency of the status quo. The questions which we unthinkingly pose have to be questioned, for, as Bourdieu continues in the following sentence: 'There is no way out of the game of culture; and one's only chance of objectifying the true nature of the game is to objectify as fully as possible the very operations which one is obliged to use in order to achieve that objectification.'[4]

Indirectly and abstractly, Bourdieu was moving towards an explanation of the purpose of *La Distinction* in relation to his previous work. In North Africa in the late 1950s, he had observed the cultures of Algerian tribes and had observed the processes of cultural adaptation amongst those tribespeople who were forced to leave the countryside to settle in Algiers. He had written a 'sociology' of Algeria and produced two other books analysing processes of acculturation in Algeria. In one of these – *Travail et travailleurs en Algérie* – he wrote a short section in which he articulated his disquiet about the role of the colonial anthropologist,[5] but his work was what he was later to call 'objectivist' on two counts. First of all, he was unalterably an outsider by virtue of his French nationality, but, secondly, he constructed detachment by writing up some of his research findings in ways which deliberately situated them within the constructed discourse of anthropology by addressing issues, such as that of 'honour', which were of theoretical relevance to that discipline.

Bourdieu's return to France at the beginning of the 1960s removed the first obstacle to 'insider' research and his 'Célibat et condition paysanne' (1962)[6] was a self-imposed methodological test in respect of insider/ outsider issues in that he sought to analyse aspects of the culture of the region in which he had been brought up. Coming to terms with the objectivism imposed by established academic disciplines was more difficult. Bourdieu carried out research on the cultural interests and competences of students. The book which was the outcome of this research – *Les Héritiers* (1964)[7] was subtitled: *les Étudiants et la culture*. In the terms discussed above, *Les Héritiers* privileged the relationship between education and culture, assuming that it was the function of the educational system to accommodate diverse regional and class cultures, without sufficiently asking whether educational institutions already embodied one particular, dominant class culture. Bourdieu analysed the cultures of students, but he did so in order to comment on the relationship between these cultures and those transmitted in educational institutions, to comment on the extent to which students who lacked the necessary 'cultural capital' were consigned to failure. Bourdieu's proposed solution – advocating 'rational pedagogy' whereby teachers would more efficiently transmit standardised course content by being trained to be sociologically sensitive to the cultural origins of their students – was one which continued to privilege an educational definition of culture within a social situation that was intrinsically multicultural.

The Development of an Autonomous Sociology of Culture

Bourdieu carried out two large research projects in the 1960s which could almost be said to be 'cultural studies' – one on museums and the other on photography – but his orientation was still dominantly educational, particularly in relation to museum attendance where the proposed solution to cultural exclusion was still that schools should perform the pedagogic function that would make museums more generally accessible. Bourdieu went some way to remedying the faults of *Les Héritiers* in *La Reproduction* (1970),[8] but the argument was made very abstractly. Society was seen as a series of 'arbitrary', that is to say, non-referential, socially constructed, or relative, cultures which were in competition with each other and in which dominance was secured, not as the result of any intrinsic merit or superiority, but only, *force majeure*, as a result of a power struggle between institutions possessing 'arbitrary', that is to say, non-intrinsic, socially endowed, authority. The curriculum taught in state-controlled schools was just one example of the imposition of arbitrary content by arbitrary authority. For the first time, Bourdieu was beginning to establish a theoretical basis for liberating the study of culture from its hitherto sub-servient function within the study of education. Whereas his studies of the cultural tastes of students had been subordinated to the consideration of the appropriate form of pedagogy to be adopted within the educational system, Bourdieu began, instead, to develop a conceptual framework for analysing sociologically the distribution of diverse cultural tastes for themselves. The conceptual work began with 'Champ intellectuel et pro-jet créateur' (1966)[9] which, significantly, was published in a number of *Les Temps modernes* devoted to the problems of structuralism. At the same time that Bourdieu was rejecting the notion that the educational system should actually be privileged in structuring or reproducing culture within society, he was also rejecting a methodology which supposed that a detached, structuralist analysis of societies and cultures could adequately explain them. In the early 1970s, Bourdieu refined his concept of 'field' in such a way as to go beyond structuralist explanation. Agents are involved in the construction of the 'fields' within which their actions have meaning and receive recognition. Historical sociology enables us to understand the 'genesis and structure' of competing cultural fields. The ways in which people adopt different tastes or cultural affiliations are not to be under-stood by generating a *post hoc* interpretative correlation between these tastes and social conditions. This was the attempt, rejected by Bourdieu, most exemplified in France in the 1960s in the work of Lucien Goldmann. Rather, they are to be understood, not as *reflections* of class positions but, instead, as evidence of social position-taking in action. Importantly, Bourdieu also argued that this position-taking occurs, as it were, at two levels. People secure recognition for themselves within the assumptions of one field, but they also 'trade' that recognition for recognition within a different field altogether. Position-taking occurs, in other words, both within and between fields and, in this second, meta-context, people deploy 'strategies of reconversion'.

The development of Bourdieu's theoretical framework is described in more detail in Chapters 2 and 3. The important point here is that in ex-tricating the analysis of culture from a pedagogical context, Bourdieu cer-tainly did not wish to relinquish a sociological perspective. In 1975, he launched his journal – *Actes de la recherche en sciences sociales*. The prefa-tory article in the first number – 'Méthode scientifique et hiérarchie sociale des objets'[10] – made it clear that the journal was to be innovative in being prepared to apply social scientific method comprehensively to all possible social and cultural phenomena. As partial exemplification of this commit-ment, Bourdieu's 'Anatomie du goût'[11] appeared the following year and the culmination of this strand of Bourdieu's work was the publication of *La Distinction*.

The Changing English Field of Reception – from 'Education' to 'Cultural Studies'

It is clear that Bourdieu's analyses of culture were produced as affirmations of the approach to social scientific research outlined in *Le Métier de sociologue* (1968).[12] Nevertheless, Bourdieu has played the 'game of culture' that he has observed. There is no more escape from that game for him than for anyone else. His productions have, therefore, been elements in his strategic position-taking – within and between fields. Like everyone else, he has been caught up in situations which have meant that his achievements have been the consequence both of his own structuring and of the structuring imposed upon them by various fields of reception or consumption. Whilst, in the 1970s, he was laying the foundations for establishing a sociology of culture that could be independent of the sociology of education, within the English and American fields of reception he acquired a reputation as a sociologist of education. In the UK, specifically, Bourdieu's name was linked with the 'new directions for the sociology of education' movement as a result of the publication of two of his articles in M.F.D. Young's *Knowledge and Control* (1971).[13] As a force for radical change, this movement was exhausted by the late 1970s. During that decade, interestingly, both the political Left and Right sought to over-privilege the role of educational change in securing social reform. The shift from Mrs Thatcher's endeavours as Minister of Education in the early 1970s – proposing curricular reforms in her White Paper, *A Framework for Expansion* (1972) – to her attempt to enforce economic sanctions over university affairs after her election as Prime Minister in 1979, parallels the waning of the influence of the 'new directions' movement. Throughout the 1970s, however, there was, in the UK, another context for Left-wing social and political criticism which apparently had little contact with the 'new directions' movement in education. The main leaders of the 'New Left' were primarily either historians or literary critics – Richard Hoggart, Raymond Williams, Stuart Hall, Eric Hobsbawm, E.P. Thompson and Francis Klingender. This is not the place to go into any detail about the work of this group and of those associated with them. I return to this 'field' – constructed through a network of social and intellectual contacts between the Centre for Contemporary Cultural Studies at Birmingham and the May Day Manifesto group that congregated around Williams in Cambridge and London – as a 'field of reception' for Bourdieu's work in Chapter 8. For the moment, my point is that, within the UK, a 'field' of Cultural Studies was established which derived its intellectual inspiration from the humanities rather than the social sciences.

Bourdieu had cited Williams' *Culture and Society* in 'Champ intellectuel et projet créateur' and he had also participated in J.-C. Passeron's production, in 1970, of a translation of Hoggart's *The Uses of Literacy*.[14] Passeron's prefatory 'presentation' of his translation sought to appropriate Hoggart as a proto-sociologist of culture even though Hoggart never had any sociological pretensions. In short, the affinity between the two types of cultural analysis was strained. Indeed, in 1971 Williams wrote an obituary of Lucien Goldmann[15] in which he regretted that his premature death had prevented the development of sympathetic intellectual exchanges. Williams sought to introduce to English literary criticism the kind of Marxist structuralist method practised by Goldmann which Bourdieu had already rejected. Later in the decade, Williams was to produce his own critical evaluation of Marxist analyses of literature. In the Introduction to his *Marxism and Literature* (1977) Williams describes how he had first encountered Marxist literary argument when he came to Cambridge in 1939 to study English literature. He recalls how his 'experience of growing up in a working-class family' had led him 'to accept the basic political position' which Marxist analysis 'supported and clarified'.[16] Williams goes on, however, to show how the practice of Marxist cultural criticism had failed to do justice to his experience of culture. He writes:

> Instead of making cultural history material, . . . it was made dependent, secondary, 'superstructural': a realm of 'mere' ideas, beliefs, arts, customs, determined by the basic material history. What matters here is not only the element of reduction; it is the reproduction, in an altered form, of the separation of 'culture' from material social life, which had been the dominant tendency in idealist cultural thought.[17]

Williams saw the need for a cultural materialism which would discard the remnants of idealist *Kulturgeschichte*. Marxist materialism had not been materialist enough in respect of culture. Marxist thought, if not the thought of Marx, had been too mechanical and had not recognised that cultural products are expressive of whole ways of life. In developing the notion of a 'structure of feeling' as a way of describing this organic integration of previously separated base and superstructure components, Williams sought to make all culture conform to his primary experience of working-class culture. What Terry Eagleton had already argued in respect of Williams' *Culture and Society* – that it was 'in reality an idealist and academicist project'[18] – was also true of the transformed Marxism of Williams' *Marxism and Literature*. Williams safeguarded the idealist cultural values he had espoused as a result of working as a cultural critic simply by calling them material and by claiming that the forms of high culture were constituted as holistically as those of an idealised working-class culture. In trying to totalise working-class culture, Williams surrendered the possibility of understanding competing cultures. Williams' cultural materialism was a sophisticated amalgamation of materialist and organicist elements of nineteenth-century cultural thought but, as such, it failed to think outside the tradition which had generated it. It failed to open up the possibility of a scientific analysis of material culture.

Williams was well aware of the competing senses in which the word culture has been used. In 1976, he published his *Keywords: A Vocabulary of Culture and Society*.[19] In the entry on 'culture', Williams argued that '. . . *culture* was developing in English towards some of its modern senses before the decisive effects of a new social and intellectual movement'.[20] The change in meaning, in other words, is tacitly explained causally by a new social and intellectual movement which, Williams continues, occurred mainly in Germany. It was Herder, Williams argues, who, in his *Ideas on the Philosophy of the History of Mankind* (1784–91), attacked the notion that 'civilisation' or 'culture' '. . . was what we would now call a unilinear process, leading to the high and dominant point of C18 European culture'[21] with the result that, in what Williams calls 'a decisive innovation', he argued that it was necessary '. . . to speak of "cultures" in the plural: the specific and variable cultures of different nations and periods, but also the specific and variable cultures of social and economic groups within a nation'.[22]

Williams convincingly suggested that it was at the end of the eighteenth century that the word 'culture' accommodated a social anthropological interest in 'cultures' as well as an earlier meaning dominantly associated with the idea of 'civilisation'. He also recognises a third usage which is 'in fact relatively late'. This is: '. . . the independent and abstract noun which describes the works and practices of intellectual and especially artistic activity. This seems often now the most widespread use: *culture* is music, literature, painting and sculpture, theatre and film.'[23]

Williams' attempted social history of semantic change successfully identified the moment in which emerged an interest in 'folk culture' and in the social anthropological analysis of cultural practices and, equally, the moment in which certain cultural forms assumed a sense of superiority as 'culture' over 'cultures', but he wrote about these changes from within the discourse of 'culture'. He could talk about the emergence of different meanings but only from within a conceptual framework concerning 'culture' that the approach attributed to Herder would seek to place relativistically as simply one framework amongst many.

Producing a Scientific Sociology of Culture

There was no way out of the game of culture for Williams but, in Bourdieu's terms, he did not acknowledge reflexively the extent to which he had been initiated intellectually into a partisan position within the game. By contrast, Bourdieu tried to play the game of culture by analysing cultures – including 'culture' or 'high culture' from outside the 'culture' tradition and, instead, from within a scientific tradition.[24] He sought to deploy the credentials he had already acquired in sociological research in the field of cultural analysis. As a producer of cultural researches, Bourdieu placed himself outside the tradition of cultural analysis which confirms itself by never questioning its own value – by deliberately presenting himself as a scientist. Rejecting – or, rather, recognising the historical reasons for – the comfortable demarcation between *Kulturwissenschaft* and *Naturwissenschaft*, Bourdieu undertakes a scientific analysis of cultural forms and of the internal critical practices by which they are sustained. He has described himself as being in the epistemological tradition established by Claude Bernard in French life sciences towards the end of the nineteenth century. This tradition sees itself as being both anti-positivist and anti-metaphysical. It emphasises the continuous application of method more than the formulation of laws. It emphasises experimental testing more than empirical observation. It is neither materialist nor idealist, but presents itself as 'naturalist'. In practice, this means that all thought in terms of the mind/body dualism has to be discarded in natural science as being an antiquated hangover of the concepts developed in medieval scholasticism. 'Natural' phenomena have to be confronted without these kinds of anachronistically philosophical preconceptions and they have to be confronted as they are by constructing analytical concepts which seem intrinsically appropriate and can be tested and refined. Naturalist scientists are naturally present with the natural phenomena on which they conduct experiments. Working hypotheses are artificial devices for generating testable findings. 'Science' is not static, or final, or absolute. Hypotheses are the products of historical, cultural conditions and they generate findings which culturally affect the production of subsequent hypotheses. The field of 'science' is one of the plurality of competing 'cultures' within society but, within the game of culture from which there is no escape, it provides a vantage point from which the assumptions of 'culture' can be analysed.

Mobilising 'Cultural Studies' Strategically

The point of the scientific intervention, for Bourdieu, is to show the ways in which cultural value judgements are deployed spuriously to legitimise social distinctions. This demonstration can only be achieved by conducting sociological analysis subversively but, equally importantly, the subversive critique of 'culture' can only be effective if, like a Trojan horse, it gains currency within the field which it criticises. It is significant, therefore, that there was an apparent *approchement* between Bourdieu and his associates and the writers of the English New Left who were in the process of establishing the new field of Cultural Studies. Translations of the work of Thompson, Williams, Hobsbawm and Klingender appeared in the *Actes de la recherche en sciences sociales* between 1976 and 1978.[25] This accommodation by Bourdieu of elements of English 'New Left' 'cultural studies' was matched by an English response. Referring specifically to Bourdieu's 'Sur le pouvoir symbolique' (1977)[26] which, as yet, was only available in English translation as a stencilled, internal paper of the Centre for Contemporary Cultural Studies,[27] Stuart Hall, at the end of his 'The hinterland of science: ideology and the "Sociology of knowledge"' (1978),[28] implied that Bourdieu's work potentially offered a way forward for cultural theory beyond the conflicting legacies of wholly internal or wholly external analyses of symbolic systems.

Importantly, the following year (1980), the journal *Media, Culture and Society* devoted a number to the work of Bourdieu in which were published some prepublication selections from the translation of *La Distinction*[29]; a translation of 'La production de la croyance: contribution à une économie des biens symboliques' (1977)[30]; as well as a short bibliography of Bourdieu's work and an article by Nicholas Garnham and Raymond Williams.[31] Entitled 'Pierre Bourdieu and the sociology of culture', this article was the most significant indication that the appropriation of Bourdieu's work in England had shifted from the field of educational analysis to the field of cultural studies.

The translation of the full text of *La Distinction* was published in 1984. By this time, 'Cultural Studies' was beginning to establish itself as an academic field within British universities. As it became an increasingly popular 'subject' – generating an autonomous discourse and a discrete field of criticism and inquiry – the conjunction of the 1960s and 1970s between Left-wing politics and cultural study began to wane. Significantly, Stuart Hall moved from Birmingham in 1979 to become Professor of Sociology at the Open University, whilst, in 1983, Raymond Williams retired from his post at Cambridge after the publication of *Towards 2000* and, for the rest of his life until his death in 1988, was to turn dominantly to the writing of novels.[32] Bourdieu's work was to become assimilated within an intellectual field that was becoming pathologically depoliticised. In the same period, Bourdieu's own situation had changed. After his appointment to the Chair of Sociology at the Collège de France, Paris in 1981–82, he became increasingly interested in the relationship between the cultural capital that he had acquired personally and the institutionalised capital embodied in the institution which employed him. His new position enabled him to reflect upon – and apply to himself – those issues that he had discussed in the section of *La Distinction* entitled 'Culture and politics'. Whereas, in the 1960s, Bourdieu had argued that the state-controlled education system was an instrument for imposing a dominant culture and of excluding the many functionally satisfactory, but dominated, cultures existing within society, by the 1980s he was more inclined to regard the political system and its associated political discourse as more powerful instruments of domination. He had shifted from the analysis of cultures within an educational frame of reference to the analysis of cultural diversity in relation to political participation. The 'autonomisation' of Cultural Studies is a political phenomenon which, in Bourdieu's view, has to be analysed as such sociologically.

Whilst Bourdieu was assembling the findings of some of his earlier research to expose, in *La Noblesse d'état* (1989),[33] the mechanisms by which dominant educational capital converted into dominant political power within the specific French social system, Polity Press began the process which would 'market' Bourdieu as a social theorist of global significance. Bourdieu's *Homo Academicus* (1984)[34] was translated into English in 1988, and the translation was offered with a 'Preface to the English edition'[35] in which Bourdieu somewhat nervously sought to guard against the possibility that his works would become socially decontexted intellectual commodities. The

increasingly widespread international translation of his work forced Bourdieu to reflect systematically in respect of his own cultural production – in
precisely the terms that he had outlined objectively as early as 1966 in
'Intellectual Field and Creative Project' – on the relationship between the
meanings of texts as products of the trajectories of authors and their meanings as free-standing items within a field of reception.

The game of culture that Bourdieu, in part, plays and which, in part,
plays him, has become increasingly complex. As someone who was insis-
tent that he was intent on producing sociological analyses of culture, he
nevertheless colluded in, or acquiesced in, a process which inserted his
texts within the field of cultural study. The shift in his attitude towards
Flaubert, discussed in Chapter 4, is indicative of his own changing intellectual strategy. At first, Flaubert was found guilty of distorting his social
perceptions by inserting them, as fictions, within a literary cultural field.
Bourdieu came to acknowledge, however, that interventions made within
cultural fields – including the novels of Flaubert – might possess greater
potential for effecting social and political change than supposedly 'scientific' interventions made within a field of social science which is increasingly
subjected to state apparatuses or system worlds which sponsor it finan-
cially. Bourdieu moved away from the view that insertion within an autonomous cultural field implied an aesthetic escape from social engagement
towards the view that the constructed autonomy of the cultural field could
be deployed more effectively for political purposes than could a social
science field whose autonomy had become dangerously weak. The key was
to ensure that the autonomy of the cultural field should be a functional
autonomy and should not become self-indulgently detached from politics.

This tension explains the way in which Bourdieu has tried to play the
game of the autonomous field of reception offered to him by Cultural
Studies whilst at the same time asserting his dominantly social and political
commitments. Within the market of Bourdieu's symbolic goods, the situation is confused by the detemporalising effect of the production of translations of some of his texts: the translation of *La Noblesse d'état* (1989) did
not appear until after Polity had published English versions of the two texts
of the 1960s (*L'Amour de l'art* (1966)[36] and *Un art moyen* (1965[37])) which
can be characterised as 'precultural study' studies of culture – *The Love of
Art* (1990)[38] and *Photography* (1990).[39] The political control exercised over
cultural study within Bourdieu's field of production was, therefore, missed
initially as the chronologically indifferent republications of *The Love of Art*
and *Photography* seemed to confirm that Bourdieu was now a contributor
within the field of Cultural Studies. Presumably, Bourdieu himself colluded
in the timing of the publication, by Polity Press, of a collection of his essays
under the title of *The Field of Cultural Production* (1993).[40] It was only as a
result of the publication of *Les Règles de l'art* (1992)[41] – translated in 1996
as *The Rules of Art*[42] – and of *Libre-Échange* (1994)[43] – translated in 1995
as *Free Exchange*[44] – that it became clear that, like Zola, Bourdieu was
seeking to deploy strategically in the political sphere the capital that he had

accumulated through his cultural studies and that, like Hans Haacke, he was interested in the capacity of art to instigate subversive social criticism.

Explicating Bourdieu's Sociological Contribution to the Study of Cultures

The bulk of this book was written between 1994 and 1996. It was commissioned and commenced during the temporal hiatus generated by the cross-Channel and transatlantic translation of *Les Règles de l'art* and *Libre-Échange* described above. It was commissioned to be an assessment of Bourdieu's contribution to cultural analysis which would itself be located within the field of cultural criticism. In Bourdieu's own terms, therefore, it was due to be the kind of criticism from within a discourse which has the over-riding, but covert, purpose of sustaining the legitimacy of that discourse. To borrow the distinction made by Bourdieu in 'On symbolic power' that was favourably received by Stuart Hall, my commission was to analyse Bourdieu's work in terms of the 'internal relations' within the field of cultural study – to analyse his work as 'structured structure' – rather than to see it in its external context and understand it as a 'structuring structure'. The essence of the argument advanced by Bourdieu in 'On symbolic power' and, indeed, the essence of his poststructuralist analysis of culture in general, is that we must go beyond these alternative stances and should seek to establish a synthetic position which accepts that cultural forms are susceptible to analysis both as *forms* in themselves and as social *constructs*. As a consequence of my acceptance of Bourdieu's synthetic solution – one which places what formal criticism can say about cultural products in an analytic alliance with what socioeconomic history may say about the conditions of that production without subscribing to materialist determinism – it became necessary myself to adopt a double stance. In taking three distinct areas of Bourdieu's cultural analysis – his discussions of Flaubert, fashion and Manet – I have tried to consider Bourdieu's work in relation to the work of other contributors to the cultural subfields of literature, fashion and art. These analyses that are internal to the subfields are, however, presented in such a way as to show that this conceptual framework belongs to our field of reception whilst, for Bourdieu, the production of his analyses was consistent with a wholly different agenda. The book offers an introductory account of Bourdieu's career and also an exegesis of his main concepts, but the intention is that these sections should provide sufficient detail to indicate that Bourdieu's career trajectory and his conceptual development interact and mutually constitute each other. The intention is that, jointly, these sections should show that Bourdieu's specific cultural analyses are the means by which he transforms his personal cultural position. The book is organised in such a way, in other words, to allow the reader to appreciate Bourdieu's cultural analyses both as 'structures' and as elements in his own 'structuring' or position-taking activity.

Bourdieu's discussions of Flaubert, Courrèges and Manet – considered in Chapters 4, 5 and 6 – are objective but they are also crucially self-regarding. Not only is the content of the analyses self-regarding but, for Bourdieu, the form of the analytical activity is also performative. He considers the consequences of Flaubert's transformation of social observation into cultural form, but, at the different moments at which Bourdieu was making an objective analysis of the relative merits, in the case of Flaubert, of social scientific or creative representations, Bourdieu was making a contextually contingent assessment of these same relative merits in his own case and, additionally, allowing the submission of his analyses to differing fields of reception to be an enactment in practice of the conclusions reached theoretically and vicariously within the texts. Just as Bourdieu argues, against Sartre, that Flaubert's Frédéric in *L'Éducation sentimentale* is not an autobiographical self-representation but, rather, a constructed persona through whom Flaubert explored experimentally, in fiction, a range of potential social trajectories that he might, in fact, adopt, so Bourdieu's analyses of Flaubert are similarly exploratory rather than representational.

In short, producing cultural analyses is one of the ways in which Bourdieu has played the game of culture. The analyses and the game-playing are reciprocally related and inseparable. In practical terms, my attempt to offer a synthetic account of Bourdieu's contribution to the analysis of culture has resulted in an organised argument which can be summarised briefly for the guidance of readers.

The Structure of this Book

Part I ('The career') contains one chapter which provides an outline of Bourdieu's career as, in his own terms, an intellectual 'trajectory' manifesting a series of strategic developments, sometimes 'planned' and sometimes 'random'.

The career is presented in three phases – the 'intellectual apprenticeship' from 1950 to about 1970; 'from *lector* to *auctor*' during the 1970s; and the 'politics of self-presentation' in the period since his appointment to the Chair of Sociology at the Collège de France in 1981–82. This account is not to be read as the biographical 'background' to his work. The purpose is not to present an objectified or fixed version of the relationship between Bourdieu's works and his career but, rather, to provide the basis for an understanding of the dynamic pragmatism underlying all the work of Bourdieu which is to be examined in the rest of the book. Subsequent chapters are to be read with reference to this introductory historical contextualisation.

Part II ('The concepts') contains two chapters which provide an account of the key concepts which Bourdieu has developed and which have shaped his empirical findings and the way in which he has conceptualised society. Bourdieu has insisted that these concepts are historically contingent and have been deployed strategically. These chapters seek to clarify the meanings of the concepts and to evaluate them whilst still accepting Bourdieu's view that, for him, they have always been tools of investigation and should only be used pragmatically by others in full knowledge of the complexity of conceptual transfer and not replicated routinely. This means that the pragmatism of their genesis as well as of their potential use has to be appreciated. The first chapter initially discusses what Bourdieu might mean by a 'concept' and then outlines the development of his use of, amongst others, 'habitus', 'field' and 'cultural capital'. These are certainly operational concepts that have performed slightly different functions for Bourdieu at different points in his career. The second chapter considers the development of Bourdieu's use of 'reproduction' in the context of the contemporary thinking about 'production' and 'consumption' or 'reception'. It asks whether, for Bourdieu, 'reproduction' is more than a conceptual tool for understanding social processes and is, instead, in spite of his disclaimers, more nearly an explanation of social reality.

If Part II isolates Bourdieu's conceptual activity, Part III ('The case studies'), consisting of three chapters, explores the ways in which the concepts have functioned in providing an approach to cultural forms. It is not possible, however, to maintain a clear distinction between concept and object. Bourdieu's concepts are not *applied* to self-existent facts because, for him, there is a constant reciprocity between observed phenomena and the language in which observation is expressed. Bourdieu's concepts develop, are refined, as they are used. Separate chapters isolate Bourdieu's work on Flaubert, fashion and Manet, partly to show his analysis in action and partly to extract from his multidisciplinary practice some contributions made by Bourdieu which can be compared with other contributions in the established fields of literary and art criticism. These are, therefore, artificially constructed case studies of Bourdieu's practice – partially circumscribed by discipline boundaries which he refuses to accept. At the same time, the chapters seek to do justice to this refusal. They suggest the ways in which these paradigmatic studies are most significant as evidence of an intellectual style which should be recognised as the true Bourdieu paradigm. They demonstrate that it should be clear from what Bourdieu says about Manet or Flaubert or Zola that he wants, like them, to sustain the affinities between cultural production and scientific naturalism, which means that Bourdieu wants to carry on producing objects and does not want to contribute to any 'definitive' objectification of those artists who are his models. Relating to the discussions in Part I and Part II, the chapters of Part III show the ways in which Bourdieu's thinking about individual artists has shifted both in relation to his developing career and in relation to his continuing refinement of his concepts.

The corollary of Bourdieu's view of the mutually reinforcing integrity of his career and his concepts is that he renders his work abstractly uncriticisable or, put another way, that he obliges all criticism of his work to be *ad hominem* criticism. Bourdieu seeks to elicit a response to the package of his life and work and to deny the possibility that the work can usefully be extracted and subjected to impersonal criticism. The two chapters in Part IV ('The criticisms') explore the criticisms of Bourdieu that have been made and examine the validity of his strategic evasion of criticism. The first chapter summarises the main lines of criticism that have been advanced in the secondary literature. The presentation is not comprehensive, but it takes a range of significant arguments, evaluates them and, in doing so, seeks to clarify Bourdieu's position. The second chapter considers the case Bourdieu has offered in self-defence against criticism and then seeks a way out of the apparent impasse whereby debate and disagreement about the value of Bourdieu's work seem logically interminable.

The last chapter attempts to summarise the development of the argument in the text and to reach a judgement of Bourdieu's work. If, as the book argues, Bourdieu's cultural analyses and findings were, and still are, integrally related to his social position-taking, but if it is also possible, as the book demonstrates, tactically to appreciate them both as functioning conceptual *objects* and as components of his subjective, socio-genetic trajectory, is it not, nevertheless, illegitimate or undesirable to propose a divided response to his life and work? Bourdieu has sought to live, or incorporate, his concepts, but is it open to us to take critical advantage of the disembodied concepts without reference to any ethical judgement of his career – or does this inclination to treat his concepts autonomously amount to a form of idealism and constitute, therefore, a complete rejection of his unified intellectual and existential project? Is it defensible to adopt the relativism of Bourdieu's cultural analysis whilst simultaneously 'bracketing' a relativist analysis of its cultural provenance? Pursuing these questions, the Conclusion argues that it is not possible to disintegrate Bourdieu's life and work. It argues for a pragmatic response – not to his disembodied concepts but to his paradigmatic life of creative conceptualisation.

Post-Script

The game of culture is not static. It is one which is inescapably changing, generating its own dynamism like an internal combustion engine. Having carried out his intellectual reconnaissance of the relations between culture and politics, and having increased his cultural capital as a result of his interventions in the field of Cultural Studies, Bourdieu has recently embarked on a process of reconversion, offering the authority that he has acquired intellectually in the political service of the socially, politically and culturally dominated members of society.

In an interview of October, 1992, about *Les Règles de l'art*, entitled 'Tout est social!',[45] Bourdieu argued that the research that he had directed leading to the publication of *La Misère du monde* (1993)[46] was not unconnected with the interests underlying *Les Règles de l'art*. He claimed that he was trying to use literary form to allow the dispossessed of French society to have a political voice. This marks a shift away from a concentration on the political potential of collective intellectuals towards an attempt to find grounds for collective action which unite intellectuals and non-intellectuals.

One of the bases for such collective action is the conviction that social solidarity between individuals in society has been undermined by the distorting affects of media coverage which, in turn, is a consequence of the effects of an unregulated market economy. Related is the view that neo-liberal politics are the consequence of the world dominance of Anglo-Saxon ideologies based on the elevation of individual freedom rather than collective welfare. The recent article (with Loïc Wacquant): 'Sur les ruses de la raison impérialiste'[47] is a diatribe against the way in which particular American ideologies masquerade as universal truths.

Since *La Misère du monde*, Bourdieu has sought to transpose what he called the 'social maieutics' of that text from the formal, written, sphere to the sphere of direct political action. After supporting the striking railway workers in December 1995, Bourdieu established a social movement entitled 'Raisons d'agir', backed by a publishing venture – Liber-Raisons d'agir. His first publication followed from the identification of the media as significant culprits in relation to our current social and political malaises. *Sur la télévision, suivi de l'emprise du journalisme* was published in December 1996.[48] Two other texts by associates followed in 1997: ARESER (Association for Reflection on Higher Education and Research): *Quelques diagnostics et remèdes urgents pour une université en péril*, and S. Halimi: *Les Nouveaux Chiens de garde*. In 1998, other associates have produced *Le 'Décembre' des intellectuels français* and Bourdieu has published a collection of his own speeches and interventions, assembled from the period between 1992 and 1998: *Contre-feux*.[49] Within this period, Bourdieu has also published *Méditations pascaliennes* (1997)[50] in which, amongst other things, he has presented himself as a reluctant intellectual and has tried to deconstruct the academic gaze in order to liberate the possibility of collective social action which is not contaminated by artificial academic and status distinctions.

Bourdieu has also recently published *La Domination masculine* (1998)[51] which has generated debate in Paris. Part of the same debate has also been the publication of a book which attempts to put the brake on Bourdieu's political influence. This is J. Verdès-Leroux: *Le Savant et la politique: essai sur le terrorisme sociologique de Pierre Bourdieu*.[52] Although this text offers analysis of Bourdieu's earlier work, it seems to be mainly motivated by the views, first, that Bourdieu is too influential, and, more significantly, that he has transgressed hallowed boundaries between the scientific and the political.

Bourdieu is currently deploying in the political field the cultural capital that he has acquired through his scientific research. In my view he is doing this legitimately precisely because his present actions follow logically from and seek to actualise the theory of practice which first brought him intellectual authority. There is no abuse of authority for its own sake but a coherent implementation of a life-long strategy. Writing in 'Sur les ruses de la raison impérialiste' (1998), Bourdieu (and Wacquant) now cite the spread of 'Cultural Studies' as one example of the general pathology whereby concepts and social movements acquire artificial status and currency in a field of international intellectual exchange that has become divorced from their particular conditions of production. Bourdieu and Wacquant argue:

> Thus it is that decisions of pure book marketing orient research and university teaching in the direction of homogenisation and of submission to fashions coming from America, when they do not fabricate wholesale 'disciplines' such as *Cultural Studies*, this mongrel domain born in England in the 70s, which owes its international dissemination (which is the whole of its existence) to a successful publishing policy.[53]

This attack on 'Cultural Studies' here has two elements. The authors complain that it is a commercial product and, separately, that it was, in origin, a mongrel construct. I have suggested in this Introduction that this second point does not represent a new position for Bourdieu. He has consistently seen himself as a sociologist of cultural phenomena and has, therefore, believed that the development of 'Cultural Studies' as a discipline has illustrated a methodological error in that it has allowed the object of inquiry to prescribe the framework within which it is conceived. I have also suggested, however, that Bourdieu has acquired cultural capital as a result of the insertion of his texts in the field of commercial exchange that he now disowns. What we see in 'Sur les ruses de la raison impérialiste', therefore, is Bourdieu seeking to regain control over his international *griffe* or brand-label (to use the terminology used by Bourdieu in relation to fashion – as discussed in Chapter 5), to reassert that cultural analyses are instruments of strategic action in particular situations and not repositories of universal explanation.

In the light of Bourdieu's new moves within the game of culture, this book offers the opportunity to observe the ways in which Bourdieu's cultural analyses were integral to a developing theoretical understanding of the relations between culture and politics – the publication and dissemination of which within the cultural field have provided him with the power to enact it through direct action in the political sphere.

Notes

1. P. Bourdieu (1979) *La Distinction. Critique sociale du jugement*, Paris, Éditions de Minuit.
2. P. Bourdieu (1984) *Distinction, A Social Critique of the Judgement of Taste*, London, Routledge & Kegan Paul, 12.
3. *Ibid.*, 11–12.
4. *Ibid.*, 12.
5. See the Foreword to the second part of P. Bourdieu *et al.* (1963) *Travail et travailleurs en Algérie*, Paris and The Hague, Mouton, 257–67.

6. P. Bourdieu (1962) 'Célibat et condition paysanne', *Études rurales*, 5–6, 32–136.
7. P. Bourdieu (with J.-C. Passeron) (1964) *Les Héritiers. Les Étudiants et la culture*, Paris, Éditions de Minuit.
8. P. Bourdieu (with J.-C. Passeron) (1970) *La Reproduction. Éléments pour une théorie du système d'enseignement*, Paris, Éditions de Minuit.
9. P. Bourdieu (1966) 'Champ intellectuel et projet créateur', *Les Temps modernes*, 246, 865–906.
10. P. Bourdieu (1975) 'Méthode scientifique et hiérarchie sociale des objets', *Actes de la recherche en sciences sociales*, 1, 4–6.
11. P. Bourdieu (with M. de Saint Martin) (1976) 'Anatomie du goût', *Actes de la recherche en sciences sociales*, 5, 2–112.
12. P. Bourdieu (with J.C. Chamboredon and J.-C. Passeron) (1968) *Le Métier de sociologue*, Paris, Mouton-Bordas, translated (1991) as *The Craft of Sociology*, Berlin and New York, de Gruyter.
13. P. Bourdieu (1971) 'Intellectual field and creative project' and 'Systems of education and systems of thought' in M.F.D. Young, ed. *Knowledge and Control. New Directions for the Sociology of Education*, London, Collier-Macmillan.
14. R. Hoggart (1970) *La Culture du pauvre* (présentation de J.-C. Passeron), Paris, Éditions de Minuit.
15. R. Williams (1971) 'Literature and sociology: in memory of Lucien Goldmann', *New Left Review*, 67, 3–18.
16. R. Williams (1977) *Marxism and Literature*, Oxford, Oxford University Press, 1.
17. *Ibid.*, 19.
18. T. Eagleton (1976) *Marxism and Literary Criticism*, London, Routledge, 25.
19. R. Williams (1976) *Keywords: A Vocabulary of Culture and Society* (Fontana Communications Series), London, Collins.
20. *Ibid.*, 88.
21. *Ibid.*, 89.
22. *Ibid.*
23. *Ibid.*, 90.
24. For a more detailed discussion of the differences between Williams and Bourdieu, see my (1997) 'Ways of knowing cultures: Williams and Bourdieu', in J. Wallace *et al.*, eds. *Raymond Williams Now. Knowledge, Limits and the Future*, London, Macmillan, 40–55.
25. E.P. Thompson (1976) 'Modes de domination et révolutions en Angleterre', *Actes de la recherche en sciences sociales*, 2–3, 133–51; R. Williams (1977) 'Plaisantes perspectives. Invention du paysage et abolition du paysan', *Actes de la recherche en sciences sociales*, 17–18, 29–36; E. Hobsbawm (1978) 'Sexe, symboles, vêtements et socialisme', *Actes de la recherche en sciences sociales*, 23, 2–18; F. Klingender (1978) 'Joseph Wright de Derby, peintre de la Révolution industrielle', *Actes de la recherche en sciences sociales*, 23, 23–36.
26. P. Bourdieu (1977) 'Sur le pouvoir symbolique', *Annales*, 3, 405–11.
27. Translated by Richard Nice (who was working at CCCS at that time) in *Two Bourdieu Texts*, CCCS stencilled Papers no. 46 (1977). This translation was subsequently published in *Critique of Anthropology*, (1979), 4, 77–85; whilst a different translation (by C. Wringe) was published in D. Gleeson, ed. (1977) *Identity and Structure: Issues in the Sociology of Education*, Driffield, Nafferton Books, 112–19.
28. S. Hall (1978) in S. Hall (1978) *On Ideology*, London, CCCS/Hutchinson.
29. 'The aristocracy of culture' – translation of *La Distinction*, 9–61 – in *Media, Culture and Society*, (1980), 2, 225–54; 'A diagram of social position and lifestyle' – translation of *La Distinction*, 139–44 – in *Media, Culture and Society*, (1980), 2, 255–9.
30. P. Bourdieu (1977) 'La production de la croyance: contribution à une économie des biens symboliques', *Actes de la recherche en sciences sociales*, 13,

3–43; translated by R. Nice as 'The production of belief: contribution to an economy of symbolic goods', *Media, Culture and Society*, (1980), 2, 261–93.

31. N. Garnham and R. Williams (1980) 'Pierre Bourdieu and the sociology of culture', *Media, Culture and Society*, 2, 209–223.
32. For detail and comment on this phase of Williams' life, see F. Inglis (1995) *Raymond Williams*, London, Routledge, Chap. 12, 266–96.
33. P. Bourdieu (1989) *La Noblesse d'état. Grandes Écoles et esprit de corps*, Paris, Éditions de Minuit.
34. P. Bourdieu (1984) *Homo Academicus*, Paris, Éditions de Minuit.
35. P. Bourdieu (1988) *Homo Academicus*, Oxford, Polity Press, xi–xxvi.
36. P. Bourdieu (with A. Darbel and D. Schnapper) (1966) *L'Amour de l'art. Les Musées d'art et leur public*, Paris, Éditions de Minuit.
37. P. Bourdieu (with L. Boltanski, R. Castel and J.C. Chamboredon) (1965) *Un art moyen. Essai sur les usages sociaux de la photographie*, Paris, Éditions de Minuit.
38. P. Bourdieu (with A. Darbel and D. Schnapper) (1990) *The Love of Art, European Art Museums and Their Public*, Oxford, Polity Press.
39. P. Bourdieu (with L. Boltanski, R. Castel and J.C. Chamboredon) (1990) *Photography, A Middle-Brow Art*, Oxford, Polity Press.
40. P. Bourdieu (ed. and int. by R. Johnson) (1993) *The Field of Cultural Production. Essays on Art and Literature*, Oxford, Polity Press.
41. P. Bourdieu (1992) *Les Règles de l'art. Genèse et structure du champ littéraire*, Paris, Éditions du Seuil.
42. P. Bourdieu (1996) *The Rules of Art. Genesis and Structure of the Literary Field*, Oxford, Polity Press.
43. P. Bourdieu and H. Haacke (1994) *Libre-Échange*, Paris, Éditions du Seuil.
44. P. Bourdieu and H. Haacke (1995) *Free Exchange*, Oxford, Polity Press.
45. P. Bourdieu (1992) 'Tout est social!', *Magazine littéraire*, 303, 104–11.
46. P. Bourdieu *et al.* (1993) *La Misère du monde*, Paris, Éditions du Seuil.
47. P. Bourdieu and L. Wacquant (1998) 'Sur les ruses de la raison impérialiste', *Actes de la recherche en sciences sociales*, 121–22, 109–18.
48. Translated as *On Television* (1998), Oxford, Polity Press.
49. Translated as *Acts of Resistance* (1998), Oxford, Polity Press.
50. P. Bourdieu (1997) *Méditations pascaliennes*, Paris, Éditions du Seuil.
51. P. Bourdieu (1998) *La Domination masculine*, Paris, Éditions du Seuil.
52. J. Verdès-Leroux (1998) *Le Savant et la politique. Essai sur le terrorisme sociologique de Pierre Bourdieu*, Paris, Grasset.
53. P. Bourdieu and L. Wacquant (1999) 'On the cunning of imperialist reason', *Theory, Culture and Society*, 16, 1, 47.

Part I

THE CAREER

---

1 An insider/outsider Frenchman

Bourdieu's career to date can usefully be divided into three phases, and these can be briefly stated before giving a detailed account.

There was, first of all, an introductory period between 1950 and 1970 in which he trained as a philosopher and gradually made his way intellectually towards sociological practice by way of ethnographic fieldwork. Although there was a philosophical origin for those things that he found empirically interesting or problematic, intellectual circumstances ensured they were formulated in the current anthropological frame of thinking. Bourdieu was interested in doing practical phenomenology, but his early work appeared to be influenced by what contemporary American anthropologists were calling 'acculturation' studies and to be relating itself uneasily to the prevalent French practice of Lévi-Strauss. In this period, therefore, Bourdieu established himself as a cultural anthropologist who was prepared to apply anthropological methodologies to the analysis of contemporary French culture.

Although there is no clear-cut rupture with this introductory period, it is possible, nevertheless, to suggest that it was from 1968 that Bourdieu developed an ideology of science and presented himself as a scientific practitioner. In this second period, through the 1970s, Bourdieu directed a research centre, established his own research journal and, through both, inspired the work of a team of colleagues and collaborators. It was in this period that he fully articulated an epistemological approach which sought to supersede structuralism without cancelling out its achievements, and constructed a conceptual apparatus to be deployed in a range of inquiries. These inquiries were not only social scientific ones. He had always been interested in art and literature or in conventional cultural history as well as in contemporary cultural practice. From the late 1960s, he led a research seminar which sought to analyse late nineteenth-century French cultural history with the same kind of scientific rigour and the same concepts as were being used in analysing, for instance, the contemporary attitudes and values of the patrons of large industrial and commercial firms.

The third period can be said to have begun with Bourdieu's appointment to the Chair of Sociology at the Collège de France, Paris, in 1981–82. His work has become less rooted in corporate research activity. He has, instead, become interested in the relationship between his personal status and power and those of the institution in which he is employed and which, in some sense, he represents. As his texts have been translated and become known internationally, he has become conscious of the disparity or tension between the universal meanings of those texts and their particular meanings as they have been associated with his personal trajectory. A reputation based on writing bestows power but there is the constant danger that misinterpretations of what is written may affect the way in which the acquired power can be exercised. Bourdieu now attempts to make his actions as an intellectual supersede his scientific practice in the same way as earlier his emphasis of reflexive practice had been designed to supersede, not negate, structuralism. He relates to contemporary culture as a person who now is the accumulated product of what he has been – both a cultural anthropologist and a social scientist. Bourdieu's observation of culture involves a rigorous analysis of the genesis of what is observed and an acceptance of the genesis of the position from which the observation is made. It is for this reason that the detailed account of Bourdieu's career which follows is to be seen as complementary to his current strategy. It is an essential element of his approach in this third phase of his career that his social and intellectual trajectories should be seen as equally constitutive of his present self and that one should not be thought to explain the other.

The Intellectual Apprenticeship

Bourdieu was born in 1930 in the Béarn in Gascony in southwest France near to the Pyrenees and the Spanish border, a region with a distinctive dialect and culture. He has argued that his capacity to be an alien observer of social relations within his home, familiar region helped him when he came to carry out ethnographic fieldwork in Algeria at the end of the 1950s.[1] Understanding the familiar culture of the Béarn posed for Bourdieu the extreme test of his capacity to construct the detachment which is the prerequisite for science.

Bourdieu has also offered an explanation of his detachment. When pressed by Wacquant in a workshop in Chicago in 1987 to overcome his reticence in giving information about his private life, Bourdieu made some revealing comments about his upbringing: 'I spent most of my youth in a tiny and remote village of Southwestern France, a very "backward" place as city people like to say. And I could meet the demands of schooling only by renouncing many of my primary experiences and acquisitions, and not only a certain accent . . . '[2] He went on to suggest that 'Anthropology and sociology have allowed me to reconcile myself with my primary experiences and to take them upon myself, to assume them without losing anything I subsequently acquired'.[3] Nevertheless, it was the particular form of schooling which, possibly, fostered Bourdieu's sociologically detached social involvement:

Reading Flaubert, I found out that I had also been profoundly marked by another social experience, that of life as a boarder in a public school [*internat*] . . . Sometimes I wonder where I acquired this ability to understand or even to anticipate the experience of situations that I have not known firsthand, . . . I believe that I have, in my youth and throughout my social trajectory . . . taken a whole series of mental photographs that my sociological work tries to process.'[4]

In these remarks of 1987, Bourdieu suggests that his schooling might explain the characteristic style of his sociological work – his practice of 'participant objectification', but, in the English Preface to *Homo Academicus* (1988), he hints at a more formal consequence. Placing the book in its pre-1968 context, Bourdieu describes how the previously dominant intellectual disciplines (including philosophy) were threatened by the 'new' disciplines ('even' sociology), and how the 'social foundations of their academic existence' were also 'under siege'. He comments:

This double criticism frequently awakens touching reactions of traditionalist conservatism in those professors who did not have the instinct and the boldness to recycle themselves in time, and in particular among those whom I call the 'oblates' and who, consigned from childhood to the school institution (they are often children of the lower or middle classes or sons of teachers), are totally dedicated to it.[5]

Although Bourdieu had the 'instinct and the boldness' to recycle himself, as someone who surely was tacitly presenting himself as an 'oblate' he did retain an engrained commitment to institutionalisation.

Like Durkheim, Lanson, Bergson, Sartre, Derrida, Foucault, Merleau-Ponty and Althusser, to name just a few 'big names', Bourdieu entered the École Normale Supérieure, Paris. Bourdieu was admitted in 1951. He was an angry young man, violently denouncing the *école* for forming the 'watch-dogs of the bourgeoisie'.[6] Dufay and Dufort quote a contemporary who recalls that Bourdieu was ' . . . animated by an extraordinary desire for revenge. He had a kind of mistrust of Parisians – which we were. Even by his thick-set physique, he seemed to proclaim his anti-Parisianism. I don't know whether he has ever overcome this resentment which inspired his fine book, *Les Héritiers* . . . '[7] Much of his anger was directed against the staff who were his teachers. The contempt which he felt is still apparent in the comments which he made in an interview in 1985: 'Philosophy as taught in the University was not very inspiring – even if there were some very competent people, like Henri Gouhier, . . . Gaston Bachelard and Georges Canguilhem'[8] and ' . . . our contempt for sociology was intensified by the fact that a sociologist could be president of the board of examiners of the competitive "agrégation" exam in philosophy and force us to attend his lectures – which we thought were lousy – on Plato or Rousseau'.[9]

Bourdieu's comments in the same interview do, however, give lots of positive indications of the way in which his thinking was developing in the 1950s. Asked what the intellectual situation was like when he was a student – 'Marxism, phenomenology and so on' – Bourdieu replied: 'When I was a student . . . phenomenology, in its existentialist variety, was at its peak, and I had read *Being and Nothingness* very early on, and then Merleau-Ponty and Husserl . . . '[10] In relation to Marxism, he commented: 'Marxism didn't really exist as an intellectual position, . . . However, I did read Marx at that time for academic reasons; I was especially interested in the young Marx, and I had been fascinated by the "Theses on Feuerbach".'[11]

Bourdieu implies that it was his reading of Sartre which pointed him towards Merleau-Ponty and Husserl, in search, in both cases, for ways out of existentialism. In the case of Husserl, he welcomed the attempt to make philosophical analysis rigorously scientific. For the same reason, he ' . . . studied mathematics and the history of the sciences'.[12] In the case of Merleau-Ponty, it was not his 'existentialism' that was the attraction: 'He was interested in the human sciences and in biology, and he gave you an idea of what thinking about immediate present-day concerns can be like when it doesn't fall into the sectarian over-simplifications of political discussion . . . '[13] It was out of a wish to avoid for himself such sectarian oversimplifications that Bourdieu avoided both the Communist Party cell run by Le Roy Ladurie in the *école* and Foucault's splinter group. His 'academic' reading of Marx was to furnish analytical detachment from everyday social issues rather than engagement with them.

In the same interview, Bourdieu both dissociates himself from the 'structuralist generation' and acknowledges that he did share with them a similar attitude towards existentialism:

> Many of the intellectual leanings that I share with the 'structuralist' generation (especially Althusser and Foucault) – which I do not consider myself to be part of, firstly because I am separated from them by an academic generation (I went to their lectures) and also because I rejected what seemed to me to be a fad – can be explained by the need to react against what existentialism had represented for them: the flabby 'humanism' that was in the air, the complacent appeal to 'lived experience' and that sort of political moralism that lives on today in *Esprit*.[14]

Bourdieu chose his words carefully when he went on to admit that he had found the work of Heidegger attractive and useful:

> I read Heidegger, I read him a lot and with a certain fascination, especially the analyses in *Sein und Zeit* of public time, history and so on, which, together with Husserl's analyses in *Ideen II*, helped me a great deal . . . in my efforts to analyse the ordinary experience of the social.[15]

Bourdieu is here suggesting that he was able to use the insights of transcendental phenomenology which had been designed to disclose the universal and the essential to offer, instead, a descriptive phenomenology of the plurality of social experiences.

Half way through his time at the *école*, in 1953, Bourdieu wrote a thesis, under the supervision of Gouhier, for a *diplôme d'études supérieures*. It was a translation of, and commentary on, Leibniz's *Animadversiones*. These, in turn, were Leibniz's critical comments on *Les Principes de la philosophie* of Descartes.[16] Alquié had published notes on the first part of this work of Descartes in 1933. It was a work in which Descartes attempted to summarise his philosophy in a series of short paragraphs so as to provide a counter-scholastic manual. Paragraphs 7 to 13 are devoted to 'The thinking self' and Alquié had noted: 'In taking as his point of departure no longer the object but the thinking subject, Descartes set philosophy on the path of idealism.'[17] It is significant that Bourdieu early in his career would have known well Leibniz's critique of this crucial Cartesian point of departure. Leibniz wrote:

> Descartes' thesis that the '*I think therefore I am*' is one of the primary truths is excellent. But it would have been only fair not to neglect other truths of the same kind . . . For I am conscious not only of my thinking self, but also of my thoughts, and it is no more true and certain that I think than that I think this or that.[18]

In these cryptic words, Leibniz opened up the possibility of a conception of history as the continuous generation of an infinity of thoughts by an infinity of thinkers rather than as the progressive refinement of an ideal Absolute.

After his *agrégation* in 1955, Bourdieu taught for a year in a provincial *lycée* in Moulins on the northern edge of the Auvergne. In 1956 he was conscripted and served for two years with the French Army in Algeria. It was in this period of national service that he wrote his *Sociologie de l'Algérie* which was published in Paris in 1958. In reading this text, it is immediately clear that Bourdieu was confronted by the problem articulated by Lévi-Strauss in 'History and anthropology': he wanted to undertake an ethnological analysis of the disappearing social organisations of Algerian tribesmen and also undertake an ethnographic study of the behaviour and attitudes of those tribesmen in their new urban situations. As ethnographer, Bourdieu's working assumption had to be that his ethnological analysis of the social historical backgrounds of his interviewees was a present, internalised force in influencing their modes of adaptation to changing conditions.

Sociologie de l'Algérie (1958), therefore, was based on secondary texts even though, undoubtedly, it was an account of people and regions with whom Bourdieu had become familiar. In relation, for instance, to the tribe to which, perhaps, Bourdieu was most 'attracted' – the Kabyles – he drew heavily on a three-volume account of the region and of the customs of its inhabitants which had been published in 1873.[19] Although all the theoretical texts referred to in the bibliography were, with the exception of Weber's *Gesammelte Aufsätze zur Religionssoziologie*, recent American publications concerned with culture and cultural change[20], the predominant impression given by the text is of an epistemological uncertainty in respect of what might be said to constitute a culture or the object of cultural study. The uncertainty is reflected in the shifts of title and chapter titles between the first edition of the text (1958), the second edition (1961) and the English translation of 1962. Lévi-Strauss had suggested that it was ethnography rather than ethnology that tended towards sociology. Bourdieu clearly wanted to produce an ethnographic study of contemporary Algerians. *Sociologie de l'Algérie* (1958), however, was an ethnological analysis of Algeria, not a sociology of the country. The chapters of the first edition are 'La culture Kabyle', 'La culture Chaouia' and so on, but, in the second edition, these have become 'Les Kabyles' and 'Les Chaouia', and the English translation consolidates this change of emphasis by adopting the title of *The Algerians*.

What was at issue here was, in part, the consequence of linguistic interference. The *Kultur* of German *Kulturgeschichte* implied the culture of a totality, of a civilisation, whereas *la culture* retained the sense of the personal culture of individuals. Bourdieu seems to have been unclear about his own emphasis. The first sentence of the 1958 text boldly states: 'It is obvious that Algeria, when considered in isolation from the rest of the Maghreb, does not constitute a true cultural unit.'[21] The Introduction proceeds to itemise many instances of cultural diversity within the geographical territory known as Algeria. Bourdieu does not define a 'true cultural unit' but, at the beginning, argues that the 'unity' of the object of study is imposed by his conceptual interest and selection: 'Algeria is specifically the object of this study because the clash between the indigenous and the European civilizations has made itself felt here with the greatest force. Thus the problem under investigation has determined the choice of subject.'[22] By the end of the chapter, however, Bourdieu is suggesting that there are inherent unities or identitities. This is true, first of all, in relation to the diversity between internal groups:

> No completely closed and, therefore, pure and intact society exists in the Maghreb; however isolated and withdrawn into itself a group may be, it still thinks of itself and judges itself by comparison with other groups. Each group seeks to establish and base its own identity on the ways in which it differs from others; the result is diversification rather than diversity.[23]

Within Algeria, different groups construct their own identities, and the same applies to the identity of 'Algeria'. Bourdieu continues:

> . . . one of the keys to the present drama may be found in the painful debate of a society which is compelled to define itself by reference to another . . . Its drama is the acute conflict within an alienated conscience, locked in contradictions and craving for a way to re-establish its own identity . . . '[24]

Groups and society are here anthropomorphised and analysed as 'beings-for-themselves' to use, deliberately, the terminology of Sartre's *Being and Nothingness*. Groups and societies are not, therefore 'totalities' to be observed, but 'totalising' entitities. This is the language of Sartre's *Critique de la raison dialectique* which was not yet published, but, whereas Sartre was to suggest a process by which free individuals might effect totalisation, Bourdieu's account of Kabyle society seems to oscillate between Hegelian idealist and materialist determinisms. On the one hand, Bourdieu praises Kabyle social organisation as an art form in a way reminiscent of Burck-hardt's celebration of the Florentine city-state: 'In the Kabyle democracy, the ideal of a democracy seems to have been realized: indeed, without the intervention of any restraint other than the pressure of public opinion, the will of the individual is immediately and spontaneously made to conform to the general will' (1961 and 1962).[25] On the other hand, he emphasises the material conditions which have fostered the flowering of human relations. The consequence of adverse physical conditions is that

> By a sort of phenomenon of compensation, to the imperfection of techniques there is a corresponding exaggerated perfection [*une perfection en quelque sorte hyperbolique ou hypertrophique*] of the social order – as if the precariousness of the adjustment to the natural environment were counterbalanced by the excellence of the social organization; as if, to counteract his powerlessness in regard to things, man had no other recourse than to develop associations with other men in a luxuriant growth of human relationships (1958, 1961, 1962).[26]

In these sentences, Bourdieu discloses the influence of Merleau-Ponty. It is in observing how men as physical beings construct themselves in a physical universe that we can phenomenologically achieve ontological disclosures.

Bourdieu's 1985 interview gives further indication of the influence of Merleau-Ponty. Asked why he began with ethnological research, Bourdieu replied that he had

> . . . undertaken research into the 'phenomenology of emotional life' [*la vie affective*], or more exactly into the temporal structures of emotional experience [*expérience affective*]. To reconcile my need for rigour with philosophical research, I wanted to study biology and so on. I thought of myself as a philosopher and it took me a very long time to admit to myself that I had become an ethnologist.[27]

The new prestige given to ethnology by Lévi-Strauss helped Bourdieu's choice of career. Bourdieu was attracted by the 'scientific humanism' of Lévi-Strauss's method, by the way in which he analysed the mythologies of American Indian tribes as 'a language containing its own reason and *raison d'être*',[28] but he reacted against the tendency prevailing at the time to see 'myth' and 'ritual' as manifestations of 'primitive' society. *Sociologie de l'Algérie* (1958) attempted to describe the social organisation of Algerian tribes without paying much attention to those myths and rituals which would have seemed to 'place' the tribes as 'backward' (to use Bourdieu's word about his own origins). It appeared as if Lévi-Strauss was isolating systems of myth and ritual, exploring their internal, relational aspects, without regard to their social functions. The transition from the first to the second edition of *Sociologie de l'Algérie* occurred

alongside the compilation of sociological information about the tribesmen who were then living in Algiers. In the second edition of *Sociologie
de l'Algérie*, Bourdieu tried to insert conventional, 'Lévi-Straussian'
analyses of myths and rituals into his accounts of historical social organisation, and then, in *Travail et travailleurs* and *Le Déracinement*, he tried
to test the extent to which the mutually reinforcing phenomena of traditional myth, ritual and social organisation had been 'incorporated' by
individuals who were adjusting to new conditions.

This meant that Bourdieu was prepared to use the insights derived from
structural analysis in a functionalist framework. It is significant that he has
recalled that, in 1958–59, he lectured in the University of Algiers on 'Durkheim and Saussure, trying to establish the limits of attempts to produce
"pure theories" '[29]. At the same time, he was considering the explanatory
usefulness of the distinction between the 'proletariat' and the 'subproletariat' in understanding the development of the Algerian war of independence as it moved into becoming a revolutionary war. There is no
evidence that Bourdieu had any sympathy for Camus' notion of continuous
rebellion rather than revolution, but he has commented explicitly that he
was driven by a desire to get away from the ideology-driven speculation
offered by Fanon in order to analyse the events which were unfolding.[30] In
1985, he summarised in the following way the views which he formulated in
several articles in the early 1960s culminating in 'Condition de classe et
position de classe' in 1966:

> . . . by analysing the economic and social conditions of the appearance of econ-
> omic calculation, in the field of economics but also that of fertility and so on, I
> tried to show that the principle behind this difference (between proletariat and
> sub-proletariat) can be traced to the domain of the economic conditions enab-
> ling the emergence of types of rational *forecasting*, of which revolutionary aspi-
> rations are one dimension.[31]

In other words, in relation both to the tendency of structuralists to abstract
mythic systems from social conditions and of the Marxists to privilege
economic explanation, Bourdieu was seeking to identify the prior conditions which could be said equally to underlie and explain those explanations offered at all points of a materialist/idealist continuum. There
remained an unresolved tension. Just as 'Algeria' was partly the construct
of the researcher and partly the construct of the inhabitants of a region of
North Africa, so the meaning of the behaviour of people who are observed
by an ethnographer is partly imposed by the ethnographer and partly generated by the people themselves. *In both cases*, the capacity to understand
meaning, to be objective about one's own motives whether in acting or in
observing, depends on the varying conditions which make varying degrees
of objectivity possible.

Bourdieu returned to Paris in 1960 after completing his empirical research. He spent one year there in which he attended the lectures of Lévi-
Strauss and worked as an assistant to Aron. From 1961 until 1964, he was to

work at the University of Lille. It was at Lille that he launched the research programmes which, separately, were to culminate in the publication of *Les Héritiers. Les Étudiants et la culture* (1964), *Un Art moyen. Essai sur les usages sociaux de la photographie* (1965), and *L'Amour de l'art, les musées d'art et leur public* (1966). In 'Célibat et condition paysanne' (1962), Bourdieu had already written up the findings of research which he had undertaken in the region where he had been brought up – the Béarn. As a 'native' who had acquired the capacity to observe the natives objectively as a result of his state-controlled schooling, Bourdieu sought to analyse the problems experienced by peasants in adapting to urbanisation and modernisation. The structure of the inquiry was similar to that of the inquiries in Algeria. In both cases, Bourdieu seems to have been intrigued by the ways in which a potent network of mutually reinforcing behaviours and attitudes ceased to cohere under the impact of external forces of change. The influence of Merleau-Ponty was still strong, particularly, in this case, of his *La Structure du comportement*. Bourdieu suggested that the network of traditional values was one of affective relations so that, for instance, the physical bearing – the awkwardness or gaucherie – of the peasants and their use of dialect rather than French were as potent distinctions in sustaining their social exclusion as any supposed differences of thoughts, ideas or beliefs.

This is the context within which *Les Héritiers* should be understood. Bourdieu sought to analyse the problems experienced by 'provincial' and 'working-class' people in adapting to becoming students in urban university institutions. Significantly, the sample consisted of students of philosophy and sociology – those who were studying what Bourdieu had himself studied just ten years before and those who were studying what Bourdieu was now teaching. The choice of intellectual discipline was a matter of relative social confidence and relative capacity to take risks. Just as the Algerian proletariat was distinguished from the subproletariat by different dispositions to make forward projections, either in terms of economic calculation or in terms of family planning, as a result of their different socioeconomic conditions, so potential students or the parents of students possess different dispositions to plan their future studies. Students possessing low prior social confidence are disposed to choose an established subject, such as philosophy, in order to acquire social status and recognition. Students possessing high prior social confidence are disposed to study a 'risky' subject such as, then, sociology, since their social investment is less bound up in educational attainment. Quite apart from the *content* of studies – the mismatch, for 'backward' students, between their indigenous culture and the knowledge culture transmitted in university curricula – Bourdieu's notion of 'cultural capital' is primarily about the social distribution of the dispositions to make variable *formal* choices.

In conducting his inquiries into students and their studies, Bourdieu's own career was in transition. His analyses of the adaptations of Algerian tribesmen and Béarnais peasants both tacitly assumed that there were irreversible processes of modernisation in operation. As someone who perceived himself to have been modernised by his education, to have achieved social recognition through intellectual attainment in philosophy, Bourdieu was disposed to see his own experience as paradigmatic. For this process to be effective, curriculum content had to remain static. Unless the educational goal posts remain fixed and the status of educational attainment is retained, investment in education is futile in securing social advance. Bourdieu was, therefore, disposed to sustain the authority of a centrally regulated and standardised state educational provision. In *Les Héritiers*, therefore, he argued that a 'rational pedagogy' should be developed which would make teachers more sociologically sensitive in transmitting a fixed curriculum to those students whose cultures prepared them differently to receive it. Bourdieu explicitly expressed his dislike of 'populism' which sought to construct curricula which were expressions of the existing cultures of learners.[32]

Exactly the same pattern applies in respect of Bourdieu's analyses of museums and art galleries. In his 1985 interview, Bourdieu recollected that when he was considering the applicability of Marxist concepts to the analysis of the behaviour of Algerian workers, he was ' . . . also working on the Marxist notion of relative autonomy in relation to the research that I was starting to carry out into art . . . '[33] The first manifestation of this strand of research was to be the publication of two short articles – 'Les musées et leurs publics' (1964) and 'Le musée et son public' (1965) – which predated the publication of *L'Amour de l'art, les musées d'art et leur public* (1966). The surveys of French museums were undertaken in 1964–65 at the request of the Study and Research Service of the French Ministry of Cultural Affairs which financed the main survey of 21 museums in France, but the project was extended to include an analysis of museums in other countries. The important point is that the focus of the research was on the *formal accessibility* of museums as institutions. Bourdieu concluded:

> In these sacred places of art such as ancient palaces or large historic residences, . . . where bourgeois society deposits relics inherited from a past which is not its own, everything leads to the conclusion that the world of art opposes itself to the world of everyday life just as the sacred does to the profane . . . [34]

but the action that this conclusion entailed was that the institutions should be deconsecrated. It was the ethos of the institutions which should be changed, not the works which they displayed, just as it was the accessibility of universities which was in need of reform rather than their curricula. This interpretation is confirmed by Bourdieu's final paragraph:

> The museum presents to all, as a public heritage, the monuments of a past splendour, instruments for the extravagant glorification of the great people of previous times: false generosity, since free entry is also optional entry, reserved for those who, equipped with the ability to appropriate the works of art, have the privilege of making use of this freedom, and who thence find themselves legitimated in their privilege . . . [35]

The message of the book is that museums as public institutions should be formally modified so as to ensure that the 'public heritage' is really available to the whole public.

At the same time, however, Bourdieu was pursuing a different line of inquiry. He was investigating the emergence of a form of artistic practice which was supremely accessible: photography. The thoughts which were to be presented, in collaboration with a team of researchers, in *Un art moyen. Essai sur les usages sociaux de la photographie* (1965) had taken shape as early as 1960 when Bourdieu had prepared monographs on the social functions of photography in a village in the Béarn, amongst workers in Renault factories, and in two photo clubs in the Lille region.[36] As he was to say in the Introduction to *Un art moyen*: 'Unlike more demanding cultural activities, such as drawing, painting or playing a manual instrument, unlike even going to museums or concerts, photography presupposes neither academically communicated culture [*la culture transmise par l'École*] . . . '[37] In a footnote, he gave figures to show 'the enormously wide diffusion that photographic practice owes to its *accessibility* (my emphasis)'.[38] As the analysis of museums was showing, consecrated art was inaccessible, but the accessibility of photography and the non-existence of prior norms and values concerning photographic practice meant that it offered the sociologist ' . . . the means of apprehending, in their most authentic expression, the aesthetics (and ethics) of different groups or classes and particularly the popular "aesthetic" which can, exceptionally, be manifested in it'.[39]

Bourdieu was opposed to the insertion of popular knowledge into the school curriculum or, perhaps, to the intrusion of popular art into the displays of established art galleries, but he was interested in examining the emergence of a new cultural form which was taking place without reference to the established mechanisms for sustaining established culture. In *Un art moyen*, Bourdieu was analysing the expressions of practical aesthetics or of aesthetics in practice. As he put it: 'Thus, most of society can be excluded from the universe of legitimate culture without being excluded from the universe of aesthetics.'[40] Whilst, therefore, Bourdieu was, on the one hand, arguing for improved pedagogy which would make a total public heritage or total culture accessible to all, he was, on the other hand, wanting to express support for the emergence of aesthetic practices belonging to multiple social groups. The possible kinds of aesthetic judgement, just like the possible kinds of economic calculation, relate to differentiated social positions. The notion that there might be 'autonomous' aesthetic judgements is at one extreme on the spectrum of possible aesthetic judgements and it corresponds with a social disposition to deny to aesthetics any practical function. Bourdieu continued:

> Even when they do not obey the specific logic of an autonomous aesthetic, aesthetic judgements and behaviour are organized in a way that is no less systematic but which start out from a completely different principle, since the aesthetic is only one aspect of the system of implicit values, the *ethos*, associated with membership of a class. The feature common to all the popular arts is their

subordination of artistic activity to socially regulated functions while the elaboration of 'pure' forms, generally considered the most noble, presupposes the disappearance of all functional characteristics and all reference to practical or ethical goals.[41]

What was true of aesthetics was also logically true of knowledge. As a sociologist, Bourdieu was observing the emergence of new cultural forms. As a university lecturer, he was aware that he was advancing new cognitive content within a traditional institutional form. For the moment, however, Bourdieu's emotional attachment to the social role of schooling, his educational conservatism, was proving useful in helping him to go beyond the explanatory achievements of structuralism. We have seen that Bourdieu has retrospectively indicated that, as early as his period of Algerian fieldwork, he had had doubts about the structural anthropology of Lévi-Strauss. These were not articulated, however, until the mid-1960s and, even then, only indirectly in non-anthropological contexts. In 1967, Bourdieu was to publish, in one volume, his translations of Panofsky's *Abbot Suger on the Abbey Church of Saint-Denis and its Art Treasures* (1946) and *Gothic Architecture and Scholasticism* (1951). The translations were followed by an Afterword in which Bourdieu characterised the orientation of the 'structuralist method' as being

> . . . generally content to establish (which is no small achievement) the homologies which develop between the structures of the different symbolic systems of a society and a period and the formal principles of conversion which allow transfer from one to another, each considered in itself and for itself in its relative autonomy . . .[42]

This relationalism of symbolic forms could be said to characterise the work of Cassirer, but, for Bourdieu, the achievement of Panofsky was that he proposed an explanation of how these homologies were actualised by living persons rather than conceived by latter-day observers. In a passage which was exactly reproduced in his 'Systèmes d'enseignement et systèmes de pensée' (1967), Bourdieu went on to argue that

> . . . Erwin Panofsky does not rest content with references to a 'unitarian vision of the world' or a 'spirit of the times' – which would come down to naming what has to be explained or, worse still, to claiming to advance as an explanation the very thing that has to be explained; he suggests what seems to be the most naive yet probably the most convincing explanation. This is that, in a society where the handing on of culture is monopolized by a school, the hidden affinities uniting the works of man (and, at the same time, modes of conduct and thought) derive from the institution of the school, whose function is consciously (and also, in part, unconsciously) to transmit the unconscious or, to be more precise, to produce individuals equipped with the system of unconscious (or deeply buried) master-patterns that constitute their culture.[43]

There is a neo-Kantian feel to this gloss of Panofsky's achievement: our perceptions of reality are regulated, but they are regulated, not by the intrinsic, universal categories of the mind, but by the thought patterns which are the social legacy of previous generations. It is the function of the school to represent this legacy and to offer it, not as a completed explanation of the world but às the raw material for new explanation. As Bourdieu wrote in 'Systèmes d'enseignement et systèmes de pensée':

> Culture is not merely a common code or even a common catalogue of answers to recurring problems; it is a common set of previously assimilated master patterns from which, by an 'art of invention' similar to that involved in the writing of music, an infinite number of individual patterns directly applicable to specific situations are generated.[44]

Already, in 1967, Bourdieu was careful to point out that the school could only exercise this kind of domination over thought in a society where it 'monopolises the handing on of culture'. He already knew, however, that this was to legitimate the total, sacred view of the world of the social minority and to marginalise the plural, profane view of the majority. The future lay with the production of photographs rather than with the preservation of museums. Equally, the future lay with the continuous generation of new thought forms rather than with the transmission of moribund learning, with the creative adaptation of the master patterns of sociological method rather than with the communication of a-temporal 'social theory'.

From *lector* to *auctor*

As a university lecturer, Bourdieu had the instinct to know, in 1967–68, that he had to 'recycle' himself. In 'Structuralism and theory of sociological knowledge' he made 'a clear-cut distinction between theory of sociological knowledge and theory of the social system'[45] and, with Passeron, he wrote, in 'Sociology and philosophy in France since 1945: death and resurrection of a philosophy without subject' (1967), an 'outline of a sociology of French sociology'.[46] In this text Bourdieu implicitly repositioned himself. The discussion of Durkheim and the Durkheimians suggests that Durkheim's *scientific* achievement was perverted by his willingness to make concessions to a university establishment which was still dominated by philosophy:

> The records of the discussions of the French Philosophical Society reveal how Durkheim had to fight on his opponents' ground, accepting the role of defendant by the very fact of offering a defence and in the end yielding to his opponents by explaining the reasons for his action in terms of the reasoning of his opponents.[47]

Durkheim's concessions enabled his work to 'provide material for routinized instruction and official pedagogism'.[48] These were the pitfalls which Bourdieu sought to avoid.

In collaboration, again, with Passeron, Bourdieu published *Le Métier de sociologue* in 1968. It was a compilation of extracts from texts which had been used in teaching and it was designed to be a handbook for students which would sustain continuous sociological practice rather than convey established social theory. It was designed to counteract routinisation of instruction, in particular the perceived routinisation of instruction in social science 'methods' associated with the contemporary ascendancy of American social scientific positivism. Bourdieu's reflexive sociological account of the relations between philosophy and sociology in postwar France had led him to argue for a sociological practice which should be constantly informed philosophically or theoretically. It should not accept the terms of philosophy, but neither should it allow itself to become a-philosophical and merely technical. *Le Métier de sociologue* assembled texts extracted from the works of, amongst others, Durkheim, Weber and Marx. It sought to show that these men were intellectual 'craftsmen' who used the master patterns of thought which were available to them to generate new knowledge – demonstrating an 'art of invention'. Texts extracted from the work of Bachelard are used but, more importantly, the rationale for the 'illustrative texts' which is offered in an extended introductory essay is explicitly derived from Bachelard's thought. Following Bachelard, sociologists are advised to construct a *science* by making a deliberate break with the everyday prenotions of the social world. The texts are to be appreciated as data in a history of epistemology after the manner proposed by Bachelard. Specifically, they are data for appreciating the social and historical conditions of the construction of social science discourse. In the terms which Bourdieu was soon to adopt, they are data for appreciating the genesis of the field of social science. Any prospective sociologist must work within the inherited boundaries of that field whilst, simultaneously, seeking to modify that field in response to current social issues in the same way as the field itself only possesses an artificial status.

It was by adopting Bachelard's view of science that Bourdieu repositioned himself within the institutional field of French academic life. Durkheim's error had been to try to model the university institution in accordance with his view of social science. Instead, Bourdieu sought simply to institutionalise social science. Durkheim's had been a 'totalising' attempt whereas Bourdieu tried to instate social scientific practice as a field of activity within a plurality of fields. This emphasis enabled him to establish a distinction between the advancement of social science practice and the transmission of social theory. There was no need for social scientific practice to be located within the field of the educational system at all.

Extending Panofsky's critique of structuralism, Bourdieu had come to see that unified phenomena or totalities such as, for instance, 'Gothic architecture' or 'Algeria', are not the products or expressions of the unifying or totalising function of a total or unified educational system. Within any society there are, instead, a plurality of systems of thought and a corresponding plurality of social systems which exist to reproduce thought. Within the plurality of intellectual/institutional systems, there is a continuous competition whereby single systems attempt to appropriate the identity of the whole. In *La Reproduction. Éléments pour une théorie du système d'enseignement* (1970), Bourdieu was to revisit the research which had led to *Les Héritiers*. The conclusion now was that the pedagogical process works throughout society in consolidating the allegiance of individuals to the social groups to which they are attracted. The pedagogical process is not limited in activity to the transmission of knowledge prescribed by the 'state' in institutions prescribed by the 'state'. Because society and state cannot be thought to coincide – since the 'state' is only a political construct of identifiable interest groups within society – state educational provision carries no socially legitimated absolute validity. It takes its place alongside other 'arbitrary' institutions dispensing self-validating arbitrary knowledge.

Objectivist social science is one such phenomenon of arbitrary knowledge. Shortly after the publication of *La Reproduction*, Bourdieu was to offer a similar poststructuralist revision of his earlier anthropological work in *Esquisse d'une théorie de la pratique, précédé de trois études d'ethnologie kabyle* (1972). For Bourdieu, social science cannot exist unless its practitioners consciously objectify what they observe within parameters which have historically been set for the field of social science. There were two main fallacies with the objectivity of structuralism. First of all, the common form of structuralism was to suppose that the behaviour of observed individuals is a reflection of an underlying structure of which they are unaware. In *Esquisse*, Bourdieu attacks Saussure's general theory of linguistics as a paradigmatic and influential instance of this fallacy: our individual *paroles* stand alone without referents, without the unconscious regulating mechanism of an underlying *langue*. However, the greater fallacy is to suppose that the detached observer can know the total system of relations which preconditions the unselfconscious actions of those observed. In a passage which was shortly to be published separately in translation as 'The three forms of theoretical knowledge' (1973), Bourdieu argued, therefore, that the methodological break required of the sociologist from primary experience in order to construct scientific objectivity has to be followed by a second break in which the sociologist must also reflect on the social conditions of the first epistemological break. This view is in complete conformity with *Le Métier de sociologue*, but it clarifies further that Bourdieu's objection was to forms of objectivism which seemed to offer *ex cathedra* accounts of totality. Bourdieu was in favour of a functional objectivity which should be at the disposal of everyone in observing the behaviour of others. It followed that the practice of sociology, like that of photography, should be accessible to all and that the objects of sociological inquiry, like the subjects of photographs, should be expressions of the ethical and class positions of the sociologists rather than contributions to the higher consecration of sociology.

As a practising researcher, Bourdieu continued to clarify his position in relation to previous practitioners, notably Weber, in 'Une interprétation de la théorie de la religion selon Max Weber' and in 'Genèse et structure du champ religieux' (both in 1971), but he was to develop and refine his own terminology to be deployed scientifically in society. He has subsequently given his own account of 'the genesis of the concepts of habitus and field'.[49] *Habitus*, in particular, was developed as a concept to explain the process by which, in a socially plural situation, all individuals internalise as a guide to their actions and attitudes, the partial structural explanations of their situations which impinge upon them partially as a consequence of those situations. Bourdieu expressed this briefly in the following way at the end of 'Structuralism and theory of sociological knowledge': ' . . . as a principle of a *structured*, but not structural, *praxis*, the *habitus* – internalization of externality – contains the reason of all objectivation of subjectivity.'[50] But the footnote to this statement is more significant. Bourdieu commented:

> Culture, which may be applied to the system of objective regularities as well as to the competence of the agent as a system of internalized models, would be a better term than *habitus*. However, this overdetermined concept risks being misunderstood and it is difficult to define exhaustively the conditions of its validity.[51]

The analysis of the subsidiary 'total cultures' of the Algerian tribes that had been offered in *Sociologie de l'Algérie* gave way to the analysis of the cultural dispositions of displaced tribesmen. Bourdieu makes it clear in 1968 that his sociological interest is not in the analysis of 'culture' but in the analysis of the multiplicity of cultural dispositions.

In 1968, Bourdieu was appointed Director of the Centre de Sociologie Européenne. Its offices were based in the Maison des Sciences de l'Homme, Paris, and it was co-funded by the governmental Centre National de la Recherche Sociologique and the École des Hautes Études en Sciences Sociales – balanced, therefore, between 'state' and 'educational' control. The logic of Bourdieu's intention to establish autonomous scientific practice outside institutionalised social hierarchies was to be realised more convincingly in the establishment, in 1975, of a journal under his direction: *Actes de la recherche en sciences sociales*. In his introductory essay, entitled 'Méthode scientifique et hiérarchie sociale des objets', Bourdieu suggested that often the status accorded socially to scientific explanations depended on the status accorded socially to the object of the research. Bourdieu's view of science and of the science to be given space in his journal was different: 'Science does not take sides in the struggle to maintain or to subvert the system of dominant classification – it takes it as an object of study.'[52] The sociology of cultural dispositions, in other words, analyses cultural value judgements without itself making any.

The contents of the early numbers of the *Actes de la recherche en sciences sociales* indicate the range of objects that were being subjected to scientific analysis by Bourdieu and by colleagues largely under his direction. The numbers of 1975 contained the analysis of the Parisian fashion industry undertaken by Bourdieu and Yvette Delsaut, published as 'Le couturier et sa griffe'; Bourdieu's 'L'invention de la vie d'artiste' about Flaubert; and Bourdieu's 'L'ontologie politique de Martin Heidegger'.

They also contained articles by Jean-Claude Chamboredon on the 'literary field'; Christophe Charle on late nineteenth-century literary production; Jean Bollack on Heidegger; and 'Le titre et le poste' co-authored by Bourdieu and Luc Boltanski. The articles are evidence of a concerted attempt to analyse material culture in a way which was not materialist in a Marxist sense but was, nevertheless, thoroughly anti-idealist.

Bourdieu's development in the first half of his career had, however, generated problems for its continuation beyond 1975. If the main task of the sociologist was to construct an object susceptible to sociological understanding, Bourdieu's inclination to make *everything* social made the conventionally discreet sphere of sociological explanation redundant. Bourdieu was interested in analysing the relations between competing fields on the assumption that all these fields are socially constructed and reproduced, but he was not interested in sustaining a second-order sociology which might be struggling for explanatory survival in competition with other 'disciplines'. Similarly, if all forms of production are thought to exemplify a mechanism of social reproduction, it was inescapable that Bourdieu's intellectual production could be situated in the process of social reproduction that he described. He was driven to locate himself ontologically within the world that he had conceptually constructed.

There were two main strategic options which might seem to have been available to Bourdieu. He could have consolidated his growing reputation by accommodating his insights to fit the rules of existing discourses and fields. He could have been thought to have been making 'interesting' contributions in the sociology of literature or of art or education, or in sociology and social anthropology. This would have meant a reduction of his ambitious intellectual project and, also, an accommodation to the routine processes of academic knowledge transmission. The alternative was to opt for a path of continuous non-disciplinary creativity, one in which he would act within the framework of the world he had constructed and would not offer that framework as if it constituted a complete, objective account of social reality.

Bourdieu seems to have made this shift – away from seeking to demonstrate that the world is entirely explicable socially to acting personally as if his demonstration were proven – towards the end of the 1970s. However dynamic and relational is Bourdieu's representation of the world of cultural tastes in *La Distinction*, it is still a *representation*. By contrast, Bourdieu's *Le Sens pratique* (1980) – his summative account of his Algerian fieldwork – is less a representation of Algeria than a *presentation* of the *self* as it had become constituted as a result of intellectual engagement with the experience of Algerian tribes.

The Politics of Self-Presentation

These are some of the considerations which lie behind the shift in Bourdieu's career which coincided with his appointment to the Chair of Sociology at the

Collège de France, Paris, in 1981–82. During the 1980s, Bourdieu carried out less empirical research than in previous decades. *Ce que parler veut dire. L'Économie des échanges linguistiques* (1982) assembled earlier articles on language; *Homo Academicus* (1984) was based on work carried out in Paris between 1968 and 1973; *Choses dites* (1987) was a collection of interviews; *L'Ontologie politique de Martin Heidegger* (1988) was a reissue of the article of 1975; and *La Noblesse d'état* (1989) combined work and thinking based on the 'Le Patronat' research project of the 1970s and the analysis of the *grandes écoles* and *classes préparatoires* which had been initially published in an article of 1981. There is a sense, therefore, in which a disintegration was occurring between Bourdieu's personal trajectory and the autonomous existence of his texts. This phenomenon has, of course, been accentuated by the translation of Bourdieu's texts into other languages, notably into English as a result of the intervention of Polity Press since its foundation in 1984. Whilst Bourdieu's texts have, in the last decade, acquired a meaning within the contemporary intellectual field and have become goods within a contemporary symbolic market, Bourdieu has himself increasingly focused his intellectual attention on his personal experience of the phenomenon which, earlier, he had analysed in respect of others – notably Flaubert, Manet and Courrèges – the phenomenon, that is, of the relations between production and reception within socially constructed cultural fields. Increasingly, therefore, Bourdieu's 'objective' accounts of contemporary culture have been openly presented as his 'objectified' account of the specific contexts within which he inserts himself and his texts.

As he came to concentrate explicitly on his own social trajectory and on his own creative project within his perception of society and its competing cultural fields, Bourdieu was first concerned in the early 1980s with the function of institutions. Bourdieu's inaugural lecture at the Collège de France, 'Leçon sur la leçon',[53] given on 23 April 1982, indicates a self-understanding which anticipates his conceptualisation of the situation of Manet. Bourdieu presents himself as a sociologist who has sociologically exposed the symbolic violence practised by higher education institutions. He knows that it is this scientific exposure which has made him eligible for a prestigious academic position, but he seeks to secure the acceptance of the college that he wishes to use its institutional traditions to institutionalise his own *anomie vis-à-vis* academicism. This interest in the function of institutions was also expressed at much the same time in 'Les rites d'institution' (1982)[54] and manifested itself in discussions of the nature of representation (in 'La représentation politique. Éléments pour une théorie du champ politique', 1981[55]) and of corporate identity (in 'An antimony in the notion of collective protest', 1986[56]).

Bourdieu was looking for a social space within which intellectuals might speak and be heard. There was a short period of apparent affinity with Habermas[57] in the mid-1980s but Bourdieu could not work with Habermas's theorised, objective 'public sphere' and needed, instead, to argue that equivalents to a 'public sphere' have been historically constructed and are in need of construction in the present. The search for space for intellectuals involved a continuing criticism of the ossified stance of academicism and of academic perspectives on the one hand (in *Homo Academicus*, 1984, but also in 'The historical genesis of a pure aesthetic', 1987[58]), and, on the other, a continuing insistence that freedom of thought might only be acquired by a full analysis and recognition of the social conditions which might make the constitution of such a field of free thinking possible – in 'Comment libérer les intellectuels libres?', 1980[59]; 'D'abord défendre les intellectuels', 1986[60]; and 'For a socio-analysis of intellectuals: on *Homo Academicus*', 1989[61]. Most recently, *Libre-Échange* (1994)[62] is at the same time a celebration of the construction of a formal space within which Bourdieu can converse with the artist Hans Haacke and, in the substance of their conversations, an account of the strategies which have to be adopted by artists/intellectuals – both Bourdieu and Haacke – to communicate their views in opposition to forms of political censure now particularly in evidence in the USA.

Increasingly, Bourdieu seemed to think that, as a sociological *writer*, the field within which his creativity should be inserted was the field of literature rather than the field of the social sciences. His institutional position was that of a professor of sociology, but he could sustain intellectual independence by writing within a literary field rather than for academic sociologists. Bourdieu's recent analyses of the literary field have, therefore, increasingly seemed like attempts to situate himself in it than to make a contribution to the future development of literary criticism. Articles such as 'Le champ littéraire' (1984[63]) and 'Existe-t-il une littérature belge?' (1985[64]) were carrying out in relation to the literary field what Bourdieu had recommended methodologically to sociologists in respect of the field of social science in *Le Métier de sociologue*.

Many of the arguments developed in these articles of the 1980s are brought together coherently in *Les Règles de l'art. Genèse et structure du champ littéraire* (1992). In his Foreword, Bourdieu aggressively opposes those who attempt to ensure that art and literature are ineffable, or contain revelations which must not be reduced by scientific analysis. He quotes Gadamer as an example of a critic of literature who ideologically will not countenance any 'reduction' of the status of the literary. This clear initial position-taking on Bourdieu's part is followed by a 'Prologue' in which he revisits his earlier analysis of Flaubert's *L'Éducation sentimentale*, and then by a systematic historical account, in Part I, of the 'three states' of the literary field.

In *Les Règles de l'art*, Bourdieu offers an interpretation of Flaubert which seems to continue where 'L'invention de la vie d'artiste' left off and, in doing so, applies explicitly to Flaubert the position that had been advanced in relation to Manet in two articles of 1987. Bourdieu now argues that Flaubert is to be definitively distinguished from his supposed persona – Frédéric – because Frédéric was represented by Flaubert as a failed writer whilst, patently, Flaubert had succeeded as a *writer*: 'Flaubert separates himself from Frédéric, from the indetermination and the powerlessness which define him, in the very act of writing the story of Frédéric, whose impotence manifests itself, amongst other things, by his inability to write, to become a writer.'[65] Bourdieu's Flaubert is no longer, as in 1975, a proto-sociologist who, fatally and at the expense of his good faith, conformed to the laws of the current literary field. Bourdieu's Flaubert is now a writer who used literary form to objectify himself by a process of auto-analysis and socio-analysis. Bourdieu now argues: 'In fact, *Sentimental Education* reconstitutes in an extraordinarily exact manner the structure of the social world in which it was produced and even the mental structures which, fashioned by these social structures, form the generative principle of the work in which these structures are revealed.'[66] In other words, Flaubert's sociological analysis enabled him both to represent the social world and also to understand the social conditions which made possible that representation in literary form. Bourdieu reads into Flaubert's achievement precisely his own project of the late 1980s.

Bourdieu goes further. He proceeds to analyse the transformations in the literary field in nineteenth-century France. In a title reminiscent of Bachelard, Bourdieu calls the first phase 'The conquest of autonomy'. In the period of the Second Empire, the dominant feature of society, according to Bourdieu, was the rise of industrialists and businessmen possessing huge fortunes and little culture who were ' . . . ready to make both the power of money and a vision of the world profoundly hostile to intellectual things triumph within the whole society'.[67] It was in this context that a literary field began to define itself in opposition to the world of money, to establish itself as a self-contained market, one of art for art's sake. Flaubert, however, was neither a realist nor an aesthete: 'He opposes both of them, and he constructs himself as much against Gautier and Pure Art as against realism.'[68] It was this that made Flaubert unique: ' . . . he produces writings taken to be "realist" (no doubt by virtue of their object) which contradict the *tacit* definition of "realism" in that they are written, that they have "style".'[69]

The new feature of *Les Règles de l'art*, however, is not simply that Bourdieu acknowledges the importance of what he calls 'realist formalism' – the positive form-making activity celebrated in the essays on Manet. It is even more that Bourdieu takes his historical account beyond the deaths of both Flaubert and Manet. In a chapter entitled 'The emergence of a dualist structure', Bourdieu outlines the state of the literary field which became established in the 1880s and continues 'up until the present time . . . '[70] The dualism referred to is between 'symbolism' and 'naturalism': ' . . . it pits an artistic and spiritualist art which cultivates the sense of mystery against a social and materialist art based on science . . . '[71] It is in this duality that Bourdieu still inserts himself. Postmodernist thinking is a form of mystification which does not say anything about capitalism or postcapitalism but, instead, participates in the valueless world which it describes. The person of the 1880s whom Bourdieu now most admires seems to be Zola. Bourdieu's view is that Zola used the dualism to construct a position for himself as a writer/intellectual rather than simply as a writer. His use of science – his interest in Bernard's biology – was not, Bourdieu suggests, significant in terms of content so much as formally: Zola used 'scientificity' as a way of securing some discourse detachment from his realist objects without adhering to the values of 'art'.[72] Most significantly, however, Bourdieu argues that Zola used his position in the literary field to intervene politically and so constitute himself as an 'intellectual' within a constituted 'intellectual' field:

> *J'accuse* is the outcome and the fulfilment of a collective process of emancipation that is progressively carried out in the field of cultural production: as a prophetic rupture with the established order, it reasserts against all reasons of state the irreducibility of the values of truth and justice and, at the same stroke, the independence of the guardians of these values from the norms of politics (those of patriotism, for example) and from the constraints of economic life.[73]

It is clear that, in *Les Règles de l'art*, Bourdieu sees himself as an inheritor of Zola's achievement. The reproduction of 'Le marché des biens symboliques', written in 1976, as the third stage of the historical progression to the present, is an indication of the extent to which Bourdieu sees the contemporary function of cultural analysis to be the construction within culture of a sphere of intellectual autonomy from which that culture can be criticised. He is supremely conscious that this autonomy has to be constantly reformed:

> It is clear in effect that the intellectual (or, better, the autonomous fields which make the intellectual possible) is not instituted once and for all with Zola, and that the holders of cultural capital may always 'regress' . . . towards one or another of apparently exclusive positions, either towards the role of 'pure' writer, artist or scholar, or towards the role of political actor, journalist, politician, expert.[74]

It is the intention of Bourdieu's writing action that he should never 'regress' to either of these alternative extremes. *La Misère du monde* (1993) and the ongoing publication of the journal *Liber* as well as of the *Actes de la recherche en sciences sociales* are all evidence of Bourdieu's continuing desire to use his analysis of the non-referential relativities of contemporary culture as a basis for making non-relative interventions in accordance with his conception of a modernist tradition.

Notes

1. P. Bourdieu (1990) *The Logic of Practice* (trans. R. Nice), Oxford, Polity Press, 16; *Le Sens pratique* (1980), Paris, Éditions de Minuit, 32–3.
2. P. Bourdieu and L.J.D. Wacquant (1992) *An Invitation to Reflexive Sociology*, Oxford, Polity Press, 204; *Réponses. Pour une anthropologie réflexive* (1992), Paris, Éditions du Seuil, 176–7.

3. Bourdieu and Wacquant, *An Invitation*, 204; *Réponses*, 177.
4. Bourdieu and Wacquant, *An Invitation*, 205; *Réponses*, 177.
5. P. Bourdieu (1988) *Homo Academicus* (trans. P. Collier), Oxford, Polity Press, xxiv.
6. F. Dufay and P.-B. Dufort (1993) *Les Normaliens. De Charles Péguy à Bernard-Henri Lévy. Un siècle d'histoire*, Paris, Éditions J.-C. Lattès, 196. The expression is taken from P. Bourdieu (1989) 'Aspirant philosophe', in *Les Enjeux philosophiques des années cinquante*, Paris, Éditions du Centre Georges Pompidou.
7. Dufay and Dufort, *Les Normaliens*, 196. Their source for this recollection is Dominique Fernandez.
8. P. Bourdieu (1990) *In Other Words. Essays Towards a Reflexive Sociology* (trans. M. Adamson), Oxford, Polity Press, 3; *Choses dites* (1987), Paris, Éditions de Minuit, 13. (The full text of this interview in German has interesting elements which are not always reproduced in the French and English texts – see 'Der Kampf um die symbolische Ordnung', *Ästhetik und Kommunikation*, 1986, 16, 143.)
9. Bourdieu, *In Other Words*, 5; *Choses dites*, 15; 'Der Kampf', 145.
10. Bourdieu, *In Other Words*, 3; *Choses dites*, 13; 'Der Kampf', 142.
11. *Ibid.*
12. Bourdieu, *In Other Words*, 4; *Choses dites*, 14; 'Der Kampf', 143.
13. Bourdieu, *In Other Words*, 5; *Choses dites*, 15; 'Der Kampf', 144.
14. Bourdieu, *In Other Words*, 4; *Choses dites*, 14; 'Der Kampf', 144.
15. Bourdieu, *In Other Words*, 5; *Choses dites*, 15; 'Der Kampf', 144.
16. First published as *Renati Descartes principia philosophiae* in Amsterdam in 1644, and published in French in Paris in 1647. Leibniz's *Animadversiones in partem generalem principiorum Cartesianorum* ('Critical remarks concerning the general part of Descartes' principles') was written in 1692 but was not published until 1844 (see G.W. von Leibniz (1965) *Monadology and Other Philosophical Essays* (trans. P. & A.M. Schrecker with an introduction and notes by P. Schrecker), Indianapolis, IN, and New York, Bobbs-Merrill, xxvi).
17. F. Alquié (1933) *Notes sur la première partie des principes de la philosophie de Descartes*, Carcassonne, Éditions Chantiers, 18.
18. Von Leibniz, *Monadology*, 25.
19. A. Hanoteau, and A. Letourneux. *La Kabylie et les coutumes kabyles*, 3 vol. 1873.
20. Herskovits, M.J. (1938) *Acculturation*, New York; Keesing, F.M. (1953) *Culture Change*, Stanford, CA, Stanford University Press; Mead, M. (1965) *Cultural Patterns and Technical Change*, New York, UNESCO (Mentor Book); Siegel, B.J. (1955) *Acculturation*, Stanford, CA, Stanford University Press; Spicer, E.H. (1955) *Human Problems in Technological Change*.
21. P. Bourdieu (1962) *The Algerians* (trans. A.C.M. Ross), Boston, MA, Beacon Press, xi, footnote 1; (1958) *Sociologie de l'Algérie*, Paris, Presses Universitaires de France, 5.
22. *Ibid.*
23. Bourdieu, *The Algerians*, xiii; *Sociologie de l'Algérie*, 10.
24. Bourdieu, *The Algerians*, xiv; *Sociologie de l'Algérie*, 10.
25. Bourdieu, *The Algerians*, 24; *Sociologie de l'Algérie*, Paris, Presses Universitaires de France (2nd edn), 25.
26. Bourdieu, *The Algerians*, 2; *Sociologie de l'Algérie* (1958), 13; *Sociologie de l'Algérie* (1961), 11 ('une perfection hyperbolique').
27. Bourdieu, *In Other Words*, 6–7; *Choses dites*, 16–17; 'Der Kampf', 146.
28. Bourdieu, *The Logic of Practice*, 2; *Le Sens pratique*, 9.
29. Bourdieu, *In Other Words*, 6; *Choses dites*, 16; 'Der Kamp', 145.
30. Bourdieu, *In Other Words*, 7; *Choses dites*, 17; 'Der Kampf', 149.
31. Bourdieu, *In Other Words*, 7; *Choses dites*, 17; 'Der Kampf', 148.

32. Bourdieu (with J-C. Passeron) (1979) *The Inheritors, French Students and their Relation to Culture* (trans. R. Nice), Chicago, IL, and London, University of Chicago Press, 72; (1964) *Les Héritiers. Les Étudiants et la culture*, Paris, Éditions de Minuit, 110.

33. Bourdieu, *In Other Words*, 7; *Choses dites*, 17; 'Der Kampf', 149.

34. P. Bourdieu and A. Darbel (1990) *The Love of Art* (trans C. Beattie and N. Merriman), Oxford, Polity Press, 112; *L'Amour de l'art. Les Musées d'art et leur public*, Paris, Éditions de Minuit, 165–6.

35. Bourdieu and Darbel, *The Love*, 113; *L'Amour*, 166–7.

36. P. Bourdieu, L. Boltanski, R. Castel, J.-C. Chamboredon and D. Schnapper (1990) *Photography. A Middle-brow Art* (trans. S. Whiteside), Oxford, Polity Press, 175, footnote 9; (1965) *Un art moyen. Essai sur les usages sociaux de la photographie*, Paris, Éditions de Minuit, 26, footnote 9.

37. Bourdieu *et al.*, *Photography*, 5; *Un art moyen*, 22.

38. Bourdieu *et al.*, *Photography*, 174, footnote 5; *Un art moyen*, 22, footnote 5.

39. Bourdieu *et al.*, *Photography*, 7; *Un art moyen*, 24.

40. Bourdieu *et al.*, *Photography*, 8; *Un art moyen*, 25.

41. *Ibid.*

42. E. Panofsky (1967) *Architecture gothique et pensée scolastique* (trans. and Postface by P. Bourdieu), Paris, Éditions de Minuit, 147.

43. *Ibid*; and (1971) 'Systems of education and systems of thought', in M.F.D. Young, ed., *Knowledge and Control. New Directions for the Sociology of Education*, London, Collier-Macmillan, 194.

44. Panofsky, *Architecture*, 151–2; 'Systems', 192.

45. P. Bourdieu (1968) 'Structuralism and theory of sociological knowledge' (trans. A. Zanotti-Karp), *Social Research*, 35, 681.

46. P. Bourdieu and J.-C. Passeron (1967) 'Sociology and philosophy in France since 1945: death and resurrection of a philosophy without subject', *Social Research*, 34, 162.

47. *Ibid.*, 170.

48. *Ibid.*, footnote 13.

49. See (1985) 'The genesis of the concepts of habitus and field (trans. C. Newman)', *Sociocriticism*, 2, 11–24.

50. Bourdieu, 'Structuralism', 706.

51. *Ibid.*, footnote 23.

52. P. Bourdieu (1975) 'Méthode scientifique et hiérarchie sociale des objets', *Actes de la recherche en sciences sociales*, 1, 6.

53. P. Bourdieu (1982) *Leçon sur la leçon*, Paris, Éditions de Minuit, (trans. in Bourdieu, *In Other Words*, 177–98 as 'A lecture on the lecture').

54. P. Bourdieu (1982) 'Les rites d'institution', *Actes de la recherche en sciences sociales*, 43, 58–63.

55. P. Bourdieu (1981) 'La représentation politique. Éléments pour une théorie du champ politique', *Actes de la recherche en sciences sociales*, 36–7, 3–24.

56. P. Bourdieu (1986) 'An antimony in the notion of collective protest', in A. Foxley *et al.*, eds. *Development, Democracy, and the Art of Trespassing: Essays in Honor of Albert O. Hirschman*, Notre Dame, IN, University of Notre Dame Press, 301–2.

57. The affinity or convergence is apparent in the questions and answers in the 'Fieldwork in philosophy' interview in Bourdieu, *In Other Words*. The interview took place in April 1985, and one of the interviewers – Axel Honneth – was, at that time, an assistant to Habermas. For more detailed discussion, see Chapter 8, pp. 125–7.

58. 'The historical genesis of a pure aesthetic', in P. Bourdieu (1993) *The Field of Cultural Production*, Oxford, Polity Press, 254–66.

59. 'Comment libérer les intellectuels libres?', in P. Bourdieu (1980) *Questions de sociologie*, Paris, Éditions de Minuit, 67–78. Translated as 'How can "free-

floating intellectuals' be set free?', in P. Bourdieu (1993) *Sociology in Question*, London, Thousand Oaks, CA, and New Delhi, Sage, 41–8.

60. P. Bourdieu (1986) 'D'abord défendre les intellectuels', *Le Nouvel Observateur*, 12–18 September, 82.
61. P. Bourdieu (1989) 'For a socio-analysis of intellectuals; on *Homo Academicus*', *Berkeley Journal of Sociology*, XXXIV, 1–29.
62. P. Bourdieu and H. Haacke (1994) *Libre-Échange*, Paris, Éditions du Seuil. Translated as (1995) *Free Exchange*, Oxford, Polity Press.
63. P. Bourdieu (1989) 'Le champ littéraire. Préalables critiques et principes de méthode', *Lendemains* (Berlin–Cologne), IX, 5–20.
64. P. Bourdieu (1985) 'Existe-t-il une littérature belge/Limites d'un champ et frontières politiques', *Études de Lettres* (Lausanne), 4, 3–6.
65. P. Bourdieu (1992) *Les Règles de l'art. Genèse et structure du champ littéraire*, Paris, Éditions du Seuil, 50; P. Bourdieu (1996) *The Rules of Art. Genesis and Structure of the Literary Field*, Oxford, Polity Press, 25.
66. Bourdieu, *Les Règles*, 59–60; *The Rules*, 31–2.
67. Bourdieu, *Les Règles*, 76; *The Rules*, 48.
68. Bourdieu, *Les Règles*, 140–1; *The Rules*, 95.
69. Bourdieu, *Les Règles*, 143; *The Rules*, 96.
70. Bourdieu, *Les Règles*, 165; *The Rules*, 113.
71. Bourdieu, *Les Règles*, 171; *The Rules*, 117–18.
72. Bourdieu, *Les Règles*, 170; *The Rules*, 116–17.
73. Bourdieu, *Les Règles*, 186; *The Rules*, 129.
74. Bourdieu, *Les Règles*, 465–6; *The Rules*, 343.

Part II

THE CONCEPTS

---

2 The socio-genesis of the thinking instruments

When we conceive something, we are involved in an active process. A concept is what we produce in the process of conceiving or conceptualisation which is retrospectively called conception. Concepts, therefore, are objects. They are thrown out in the process of conceiving and they acquire an existence which is independent of the process. Similarly, we receive things and receipts are the objective record of the process which is called reception, or we deceive people and a deceit is the objective form taken by a deception. Although we perceive things and we refer to the process of perception, we rarely talk about percepts in ordinary speech. This is perhaps because the defining characteristic of the process of perceiving is that we grasp things by being involved in them, by responding through them. The objectified products of this process should have no function in subsequent acts of perceiving. By contrast, the defining characteristic of the process of conceiving is that we seize things *with* other things. The act of conceiving is cumulative. We conceive a set of actions on a field to be a game of football because we grasp the phenomenon by using the prior concept of a game to generate the more refined concept. We use concepts socially to fix conventional meanings which affect practices. Actions, for instance, which are conceived as games acquire rules which embody and consolidate the concept. Concepts are tools by which we define and classify phenomena. They do not have intrinsic meaning. They do not represent real things but themselves acquire objective reality as they function in helping us to make sense of things and objects. Their uses are transitory. They are never destroyed but they are always superseded. They have an in-built functional obsolescence.

This account of Bourdieu's position is a way of stating that, in the terms of medieval scholasticism, he is a nominalist rather than a realist. He believes that names have reality and do not simply refer to reality. He believes that words are things rather than just the descriptors of things. This explains why his short account, published in 1985, of his use of the concepts of *habitus* and *field* is called 'The genesis of the concepts of *habitus* and of *field'*. He offers an account of the emergent functions of these concepts in his thinking. The use of 'genesis' in the title is a recognition that these, and all, concepts are constructs which have beginnings, but Bourdieu is not at all intent on privileging the meanings of original usages. Scientific theory is to be exercised rather than contemplated. It involves the continuous, practical deployment of concepts. As Bourdieu puts it himself:

> Unlike theoretical theory, a prophetic or programmatic discourse which is its own end, and which stems from and lives by confrontation with other theories, scientific theory emerges as a program of perception and of action which is disclosed only in the empirical work in which it is actualized. It is a temporary construct which takes shape for and by empirical work and which gains less by theoretical polemics than by confrontation with new objects.[1]

The purpose of this chapter, therefore, is to point to the ways in which Bourdieu has developed and used his concepts and not at all to establish definitive meanings for them.

Habitus

Published in the third period of Bourdieu's career, 'The genesis of the concepts of *habitus* and *field'* offers a retrospection on the historical development of these two key concepts. Published in the year that Bourdieu gave the interview which was subsequently issued as 'Fieldwork in philosophy'[2] and not too long before the conversations which were to be assembled as *Réponses*,[3] the article is indicative of Bourdieu's strategic insistence that both his career and his concepts were haphazard mixtures of strategy and contingency. Bourdieu first looks at his concept of *habitus*. He argues: ' . . . the notion of habitus expresses first and foremost the rejection of a whole series of alternatives into which social science (and more generally, all of anthropological theory) has locked itself, that of consciousness (or of subject) and of the unconscious, that of Finalism and of Mechanicalism, etc. . . . '[4]

He claims that it was in his 1967 'postface' to the French translations of Panofsky's *Abbot Suger on the Abbey Church of Saint-Denis and its Art Treasures* and *Gothic Architecture and Scholasticism*[5] that he first appropriated the concept for his own purposes. Whereas Panofsky had used the concept solely to explain the affinities between scholastic thinking and Gothic architecture, Bourdieu used it to account for the ways in which all social structures are generated in practice by participating social agents. Whereas Panofsky solely tried to show how our present conception of a structural relationship in one particular historical period between thought and art was not the product of our disposition to impose patterns but corresponded, instead, to an actual process inherent within the historical period, Bourdieu used the concept of *habitus* more extensively. All humans inherit dispositions to act in circumscribed ways. In this sense they possess an inherited concept of society which they then modify, generating a new concept which is apt for their conditions and experiences. For Bourdieu, the concept of *habitus* developed in similar circumstances to Chomsky's notion of *generative grammar*, but, unlike Chomsky, Bourdieu was not searching for a universal explanatory principle, only a concept with which to describe localised strategic actions.

Bourdieu explains how the concept of *habitus* enabled him to resolve a series of intellectual problems, but he rightly realises that his account of the use to him of the concept gives this function too much prominence. He comments:

> The first uses that I was able to make of the notion of habitus probably contained more or less all of that – but only in an implicit state: they were the product not of a theoretical calculation similar to the one that I have just performed . . . but of practical strategy of scientific habitus . . . [6]

It is clear that there is in Bourdieu's retrospection of 1985 an element of *post hoc* rationalisation with respect to the value of *habitus* in helping him to adopt a coherent attitude towards structuralism. The motivation for the concept was more directly practical and its development was latent in the way in which Bourdieu tried in his earliest work to reconcile existential phenomenology with cultural anthropology.

In his discussion of Kabyle culture in *Sociologie de l'Algérie* Bourdieu concluded with a subsection devoted to ' "lived" democracy and "constituted" democracy'.[7] He claimed that family solidarity provided the pattern for the solidarity of the whole society. Family and political structures were homogeneous because they were parallel, logical developments from the same underlying schema. In Kabyle society there was no need for a written 'constitution' because there already existed a harmony between public and private affairs since both shared a common generative impulse. The argument is stated at the end of the corresponding section of *The Algerians* in the following way:

> By the very reason of the intensity of communal sentiments, the rules on which the community is based do not need to be made to appear as imperatives. They permeate the living reality of manners and customs. The gentilitial democracy does not have to define itself in order to exist; perhaps it even exists with a much greater vitality in proportion as the sentiments on which it is based are less defined.[8]

Bourdieu claimed to have observed a social system that had so constituted itself that it functioned automatically and harmoniously. There was a pre-ordained order which could be perpetuated as long as the mechanisms for unquestioning socialisation could all be sustained. In other words, Bourdieu did not want to assume that the harmony of the social system was preserved by a mysteriously collective consciousness, but, rather, that the generic order had to be constantly renewed. This was a fragile condition and, by contrast, western democracy evidenced the conflict which inevitably flowed from the collapse of the mechanisms of value transmission.

Bourdieu's account of pre-lapsarian Kabyle society was the backcloth for his analyses of the cultural adaptation, the acculturation, of Kabyle workers in Algiers. He sought to observe the operation of the mechanisms for value transmission in a situation where the original coherence of the whole system had collapsed. Although he did not at this stage give the mechanism a name, it is clear that the observation of the acculturation of workers called for a concept – *habitus* – which would make sense both of the persistence of old values in new behaviour and of the ways in which new collective values were actively constructed by individuals who had been dispossessed of their places in an automatically self-harmonising system.

Talk of 'values', however, must not cause us to lose track of the corporal force of *habitus*. The adaptations that Bourdieu observed were physical as well as attitudinal and part of the use of *habitus* as a concept was that it denied this kind of body/mind separation. Bourdieu has commented that Marcel Mauss had rediscovered the corporal dimension of *hexis/habitus* '. . . as behaviour, deportment, . . . where it serves to express the systematic functioning of the socialized body'.[9] This was particularly noted in relation to dancing and it is in this context that Bourdieu first used the concept in 1962 in 'Célibat et condition paysanne'. Bourdieu describes the small country dances of his native Béarn, held either at Christmas or at the New Year, as being occasions of a clash of civilisations – between rural and urban life. The difficulties of cultural adaptation experienced by the traditional peasants are manifested in their awkward physical movements. Bourdieu comments that 'This is not the place to analyse the motor habits peculiar to a peasant from the Béarn, that *habitus* which denounces the *paysanas*, the clumsy peasant. Popular observation understands perfectly this *hexis* which is the basis for stereotypes'.[10]

The *habitus* and its Greek antecedent the *hexis* function here for Bourdieu as concepts which suggest that lapses from prior coherent value systems, whether in Algeria or the Béarn, are physically apparent. Bourdieu has noted that Merleau-Ponty did not use the concept of *habitus*,[11] but the association of Mauss's social psychological usage with the thinking of Merleau-Ponty's *La Structure du comportement*, first published in 1942, enabled Bourdieu to extend the function of the concept. Merleau-Ponty's work evaluated the opposing contributions of Pavlov's theory of conditioned reflex and of *Gestalt* psychology to the explanation of human behaviour. He concluded that behaviour is neither explicable as a response to stimuli nor as purposeful action dictated holistically. Instead, behaviour is to be understood as the physically and mentally adaptive piecemeal actions of behaving persons.[12] One of the features of Kabyle peasant life that Bourdieu had observed was that the peasants possessed no sense of constituted time. They lived in a continuous present in harmony with the rhythm of the seasons. Bourdieu was able to use the concept of *habitus* to

graft this perception to Merleau-Ponty's materialist phenomenology of behaviour. For Bourdieu, the *habitus* embodies the attitudes which we inherit, but it does not constitute a stimulus which conditions how we must
behave. This is what Bourdieu means when he says that the concept of
habitus enables him to avoid 'mechanicalism'. We do not act out mechan-
ically or automatically any dispositions which we can be said to possess
intrinsically prior to their enactment. The concept of *habitus* also enables
Bourdieu to oppose the alternative extreme of 'finalism'. We do not regu-
late our present actions by reference to any future goal. Our actions are not
purposeful but, rather, continuously adaptive.

Situation, Position and Condition

In denying that the *habitus* conditions behaviour either mechanistically or
finalistically, we are forced to consider the distinction that Bourdieu makes
between 'situation' and 'position'. It is important to realise that Bourdieu
does not contend that the *habitus* operates identically for all people. It is
not a universal entity or faculty. The best clarification of Bourdieu's thinking here is his 'Condition de classe et position de classe' (1966). Like
'Intellectual field and creative project', published in the same year, 'Condition de classe et position de classe' clarifies Bourdieu's relation to structuralism. At the beginning of the article, he writes:

> To take seriously the notion of social structure is to suppose that each social class
> owes *positional properties* which are relatively independent of intrinsic proper-
> ties . . . to the fact that it occupies a historically defined position in a social
> structure and that it is affected by relations which unite it with other constitutive
> aspects of the structure.[13]

Structuralism involves taking seriously the fact that individuals, groups or
classes occupy positions in society which are defined *in relation* to the total
structure of that society and in relation to each other. Position-taking is
adaptive. Position-taking is relational rather than intentional. Bourdieu gives
an example derived both from his researches in Algeria and in the Béarn:

> . . . you can isolate, as Weber does, in the peasant condition that which relates to
> the situation and the practice of working the soil, that is to say a certain kind of
> relationship with nature, based on dependence and submissiveness, and correla-
> tive with certain recurrent traits of peasant religious belief, or you can isolate
> that which relates to the position of the peasant in a specific social structure, an
> extremely variable position in different societies at different times, but domi-
> nated by the relationship with the citizen and urban life . . .[14]

For Bourdieu, the structural analysis which is of interest is the analysis of
social groups in different societies who occupy comparable *positions* relative to their different social structures, rather than the analysis of groups

who might be supposed to have the same intrinsic *situation*. The interesting comparison, in other words, between societies, both geographically and historically, is between the ways in which groups strategically acquire different positions rather than in the universal similarities of their situations. Nevertheless, as the passage above explicitly states, a group's capacity to adapt relationally is itself relative to its situation. A group's condition is a function both of its situation and of its position. For some groups, their condition may almost coincide with their situation which then appears to be 'natural' and legitimately to give rise to universal explanations, whilst, for other groups, their condition may almost coincide with their position such that it appears contrived and, consequently, appropriately susceptible to relational analysis.

Although individuals, groups and classes do not have fixed, objective existence, they all comprise variable mixtures of situation and position which make them unstable, possessing the potential for change. Individuals modify their situations positionally by reference to groups; groups by reference to classes; and classes by reference to the total structure of society. The position-taking is not simply by reference to a static network of relations. Position-taking accommodates both the past and the future. Although 'Condition de classe et position de classe' does not refer to the concept of *habitus*, the dynamic relationalism of position-taking does involve the *habitus*. The *habitus* of every individual inscribes the inherited parameters of modification, of adjustment from situation to position which provides the legacy of a new situation. The parameters of modification for individuals relate to the objective trajectories of the groups from which they acquire their *habitus* and of those with which they align themselves. Individuals and groups possess the capacity to gauge the upward or downward mobility of the larger groups with which they affiliate.

Bourdieu recognises that the distinction between situation and position may only be 'heuristically fertile'[15] rather than absolute. One person's situation is another person's position or, even, all persons constantly generate positions from situations and, in turn, generate new positions from those new situations. The important emphasis, however, is that situations are given or received whereas positions are actively made. Situations are static whereas position-taking is the dynamic activity that constantly destabilises situations. Bourdieu's view is that it is the position-taking which occurs within and in relation to the transiently objective situation of larger groups that brings about change. The position-taking of individuals in groups modifies the objective situation of those groups whilst, at the same time, groups position themselves as groups in relation to classes, and so on. Having rejected the form of structuralism that would make comparisons across societies between groups sharing the same intrinsic situations in favour of a form of structuralism that would compare across societies the relational positions of groups within those societies, Bourdieu goes further. He wants to understand the process of position-taking itself. It is not enough for Bourdieu, in other words, to compare situations or positions structurally at all, even if this is done in a way which attempts to offer a dynamic grid. The problem is how to avoid representing dynamism statically. Bourdieu's solution is to argue that positions are not just mathematical functions of situations that can be plotted by an external observer. Position-taking is immanently creative. It is the *habitus* that immanently transforms situations into positions. Individuals in different situations have different capacities to generate positions, but all individuals possess some capacity for positional change. The extent to which this capacity is actualised depends on random encounters with other individuals and groups, such that social trajectories can never be fully calculated or predicted by detached observers. Those who present themselves as detached observers are only indulging in their own position-taking – producing a relatively more comprehensive calculation of the relatively less calculated position-taking of others as the basis for their own position-taking.

Bourdieu argues that position-taking is always embellished. There is an element of artifice involved. The structuralism that Bourdieu opposes is based on a functionalism which supposes that there are intrinsically different functions in societies. In contrast, Bourdieu offers a view of social relations which supposes that individuals and groups artificially construct differences as part of their position-taking activity. For Bourdieu, the cultures of individuals and groups are the tokens by which they distinguish themselves in order to position themselves. Cultures are, therefore, artificial objects deployed in position-taking rather than integral parts of intrinsically differentiated situations. Consideration of the relationship between situation and position leads, in other words, towards an understanding of Bourdieu's concept of 'cultural capital'. In 'Condition de classe et position de classe', Bourdieu writes:

> A social class is never defined only by its situation and its position in a social structure, that is to say by the relations which it objectively has with the other social classes. It also owes a number of its properties to the fact that the individuals who compose it enter deliberately or objectively into symbolic relations which, in expressing differences of situation and of position according to a systematic logic, tend to transmute them into *signifying distinctions*. The relative independence of the system of actions and expressive processes or, if you like, of *marks of distinction*, thanks to which social subjects express and, at the same time, constitute, for themselves and for others, their position in the social structure (and the relation that they hold to this position) – by bringing about an expressive reduplication of the 'values' (in the linguistic sense) necessarily attached to the class position – authorises the methodological authorisation of a properly cultural order. In fact, this 'systematic expression' (in the terms used by Engels) of the economic and social order can, as such, be legitimately constituted and treated as a system and, therefore, be made the object of structural apprehension.[16]

Bourdieu is saying that abstractly formulated relations between situations and positions within social structures are actually constructed practically by participants. Practical construction reduplicates what is abstractly observable or systematically analysable. Nevertheless, the practical construction is effected by using cultural signifiers which themselves have a systemic autonomy from those relationships which enable social structures to be characterised as systems. The cultural signifiers used by subjects to reduplicate their unembellished situations and positions no more have intrinsic meaning or value than do the situations and positions which they reduplicate.

It is important to realise that, for Bourdieu, cultural value judgements and the cultural allegiances of individuals are arbitrary within an autonomous system of cultural objects. That is to say that there are 'elective affinities' within an autonomous cultural system – that our cultural 'choices' are strategically guided by our *habitus*, neither mechanistically nor finalistically determined – but situations and positions within this autonomous cultural context are not *reflections* of parallel social situations and positions. Instead, Bourdieu argues that an individual can deploy a cultural situation or position strategically to take a new social position, and *vice versa*. Neither the social nor the cultural conditions of individuals represent their true being. The notion of true being is excluded. Human society is seen by Bourdieu as a series of encounters between entities which have relational meaning within autonomous systems and also relational meaning across systems.

Cultural Capital

In order to enforce this view that culture is a currency that people use rather than an intrinsic quality, Bourdieu took hold of the concept of 'capital' as developed in economic theory and applied it to culture. The possession of money enables us to make purchases which alter our social condition. We trade the value of our situation within the economic system in order to improve our position within that system, but our personalities are not modified by the nature of the coins which we use, only, instead, by the quantity of our possessions and by the fact that the economic system operates by esteeming quantity. Similarly, our social positions are only modified by our cultural tastes in as much as the cultural system assigns more value to some tastes than to others. We are not intrinsically altered by preferring Mozart over Morrissey or Manet over Man Ray, but the judgements of value made between our preferences within the cultural system affect our position within that system and have consequences for both our economic and our social position-taking.

Gary Becker's *Human Capital*, published in 1964, reported on a research project which had commenced in 1957 and had been undertaken under the auspices of the National Bureau of Economic Research, New York. As Becker commented in his Introduction, interest in the economics of education had 'mushroomed throughout the world'[17] during this period of seven years. At governmental level, in rich and poor countries, it had become important to establish what might be the rates of return on money invested in education. One main conclusion of Becker's analysis of the economic benefits accruing to different categories of students in different kinds of American educational establishments was that

> . . . because observed earnings are gross of the return on human capital, some persons earn more than others simply because they invest more in themselves. Because 'abler' persons tend to invest more than others, the distribution of earnings would be very unequal and skewed even if 'ability' were symmetrically and not too unequally distributed.[18]

Bourdieu first used the term 'capital' in *Les Étudiants et leurs études* (1964) in order to argue that the analysis of student performance in higher education is neither a direct reflection of innate, individual abilities nor of social class. The cultures which students possess on commencing their higher studies have been accumulated during the protracted period of cultural initiation which is compulsory state schooling. Cultural position-taking has already acquired relative independence of social situation through the work of school. The degree of future aspiration which will affect performance correlates with the level of achieved position and, as an example, Bourdieu suggests that 'certain professions' are thought, from the outset, to 'suppose the possession of a capital'[19] such that students without this capital effectively exclude themselves by assuming that they are not able to compete for admission.

Bourdieu made lavish use of the concept of cultural capital in *La Reproduction* (1970) and in 'Reproduction culturelle et reproduction sociale' (1971). He was resolute in denying that scholastic success could be explained by innate ability but he was equally resolute in denying a facile, static correlation between student performance and class origins:

> Social origin, with the initial family education and experience it entails, must therefore not be considered as a factor capable of directly determining practices, attitudes and opinions at every moment in a biography, since the constraints that are linked to social origin work only through the particular systems of factors in which they are actualized in a structure that is different each time.[20]

Nevertheless, Bourdieu's concept of 'cultural capital' has often been misinterpreted. The degree of cultural capital possessed has often been taken to be a direct expression of class position. This is, however, to ignore the genesis and development of the concept. Bourdieu has explained these in his 'Les trois états du capital culturel' (1979). Here he explicitly comments on the work of Becker. The economists of education had the merit that they 'explicitly posed the question of the relationship between the rates of profit assured by educational investment and by economic investment . . .'[21] but, having raised the question of the relationship between straight, money-making, economic activity and educational or cultural investment, they were only able to analyse the relationship in economic terms. The economic system was an example of an unembellished system of monetary values comparable in practice with the abstract systems of relations constructed by structuralist sociologists. Bourdieu argued, instead, that behaviour within the economic system relates strategically with behaviour within the social and cultural systems. As a result, the economists failed to recognise the '*domestic transmission of cultural capital*'.[22] To be precise, the economists sought to analyse the extent to which investment in education might improve on the profits which 'able' people might be expected to acquire without recognising that ability is itself the consequence of investment. Explicitly citing Becker, Bourdieu comments generally that the inquiries of the economists ' . . . on the relation between "aptitude" (*ability*) in studies and investment in studies show that they are unaware that "aptitude" or "giftedness" are also the product of investment in time and in cultural capital . . . '[23] Although Bourdieu borrows economic terminology from the human capital economists, he does so, therefore, in order to suggest that the cultural sphere operates autonomously as a market and, in doing so, constitutes a system which impinges on the austerely monetary system artificially constructed by economism.

'Les trois états du capital culturel' is an important article not only because Bourdieu reflects retrospectively on the origin of the concept of cultural capital but also because, writing in 1979, he makes adjustments to it. The article demonstrates clearly the way in which the function of the concept has shifted over time in order to perform new tasks. As the title of the article suggests, Bourdieu now identifies three kinds of cultural capital. He summarises in the following way:

> Cultural capital can exist in three forms: *in an incorporated state*, that is to say in the form of the durable dispositions of the organism; *in an objectivated state*, in the form of cultural goods, pictures, books, dictionaries, instruments, machines, which are the marks either of realised theories or of criticisms of these theories, of problems, etc.; and finally *in an institutionalised state*, a form of objectivation which must be kept separate since, as can be seen in relation to scholastic titles, it confers on cultural capital the supposed capacity to guarantee completely original properties.[24]

Incorporated cultural capital is indistinguishable from the *habitus*, but Bourdieu is making it clear, for the first time, that there are cultural dispositions which are biologically transmitted. It is not the case, in other words, that the cultural dispositions of individuals are wholly artificial constructs – pawns in strategic position-taking acting in accordance with the dispositions of an essentially social *habitus*. In as much as Bourdieu had earlier implied that cultural dispositions are deployed by primarily social beings, he now seems to be denying the vestiges of a humanist, essentialist conception of selves or social beings that this would seem to suggest. The emphasis, however, is not that beings are integrally sociocultural. Rather, the emphasis – in accord with his sympathy for Gilbert Ryle's 'the ghost in the machine'[25] as expressed in 'Structuralism and theory of sociological knowledge' (1968)[26] – is that beings are integrally nothing at all. The *habitus* is an amalgam of social, cultural and economic dispositions, but no one of these dispositions has primacy in determining the configuration of the others. Beings, as objects, move randomly within predetermined parameters. The only controlling factor over individual objects, therefore, is the successive reproduction of parameters. The objects do not themselves exercise 'self'-control. The key factor about incorporated culture is, as Bourdieu proceeds to point out, that it is confined to the physical life-spans of individuals. Every incorporated culture is the unique product of unique dispositions.

Objectivated cultural capital, on the other hand, exists independently of persons possessing different incorporated cultural capitals. In origin, all kinds of objectivated cultural capital were the products of objectification as people sought to modify their incorporated cultural capital through the duration of their lives. Objectivated cultural capital acquired autonomous market value over time and, thus, present position-takers now deploy, second or third hand, the value created first hand by earlier position-takers. It was as if, writing shortly after the publication of *La Distinction*, Bourdieu was anxious to make it clear that he had not been positing *necessary*, or static and fixed, relationships between specific tastes and specific class positions. On the contrary, the objectivated cultural stock accumulated in one generation can crash in the next. The value of the objectivated cultural capital of the past has constantly to be renewed and reactivated in the contemporary market. Although objects – such as books or pictures – can be said to be the repositories of objectivated cultural capital, they have no value unless they are activated strategically in the present by those seeking to modify their incorporated cultural capital. All those objects on which cultural value has ever been bestowed lie perpetually dormant waiting to be revived, waiting for their old value to be used to establish new value in a new market situation.

Objectivated cultural capital is permanently potential, always dependent on the selections of individuals. Institutionalised cultural capital, by contrast, has an objective existence which is instrumental in constituting individuals. Institutions are consolidated social groups which have the power to prescribe or pre-empt the ways in which individuals might try to use objectivated cultural capital to modify their own incorporated cultural capital. Bourdieu refers particularly to educational institutions which are embodied value systems. By bestowing titles and awards on individuals they appear to be giving expression to the differences between those individuals. In reality, however, they are constructing differences in terms of their values and denying the validity of the differentiations made by individuals themselves. Objectivated cultural capital implies a free market with a floating currency whereas institutionalised cultural capital implies a market with fixed rates of exchange.

These distinctions were of particular importance to Bourdieu when he was about to take the Chair of Sociology at the Collège de France, Paris.

The question was whether the historical tradition of the college – its institutionalised cultural capital – would prevail over his capacity to construct his own social trajectory on the basis of his incorporated cultural capital and his deployment of his objectivated – intellectual – cultural capital, or whether he would be able to 'mobilise' the capital of the college to advance his own career. The key general question was whether all institutionalised cultural capital might properly be recognised to be a form of objectivated cultural capital. Was the value of an institution dependent on a process of continual reactualisation in the same way as the value of a picture? Might institutionalised cultural capital be deployed by individuals in the same way as objectivated cultural capital?

Although the concept of 'institutionalised cultural capital' was only articulated at the point in his career when Bourdieu was making a choice of institutional affiliation, it was, nevertheless, a legacy of the thinking of the 1960s. It was the institutions of the state which imposed standardised titles and labels on the whole population. In work of the 1970s and 1980s culminating in *La Noblesse d'état* (1989), Bourdieu attempted to show that industrial organisations and higher education institutions were the products of the strategies of their members. State organisations were the organs of the partisan groups within society who succeeded in imposing their particular interests on the whole of society by constructing and dominating the concept of the state. It was no longer enough to argue that some parts of the population could be seen to be socially excluded as a result of their cultural disadvantage in respect of the dominant culture transmitted in state educational institutions. It had to be recognised, instead, that institutions themselves are the instruments used by social groups to perpetuate their values. To that extent, the cultures transmitted within institutions are of secondary significance in relation to the divisions of social capital embodied in institutional divisions.

It was logical, therefore, that Bourdieu should publish 'Le capital social: notes provisoires' in 1980. It is important to be clear that Bourdieu is not at all reverting to an emphasis of social class determinants of social or cultural opportunity. It is better to see 'social capital' as a further, fourth, kind of cultural capital. Social capital has nothing to do with any integral personality qualities of individuals, no affinity whatsoever with individual 'charisma'. There is an autonomous market of social esteem as of cultural taste or economic power. 'Social' properties have value within a market-place which assigns them value, and they are used by individuals to develop a social position-taking that is real rather than simply artificial. Social cultural capital is deployed by possessors of incorporated cultural capital in the same way as is objectivated capital. It makes sense to suggest that whereas cultural capital is objectivated in cultural objects, social capital is objectivated in institutions.

Bourdieu writes:

> The existence of a network of bonds is not a natural datum, nor even a 'social datum', constituted once and for all by a social act of institution (represented, in

the case of the family group, by the *genealogical* definition of parent relations which is characteristic of one social formation), but the product of the work of establishment and maintenance which is necessary to produce and reproduce those durable and useful bonds that are appropriate for acquiring material or symbolic profits.[27]

Instead of referring to a 'network of bonds' (*un réseau de liaisons*), Bourdieu might just as appropriately have talked about a market or a system of social relations. Even more, he might have talked about a 'field' of social relations.

It was in the mid-1960s that Bourdieu developed the concept of 'field' to signify in abstract the formal context in which every kind of capital must acquire its particular value. At first the concept was used in parallel with the concept of *habitus* in opposition to structuralist thinking. One reading of 'Intellectual field and creative project' (1966) would be to say that Bourdieu equated 'fields' with 'structures'. He argued that nineteenth-century intellectuals had themselves constructed the market, or field, or structure within which their goods would be received and valued. By contrast, structuralist analysts tried to explicate historical texts by reference to the social structure within which they were produced as if that structure possessed an independent existence. Bourdieu introduced the notion of field to try to ensure that texts would neither be interpreted internally – without reference to any context – nor externally by reference to a *post hoc*, intellectually constructed context. Bourdieu wanted to argue that the proper externality to be understood was the externality internalised by authors themselves in the process of creating.

Field

As Bourdieu has himself implied, however, the achievement of 'Intellectual field and creative project' was limited. It transformed authors into producers of fields rather than texts and, in doing so, invited an analysis of the field of autonomous literary production in the place of an analysis of autonomous texts. Bourdieu was analysing a past literary field from a position within that field as it had been intergenerationally reproduced ever since. The notion of an 'intellectual field' was unfortunate if it implied that the construction of a field is an action peculiar to intellectuals rather than that an intellectual field is a particular manifestation of a universal process of field generation and maintenance.

It is clear from the second paragraph of 'Intellectual field and creative project' that Bourdieu was aware that he was offering an artificially autonomised literary history of literary production. It was only in the late 1960s and early 1970s that it became clear that Bourdieu was seeking to produce a science of the humanities and that, in order to do so, he was using 'field' in a way that was derived analogously from the physical sciences. Bourdieu contended that he was subscribing to the approach of modern science that Cassirer had made explicit – that it involved a '*relational* mode of thinking'[28] rather than one that supposed that it was dealing with the interactions of substances. In 1968, Bourdieu made it completely clear that he was attempting to banish humanist presuppositions from the analysis of humanist culture. In 'Structuralism and theory of sociological knowledge', he wrote:

> To remove from physics any remnant of substantialism, it has been necessary to replace the notion of force with that of form. In the same way social sciences could not do away with the idea of human nature except by substituting for it the structure it conceals, that is by considering as products of a system of relations the properties that the spontaneous theory of the social ascribes to a substance.[29]

Somewhat paradoxically, Bourdieu was influenced in his development of the concept of field by the work of Kurt Lewin. There is a logic here in that Lewin, like Bourdieu, admired Cassirer, and for the same reasons. Lewin's summary of Cassirer's achievement, published in 1949, has a Bachelardian flavour that would have been congenial to Bourdieu:

> He discloses the basic character of science as the eternal attempt to go beyond what is regarded scientifically accessible at any specific time. To proceed beyond the limitations of a given level of knowledge the researcher, as a rule, has to break down the methodological taboos which condemn as 'unscientific' or 'illogical' the very methods or concepts which later on prove to be basic for the next major progress.[30]

The paradox is that Lewin introduced the relational thinking of physics to a discipline – social psychology – which, in Bourdieu's terms, was already, by definition, substantialist. The affinity between the thinking of Bourdieu and Lewin and, yet, the fundamental difference, are both apparent in the following extract from Lewin's 'Constructs in field theory' (1944):

> One of the basic psychological concepts is that of psychological *position*. Position is a 'spacial relation of regions'; for instance, the position of a region A can be characterised by its lying in B. Examples of psychological concepts which have the conceptual dimension of position are: group belongingness of an individual, his occupational position, involvement in an activity.[31]

The affinity for Bourdieu relates to the development of notions of position-taking, social capital and social space, but Bourdieu's difference from Lewin is similar in form to his difference from the human capital economists – that human individuals are substantialised and exempted from the relationalist approach that is otherwise adopted.

Bourdieu has acknowledged that it was a reading of the chapter of Weber's *Wirtschaft und Gesellschaft* devoted to the sociology of religion that enabled him to develop his own thinking further. Although Weber's analysis 'permanently referred to the intellectual field', nevertheless it 'wasn't at all an academic commentary'.[32] Bourdieu was liberated, in other words, by the fact that the nature of Weber's analysis was not determined by the consecrated status of its object. It was possible to treat religion

scientifically rather than from within an intellectual field that was pre-
disposed to regard the existence of religion as a necessary datum.

Bourdieu proceeded to clarify the way in which religion should be analysed scientifically,[33] but the next breakthrough was the realisation that the
concept of field could best be elaborated by resolutely applying it to a wide
range of social phenomena. Although Bourdieu's work on Weber's sociology of religion had assisted him, the fact that the object of analysis,
however scientific, was religion suggests that Bourdieu was still in the
process of exorcising a research agenda that had been set by the functional
theory of stratification. The 'Davis–Moore Theory of Stratification', advanced in 1945, was still the subject of lively debate in the *American Sociological Review* well into the 1960s. Davis and Moore had insisted that their
analysis related to 'the system of positions, not to the individuals occupying
those positions'.[34] They contended, however, that the system of positions
in society was functionally necessary. They argued: 'As a functioning mechanism a society must somehow distribute its members in social positions
and induce them to perform the duties of these positions.'[35] And, amongst
the major, necessary societal functions, they listed religion, claiming that
'The reason why religion is necessary is apparently to be found in the fact
that human society achieves its unity primarily through the possession by
its members of certain ultimate values and ends in common'.[36]

There are respects in which 'system' and 'field' function similarly as
concepts. It was, therefore, crucial that Bourdieu should dissociate himself
from any reading which might suggest that he conceived of society as made
up of fixed fields which were functionally inter-related – with their respective roles allocated by some transcendent, controlling entity which was
'society'. This explains why, as Bourdieu puts it,

> There remained only the need to put to work this thinking tool defined in this
> manner in order to discover, by applying it to different fields, the specific proper-
> ties of each field: haute couture, literature, philosophy, politics, etc. . . . as well as
> the invariables which a comparison of the different universes treated as 'particu-
> lar instances of the possible' might reveal.[37]

Bourdieu was explicit in 'Les stratégies de reconversion' (1973) that fields
are not functional invariables, although they may possess common, invari-
able characteristics. Hence his constant attention to the 'genesis' of fields as
well as to their perpetuation. The capital which individuals transfer between fields does not have a fixed exchange rate. The strategic movement
of capital between fields takes place simultaneously with a strategic re-
valuation of old fields or regeneration of new. Fields are simply parts of the
infinitely fluid game. Individuals with individual *habitus* act and react in a
continuous present, neither influenced by the past or the future. In effect,
the *habitus* defines the sphere of operation of human automata. Some
degree of capital is associated with the *habitus*, but, by and large, objects
which acquire value in independent fields – cultural, social or economic
value in their respective fields – accrete to individuals transiently. The

objectivated capital which temporarily adheres to the incorporated cultural capital of individuals has constantly fluctuating value since the judgements of value within independent fields are constantly changing and, at the same time, the relations between fields and the relative value of the values of those fields are also perpetually contingent. The temporary adhesion of objectivated capital to incorporated capital enables individuals to occupy a position in the social structure, but that position immediately becomes a situation and, as such, a stepping-stone for further position-taking.

Bourdieu's relational concepts, therefore, are ways of talking about a relational world. It is a vision of society as one of continuous creation or production. Only the concept of *habitus* prevents total contingency. There is a constant tension between the urge to create and the urge to conserve, between the tendency of the *habitus* to deploy objectivated cultural capital creatively or to be constrained and conditioned by the legacy of institionalised cultural capital. In any society, in other words, there is tension between production and reproduction.

Notes

1. P. Bourdieu (1985) 'The genesis of the concepts of *habitus* and of *field*', *Sociocriticism*, 2, 11.
2. The interview with A. Honneth, H. Kocyba and B. Schwibs was given at Paris in April 1985, and published in German under the title of 'Der Kampf um die symbolische Ordnung' in *Asthetik und Kommunikation*, (1986), 16, nos. 61–2. It was collected in P. Bourdieu (1987) *Choses dites*, Paris, Éditions de Minuit, and in translation in P. Bourdieu (1990) *In Other Words*, Oxford, Polity Press.
3. The conversations, described by Loic Wacquant as the Chicago and the Paris Workshops of Winter/Spring 1987–88, were published in P. Bourdieu with L.J.D. Wacquant (1992) *Réponses*, Paris, Éditions du Seuil; translated as P. Bourdieu and L.J.D. Wacquant (1992) *An Invitation to Reflexive Sociology*, Oxford, Polity Press.
4. Bourdieu with Wacquant, *Réponses*, 12–13.
5. E. Panofsky (1967) *Architecture gothique et pensée scolastique* (trans. and with a Postface by P. Bourdieu), Paris, Éditions de Minuit.
6. Bourdieu, 'The genesis . . . ', 13–14.
7. See 'Démocratie "vécue" et démocratie "constituée" ', in P. Bourdieu (1958) *Sociologie de l'Algérie*, Paris, PUF, 'Que Sais-je?' collection, no. 802, 27–30.
8. P. Bourdieu (1962) *The Algerians*, Boston, MA, Beacon Press, 23–4.
9. Bourdieu, 'The genesis of . . . ', 14.
10. P. Bourdieu (1962) 'Célibat et condition paysanne', *Études rurales*, 5–6, 99. On this same page, Bourdieu refers to an anecdote told by Mauss in a communication to the Société de Psychologie, 17 May 1934, and published in the *Journal de Psychologie Normale et Pathologique*, (1935), 35, 271–93. In the same article, entitled 'Body techniques', Mauss wrote:

> Hence, I have had the notion of the social nature of the '*habitus*' for many years. Please note that I use the Latin word – it should be understood in France – *habitus*. The word translates infinitely better than '*habitude*' (habit or custom), the '*exis*', the 'acquired ability' and 'faculty' of Aristotle (who was a psychologist). It does not designate those metaphysical *habitudes*, that mysterious 'memory', the subjects of volumes or short and famous theses. These 'habits' do not vary just with individuals and their imitations; they vary

especially between societies, educations, proprieties and fashions, prestiges. In them we should see the techniques and work of collective and individual practical reason rather than, in the ordinary way, merely the soul and its repetitive faculties (M. Mauss, trans. B. Brewster (1979) *Sociology and Psychology. Essays*, London, Routledge & Kegan Paul, 101).

11. Bourdieu, 'The genesis of . . . ', 14.
12. 'We are upholding no species of vitalism whatsoever here. We do not mean that the analysis of the living body encounters a limit in irreducible vital forces. We mean only that the reactions of an organism are understandable and predictable only if we conceive of them, not as muscular contractions which unfold in the body, but as acts which are addressed to a certain milieu, present or virtual: the act of taking a bait, of walking toward a goal, of running away from danger' (M. Merleau-Ponty (1965) *The Structure of Behaviour*, trans. A. Fisher, London, Methuen, 151).
13. P. Bourdieu (1966) 'Condition de classe et position de classe', *Archives européennes de sociologie*, VII, 201.
14. *Ibid.*, 201–2.
15. *Ibid.*, 202.
16. *Ibid.*, 212.
17. G.S. Becker (1964) *Human Capital. A Theoretical and Empirical Analysis, with Special Reference to Education*, New York, National Bureau of Economic Research, xv.
18. *Ibid.*, 153.
19. P. Bourdieu and J.-C. Passeron (1964) *Les Étudiants et leurs études*, Paris, The Hague, Mouton, Cahiers du Centre de Sociologie Européenne, 1, 46.
20. P. Bourdieu and J.-C. Passeron (1977) *Reproduction in Education, Society and Culture*, London and Beverly Hills, CA, Sage, 88.
21. P. Bourdieu (1979) 'Les trois états du capital culturel', *Actes de la recherche en sciences sociales*, 30, 3.
22. *Ibid.*
23. *Ibid.*
24. *Ibid.*
25. Developed in G. Ryle, *The Concept of Mind*, 1949.
26. See P. Bourdieu (1968) 'Structuralism and theory of sociological knowledge', *Social Research*, 35, 690.
27. P. Bourdieu (1980) 'Le capital social. Notes provisoires', *Actes de la recherche en sciences sociales*, 31, 2.
28. Bourdieu, 'The genesis of . . . ', 16.
29. P. Bourdieu (1968) 'Structuralism and theory of sociological knowledge', op. cit. 692.
30. K. Lewin (1949) 'Cassirer's philosophy of science and the social sciences', in P.A. Schilpp ed. *The Philosophy of Ernst Cassirer*, Evanston, IL, Library of Living Philosophers, 275.
31. K. Lewin (ed. D. Cartwright) (1952) *Field Theory in Social Science. Selected Theoretical Papers*, London, Tavistock Publications, 39.
32. Bourdieu, 'The genesis of . . . ', 17.
33. See P. Bourdieu (1971) 'Une interprétation de la théorie de la religion selon Max Weber', *Archives européennes de sociologie*, XII, 1, 3–21; P. Bourdieu (1971) 'Genèse et structure du champ religieux', *Revue française de sociologie*, XII, 3, 295–334.
34. K. Davis and W.E. Moore (1945) 'Some principles of stratification', *American Sociological Review*, X, 2, 242.
35. *Ibid.*
36. *Ibid.*, 244.
37. Bourdieu, 'The genesis of . . . ', 18.

3 Production, reception and reproduction

In 'Structuralism and theory of sociological knowledge' (1968), Bourdieu argued that

> . . . the plurality of theories of the social system must not conceal the unity of the meta-science upon which all that in the former stands out as scientific is founded; scholars such as Marx, Durkheim and Weber, totally different in their views of social philosophy and ultimate values, were able to agree on the main points of the fundamental principles of the theory of knowledge of the social world.[1]

This was also the principle which underpinned the collection of extracts of sociological writings which, with Passeron and Chamboredon, Bourdieu assembled in the same year in *Le Métier de sociologue*. There was a sociological way of conceptualising that unified the practice of sociology in a way which was much more important than any possible unity of conceptions of society. We have seen in the last chapter that Bourdieu has tried to maintain this position in his retrospective accounts of the development of his working concepts.

At about the time, however, that Bourdieu was refining his concept of cultural capital to contain the notion of its existence in an institutionalised form, he was also reflecting on the relationship between description and prescription in 'Décrire et prescrire' (1981). Whereas he had earlier supposed that concepts became objects and could thus be thought of as components of 'objectivated cultural capital', he was now prepared to consider that concepts might become embedded and institutionalised. The consequence of his deployment of his social capital to mobilise support might be that society might be thought actually to be as he conceptualised it. Concepts could not represent things as they really are, but they could impose themselves as reality. Through the 1970s, it began to feel as if the concepts of *habitus*, or 'cultural capital', or 'field' were becoming more than ways of sociological knowing. Having plucked these objectivated concepts from their disparate contexts in Mauss, or Becker, or Lewin, Bourdieu had individually moulded them to constitute an interlocking system of ideas. They had become conceptions of society. They were acquiring an institutionalised status that matched his new institutional position. Bourdieu proceeded to work *as if* his concepts were true rather than continuing to work with concepts as infinitely adaptable instruments for grasping infinitely changing realities.

In seeking to secure public recognition for the conceptual meanings that he had privately constructed, Bourdieu had to overcome some rival conceptualisations which were already firmly institutionalised or which possessed new currency. Bourdieu's notion of 'reproduction' in culture and society developed not so much as a concept to be deployed empirically but as a conception to be adopted in opposition to Marxist or neo-Marxist theories of production on the one hand and, on the other, to idealist theories of artistic and literary reception.

Production

As we have seen, Bourdieu read Marx as a student 'for academic reasons'; was 'especially interested in the young Marx'; and had been 'fascinated by the 'Theses on Feuerbach'.[2]

What McLellan has described as Marx's 'summary statement of the materialist conception of history, which has become – often too exclusively – the 'classical' exposition of this idea',[3] reads as follows:

> In the social production of their life, men enter into definite relations that are indispensable and independent of their will, relations of production which correspond to a definite stage of development of their material productive forces. The sum total of these relations of production constitutes the economic structure of society, the real foundation, on which rises a legal and political superstructure and to which correspond definite forms of social consciousness. The mode of production of material life conditions the social, political, and intellectual life process in general. It is not the consciousness of men that determines their being, but, on the contrary, their social being that determines their consciousness.[4]

This famous passage from the *Preface to a Critique of Political Economy* is a crucial statement. It was responsible for the institutionalisation of the concept of 'production' in orthodox Marxist thinking – an institutionalised form of cultural capital in relation to which Bourdieu had to adopt a position in the 1960s.

Marx posited two kinds of production. As social beings, individuals generate structures of objective relations which, as such, acquire a force that is independent of the wills of the originating individuals. This is presented as a general, a-historical principle, but the form taken by these objectified structures 'corresponds to' definite stages in the development of material production. The principle of objective production is a-historical but the forms taken by the objectivations are determined historically. Because the relations of production directly reflect the levels of material production, they constitute the 'economic structures' of society. The constructed economic structures become the 'real foundation' for the second kind of production. Legal and political superstructures rise in correspondence with base economic structures and, in turn, forms of consciousness correspond to these superstructures. As a result of this process of two-tiered production, Marx was able to bypass the mediating function of economic structures to claim that social being determined consciousness.

There was a hint of the influence of social contract theory behind Marx's willingness to posit a state of natural, material production prior to the construction of economic structures. In opposition to Marx's theory, however, Bourdieu's anthropological research amongst Algerian tribes had suggested that material production and social organisation were successfully integrated without the need for economic structures at all. There was little evidence that the exercise of the law or of authority within the tribe, kinship practices, the ownership of property, the exchange of goods, agricultural production and consumption, religious beliefs or ritual and myth-making activities constituted, any of them, separate structures, some of which could be said to be infrastructures and some superstructures. Rather, Bourdieu observed the coherent whole to be the product of social agents who were able to sustain that harmonious coherence intergenerationally for as long as material production remained unchanged. Hence he was able to characterise Kabyle society as 'lived' rather than 'constituted' democracy.

Although Marx emphasised that the consciousness of men did not determine their being, elsewhere in his writing he did insist that men are distinguished from animals by their capacity to reflect consciously on their actions. In his *Economic and Philosophic Manuscripts of 1844* Marx made a distinction between instinctive and rational production. He wrote:

> The animal is immediately identical with its life-activity. It does not distinguish itself from it. It is *its life-activity*. Man makes his life-activity itself the object of his will and of his consciousness. Admittedly animals also produce. They build themselves nests and dwellings, . . . But an animal only produces what it immediately needs for itself or its young. It produces one-sidedly, while man produces universally. It produces only under the dominion of immediate physical need, while man produces even when he is free from physical need and only truly produces in freedom therefrom. An animal produces only itself, while man reproduces the whole of nature.[5]

In contrast, the influence of Merleau-Ponty led Bourdieu to emphasise the corporality of human behaviour and to emphasise the role of consciousness as an instrument of adaptibility. Marx's distinction between 'human' and 'animal' behaviour was too facilely dualistic. Bourdieu was inclined to be more Marxian than Marx: the position of persons on a spectrum of animal/human behaviour is itself a function of their real condition – their instinctiveness or their consciousness are determined by their social being rather than the reverse. Equally, the capacity to universalise is not one which distinguishes men from animals but only some men from others corresponding with their social condition. It follows, finally, that the production of 'art' is not an activity which distinguishes the human but, rather, there is a spectrum of arts and artifacts corresponding to the social conditions of their producers.

The legacy of Marx's thought about production, therefore, was confused. A doctrinaire Communist interpretation that insisted rigidly on a mechanical relationship between economic bases and cultural superstructures prevailed in Germany until it was challenged there for a short while from the late 1920s until 1933 by the Frankfurt School. In spite of his idealist philosophical leanings, Lukacs adopted this ideological position in the work that he did in the USSR between 1933 and 1944. It was against this doctrinaire position that Sartre began to formulate a form of Marxist existentialism which endeavoured to graft a belief in the role of human consciousness in the production of society on to the tradition of dialectical materialism that was still upheld by the political Stalinists.

Marx's *German Ideology* and *Paris Manuscripts of 1844* did not appear in French until 1937 and were largely ignored until after 1945. Poster has emphasised the role played by Jean Hyppolite in introducing the work of Hegel and Marx to France from his translation of Hegel's *Phenomenology of Spirit* (between 1939 and 1941) through to his *Études sur Marx et Hegel* (1955). The recent availability of some of the works of the young Marx and Hyppolite's Hegelian representation of Marx combined to prepare the way for a revision of doctrinaire Marxism. Whereas the doctrinaire position still emphasised that superstructures were determined by economic bases, mind by matter, in opposition there was a renewed interest in explaining the mechanisms of a historical dialectic.

Sartre's *Critique de la raison dialectique* was published in 1960 in Paris. After the war there had been a series of Communist attacks on Sartre's existentialism culminating in Lukacs's *Existentialisme ou marxisme* (1948). Sartre contended that existentialism advocated the exercise of freedom whilst the French Communist Party required unquestioning acceptance of the dogma of dialectical materialism. Wishing, nevertheless, to be politically engaged and sympathetic to the political goals of the Communists, Sartre sought to work out a philosophical position which reconciled his belief in freedom with his commitment to a progressive and materialist view of history. Sartre did not want to ignore the role of writers and intellectuals in effecting the progress of materialism. This meant that, for Sartre, the production of art was instrumental in the process of producing social change. Whereas Lukacs had conceived the function of a novelist like Scott as being almost unconsciously to articulate the hidden forces in society which were driving it forward, Sartre, by contrast, sought to emphasise the role of the writer in bringing historical changes *into existence*. Instead of seeing the writer as a participatory facilitator of materialist change, Sartre saw the writer as a detached, idealist mentor who is capable of transcending his own social situation and of projecting his transcendent vision by co-opting the free participation of readers. Consequently, for Sartre, novels were not to be seen as inert 'totalities' offering representations of complete and completed realities, but as 'totalisations' – moments in the process of bringing the writer's transcendence of his own situation into social existence through the constantly renewable 'completions' made by readers.

Like the Hegelian young Marx, Sartre presented the production of art as the action of consciousness which operated as a go-between between mind and matter in the dialectically materialist progress of history. In wanting to combat the view that art is a mechanical, superstructural *reflection* of material conditions, Sartre argued that art – operating through consciousness – is active in shaping the material world. Sartre sustained a dualistic attitude which, therefore, refused to admit that art functions *within* society, sometimes reflectively and sometimes proactively.

Bourdieu was later to use his response to Sartre's five-volume study of Flaubert, *L'Idiot de la famille, 1821–57*, published between 1966 and 1972, to articulate fully a critique of Sartre's account of social and cultural production.[6] In the mid-1960s, however, Bourdieu recognised that Touraine's ideas of agency and social action implied a view of the production of society that was akin to Sartre's. 'Une sociologie de l'action est-elle possible?'[7] (1966) was a review of Touraine's *Sociologie de l'action* (1965).[8] Bourdieu quotes Touraine's view that 'Through labour, man constructs, out of nature and against nature, a social world; he creates a universe of human products and becomes conscious of himself in his relation with these works'.[9] For Touraine, 'men make their own history'[10] through labour just as, for Sartre, they do so through the exercise of rationality. The agents of this productivity are 'historical subjects', but, according to Bourdieu, they are not empirical agents so much as manifestations of, in Touraine's words, 'the emergent structure of a totalizing activity, the unity of the dialectical movements of historical action'.[11] It is readily possible to see why Bourdieu was anxious to clarify that Touraine's conception of socially productive labour was different from his own emergent view of social practice or 'le sens pratique'. Bourdieu commented in conclusion that 'The historical subject secularizes the Hegelian Spirit, or matches the determinisms of the dialectical reason of J.P. Sartre, but the fundamental objective is the same'.[12]

The Marxisms of Sartre and Touraine were different in privileging the sociohistorical function of, for the former, intellectuals and, for the latter, labour, but they were both attempts to offer a new interpretation of dialectical materialism. Sartre and Touraine both tried to offer an explanation of the ways in which conscious human action contrived to actualise a historical process which was, in any case, independently necessary. The notion of dialectical progress required that the terms of the dialectic should have autonomous existence. Autonomous, 'free' agents related dialectically with autonomous matter. Producers were separate from their productions.

It is clear that Bourdieu's developing concepts – particularly of *habitus* and 'field' – were directly antagonistic to Hegelianised versions of Marxism. The concept of 'field' was to provide a substitute for Marx's 'economic structures' in mediating between beings and superstructures. For Bourdieu, there was only ontological base and objectivated fields. The concept of *habitus* enabled Bourdieu to insist, however, that beings are not essences but have biological existence. The producers of structures do not have autonomy. They produce in accordance with the ways in which they themselves were produced and in relation to produced structures. Producers necessarily reproduce, not in the sense that they replicate something that has already existed but in the sense that they are caught up in a process of constant reproduction. Bourdieu's theory of reproduction is a Marxist theory of production from which the dialectic has been exorcised.

Whilst Bourdieu was moving towards a theory of reproduction in opposition to the revisionist Marxist theories of production, another view of Marx was gaining ascendancy. In the early 1960s, Althusser initiated a new approach to the study of Marx. Reacting against the postwar Hegelian, existentialist and phenomenological readings of Marx, Althusser systematically applied, instead, an analytical procedure derived from Bachelard to the study of Marx's texts. In *Pour Marx* (1965), Althusser assembled articles and papers written in the previous five years. His main contention was that there was a 'break' – a *'coupure épistémologique'* in Bachelard's phrase – in Marx's work at about the time of *The German Ideology* such that Marx moved from producing political philosophy to producing political 'science'. One of Althusser's main followers was Pierre Macherey who provided a contribution to Volume 1 of *Lire le Capital* (1965) which sought to analyse the way in which Marx had contrived to present *Le Capital* as 'science'. It was a detailed textual study of the opening section of Marx's text and Macherey insisted that in concentrating on this commencement

> What we have to confront right at the outset is not, as one might by deduction, the way Marx's discourse continues, but completely the opposite: what precedes it, its conditions. Thus the question posed in this reading of a paragraph seems quite simple: in what respect is Marx's discourse scientific? And can we read the *imprint* of this in the introduction?[13]

Macherey argues that Marx did not present his text as science in accordance with the way in which science was already understood. He wanted ' . . . *simultaneously* to constitute a certain idea of science and realise a scientific discourse'.[14] For this reason, according to Macherey, it is not possible to extrapolate from the text a Marxist theory of science. Rather,

> The theories go with their practice; you need to embark on the path of this practice in order to trace that of the theory which alone explains the practice. In this way we can already see in what way Marx breaks with a certain conception, a classical presentation of science.[15]

Althusser and Macherey attempted to effect an epistemological break with their contemporary philosophical context by reading into Marx the view that he had historically effected an epistemological break. For Macherey, it was the contemporary job of the philosopher to identify the discourse claims which texts might make for themselves, ' . . . to study *in what conditions*, and *for what conditions* scientific problems are posed'.[16]

It was Bourdieu's view[17] that Macherey's approach preserved the function of the philosopher as arbiter of the scientificity of social science writing or of the 'literariness' of literature. Macherey's formulation in *Lire le Capital*, however, was ambiguous. Because Macherey's analysis was *about* Marx and, therefore, by implication, about the way in which Marx constructed a science of human history which assigned primacy to the influence of the progressive transformations of the means of material production, it was assumed that Macherey's approach was itself materialist and Marxist. The title of Macherey's next book – *Pour une théorie de la production littéraire* (1966) – compounded this confusion although a reading of the text quickly clarifies the situation. In the passage quoted above, Macherey argues that it is the task of the philosopher to analyse the conditions in which scientific problems are 'posed'. He might have written 'produced', but he should have written 'constructed'. In other words, Macherey's language falsely gives the impression that he is interested in analysing – as a social scientist or social historian – the material conditions of the production of science or literature. On the contrary, Macherey is interested in analysing philosophically how *texts* construct for themselves the field or discourse within which they wish to be received. He is interested in how texts *position* themselves rather than in the socioeconomic *conditions* which might be thought to determine the parameters within which that position-taking can occur. In all this, Macherey follows Bachelard rather more than Marx.

In as much as Macherey does follow Bachelard, he says much with which Bourdieu would be in agreement. Macherey argued that it was crucial to make a distinction between ' . . . criticism as appreciation (the education of taste), and criticism as knowledge (the "science of literary production"). The former is normative and invokes rules; the latter is speculative and formulates laws. The one is an art, a technique (in the strict sense). The other is a science'.[18] Bourdieu would certainly agree with the basic distinction, although he would reject Macherey's conception of science as stated here. Bourdieu advocates a scientific analysis of culture rather than the development of 'taste' and, indeed, *La Distinction* precisely seeks to subject 'taste' to scientific scrutiny, but Bourdieu does not oppose art to science nor does he suppose that science 'formulates laws'. It should be the 'craft' of the social scientist to analyse, within the rules of his own practice, the methods of self-regulation[19] constructed by other cultural practices – whether they are rules of 'taste' or of 'science'.

Relatedly, Macherey suggests that the task of the scientist of literary production involves the construction of a new scientificity in relation to texts, distinguished from empirical literary criticism:

> Knowledge is not the discovery or reconstruction of a latent meaning, forgotten or concealed. It is something newly raised up, an addition to the reality from which it begins . . . Let us say, provisionally, that the critic, employing a new language, brings out a *difference* within the work by demonstrating that it is *other than it is*.[20]

It has to be recognised that the same principle applies to the texts under scrutiny. A newly constructed science of literature must analyse texts as themselves new constructions. This explains why structuralist thinking has been so misleading. Macherey writes:

> If we are to make sense of the concept of structure it must be with the recognition that structure is neither a property of the object nor a feature of its representation: the work does not derive from the unity of an intention which permeates it, nor from its conformity to an autonomous model.[21]

Bourdieu could not have better expressed his reservations about structuralism, rejecting, like Macherey, the notion that actions are governed either by prior structural intention or by any immanent purposiveness. The difference, of course, is that Macherey considers that *texts* behave strategically whereas Bourdieu regards 'texts' as symbolic counters deployed strategically by people in the process of maneouvring socially for positions of power and status.

Macherey does not discount the role of the author as producer, but he contends that the defining characteristic of a new, autonomous science of literature must be that it treats literature as itself autonomous:

> The specificity of the work is also its autonomy: in so far as it is self-elaborating it is a law unto itself and acknowledges only an intrinsic standard, an autonomous necessity. This is why literary works ought to be the object of a *specific science*: otherwise they will never be understood.[22]

Macherey's concentration on texts is a strategic limitation. He insists that '*autonomy must not be confused with independence*'[23] and comments that a book ' . . . is, like all products, a *second reality*, though it does have its own laws'.[24] For Bourdieu, however, this recognition is inadequate. Macherey's new science of literature is misguided because it represents 'autonomy' as an absolute, a-historical quality of 'literature'. It does not acknowledge that the extent to which art presents itself as autonomous is a function of the degree of its dependency on non-artistic conditions. By studying all literary 'production' as if it were autonomous, Macherey failed to realise that 'real' economic conditions produce variable degrees of autonomy within which various kinds of literature may then be produced.

A follower of Bachelard as much as was Macherey, Bourdieu[25] saw the need to construct a new social science of *cultural* production – one which would have the capacity to identify the social function of the whole range of cultural forms rather than one which assumed the autonomy and privileged status of Literature. A follower of the Marx whom the Althusserians sought to discredit as 'pre-Marxist', Bourdieu sought to establish a science of cultural forms in their relations to the prevailing conditions of social being rather than supposing that they were reflections of modes of material production. In doing this, Bourdieu autonomised symbolic exchange as social rather than economic exchange. In this autonomised field, cultural production operates in exchange with cultural reception.

In spite of the trappings of Althusserian radicalism, Macherey's views can be regarded as fundamentally conservative. His insistence on the construction of a science of literary production can be seen as an attempt to stabilise the significance of an unquestioned canon of texts and to keep shut the floodgates which held back a plurality of unscientific and individual textual interpretations. Macherey had no way of answering why he should not be considering fashion as discourse as scientifically as the novels of Jules Verne. It was just assumed that the novels merited the kind of philosophical attention that he advocated. His analysis of the production of literature was carried out on texts which were already socially designated as 'literature' within a wider cultural context, but that prior value judgement was not regarded as a proper object of attention. What constituted itself as literature could be philosophically determined and, hence, Macherey's approach proscribed heterodox textual interpretations.

According to Lecourt, the events of May 1968 shattered the Althusserian Marxism which had dominated the French Left throughout that decade. Describing the background to his writing of *L'Épistémologie historique de Gaston Bachelard* in the autumn of 1968, Lecourt writes in the introduction to the later English translation that, after May of that year,

> . . . there arose the ultra-left breeze which, its voice slowly growing stronger, took up the same arguments in a different tone. The very term science soon seemed suspect, on the pretext that in our society the sciences are enrolled in the service of capital: Althusser was found guilty of having wished to apply it to Marxism; this was seen as the hallmark of his theoreticism, the proof of his revisionism.[26]

The attempt made by Althusser and Macherey to amalgamate Bachelard and Marx had distorted Bachelard's historical epistemology as much as Marx's political philosophy, and Lecourt sought to 'disentangle' these elements. It was in 1968, also, that Bourdieu and Passeron published *Le Métier de sociologue* which advocated the cultivation of reflexive scientificity – the production of 'science' which remains constantly conscious of the social conditions of its existence. Bourdieu was in sympathy with Macherey's wish to emphasise the scientific explanation of literary phenomena, but this involved, as it did not for Macherey, a full sociological agenda. It entailed, first of all, a social historical analysis of the structures of tastes and value judgements which caused certain past works to be offered as 'literature' for the reception of future generations. It entailed, secondly, a sociological explanation of the different ways in which that literature is received in the present. Bourdieu's scientific agenda required, finally, that sociologists should be systematically reflexive in order to explain both their social historical constructions of the contexts of past literary production and their own peculiar positions within the structure of contemporary responses to the historical literary legacy. In Bourdieu's terminology,

Macherey was arguing that the meanings of texts had to be appreciated within the field of meaning which they themselves proclaimed. Even though Macherey wrote against the interpretation of texts, he nevertheless uncritically assumed that it was the function of philosophers, writing within the field of philosophical discourse, to interpret the fields to which texts might belong. By contrast, Bourdieu's approach enabled him to offer a sociological account of the ways in which diverse cultural products – including literary texts – were, and are, situated within their particular fields and, at the same time, to offer an identically sociological account of the contemporary status of the sociological field itself. He was able to situate his analysis of culture within culture whereas Macherey's analyses left the supremacy of philosophical discourse unchallenged. Macherey's shortcoming was that he sought to apply Bachelard's historical epistemology a-historically, whereas Bourdieu attempts to follow through the logic of Bachelard's historicity in becoming contemporaneously reflexive.

Production/Reception

Under the influence of forces similar to those which surfaced in Paris in May 1968, an approach to literature was developing in Germany that sought to understand cultural production in a completely non-Marxist manner. In 1967, H.R. Jauss gave an inaugural lecture at the University of Konstanz entitled *Literaturgeschichte als Provokation der Literaturwissenschaft* (*Literary History as a Challenge to Literary Theory*) which was published in German in 1970 and which subsequently appeared in French in 1978 in *Pour une esthétique de la réception*. With his colleague, Wolfgang Iser, whose *Der Akt des Lesens. Theorie ästhetischer Wirkung* (*The Act of Reading. A Theory of Aesthetic Response*) was published in 1976, Jauss established what was to be known as the Konstanz School of criticism. Joseph Jurt has suggested that the inaugural lecture was inspired by 'the new life which breathed in this new university beside Lake Constance, an institution destined at the time to become a German Harvard'[27] and he has indicated the strategies adopted in the early 1970s to ensure that 'reception theory' effected a paradigm shift in literary studies in higher education institutions throughout Germany. With the hindsight gained by 1985, the editor of the French translation of Iser's *The Act of Reading* – Pierre Mardaga – was prepared to argue that the novelty of the Konstanz approach to literature 'derived from the historical situation of the German universities in the 1960s'.[28] The increasing democratisation of the university institutions generated the situation in which the presumed literary canon was called into question. As Mardaga puts it: 'The question of the development of the tradition and its conservation was posed more and more pressingly mainly because the scientific approach to literature found itself increasingly incapable of coping with conflicts of interpretation.'[29] Rather than seek to establish new, philosophical grounds for differentiating 'literature' and for outlawing interpretation altogether, in the manner of Macherey, the Konstanz School sought, instead, systematically to incorporate the diversity of responses into the literary canon. Jauss's inaugural lecture was the key manifesto. It was no longer possible, he claimed, to write the kind of literary history offered by those late nineteenth-century critics whose goal had been ' . . . to represent, through the history of the products of its literature, the essence of a national entity in pursuit of itself'.[30] Nationalistic literary history was no longer possible and, consequently, it was no longer possible to practise positivist literary historical research that assumed that the facts of a nation's literary history existed independently of historical value judgements. Jauss argued that

> In effect, the value and status of a literary work are neither deducible from the biographical or historical circumstances of its conception, nor from the simple place which it occupies in the evolution of a genre, but from criteria which are much more difficult to handle: the effect produced, 'reception', the influence exercised, and the value recognised by posterity.[31]

Jauss proceeded to present his theory of reception as a middle way between, on the one hand, the extraneous, mimetic orientation of Marxist theory and, on the other, the internal, textual focus of the formalists. Jauss proposed seven guiding theses. He insisted, first of all, that the historian of literature 'must himself always become again a reader before being able to understand and situate a work'.[32] This involves 'founding his own judgement on his consciousness of his situation in the historical chain of successive readers'.[33] Jauss takes care differently in his second thesis to ensure that the interpretation of the contemporary reader historian cannot be wilfully individualistic. Not only must the present reader be aware of his position in the tradition of previous readers, but he must also reconstruct the *horizon d'attente* – the attention parameters – of the first public of the work, a reconstruction which, for Jauss, involves, amongst other things, an appreciation of the prior knowledge of the work's genre that might be presupposed in its first readership. By reconstructing this *horizon d'attente*, Jauss argues, in the third thesis, that the historian establishes the data by which he can gauge the extent to which a work succeeds in its effect in changing the horizon out of which it emerged. The impact of the work, its immediate or posthumous reputation, become criteria for evaluating its achievement. Most importantly, the reconstitution of the horizon ensures that evaluative criteria are not anachronistically employed or, even more, that there is no critical recourse to a-temporal aesthetic qualities inherent in works that are accessible a-temporally to readers at all times.

Without referring further to Jauss's remaining theses, it is immediately clear that the extraordinary programme which he proposed was a blueprint for a new academic exclusivity. Threatened both by the disrespect of the young generation of students for the established literary canon and by their interpretative libertarianism, an academic scholar sought to legitimate his academicism by arguing that a correct way of receiving a text might be attained by knowing the history of all previous receptions. For Jauss, the meanings of texts are produced by readers. The texts do not reflect the material conditions of their production as in doctrinaire Marxism, nor do the intersubjectively acquired meanings derived from the encounter between authors and readers impose themselves dialectically, as for Sartre, on material history. Instead, readers are members of an autonomous, transhistorical community. Textual readings are cocooned. Current readings are informed by past readings without, in either case, any reference to their social conditions. Jauss's field of literature, to use Bourdieu's term, is entirely self-referential.

Although normally regarded as the co-founder of 'reception theory', Wolfgang Iser distanced himself from the original manifesto statement of his senior colleague. In the Preface to *Der Akt des Lesens*, Iser was quite explicit that his book offered a theory of aesthetic response (*Wirkungs-theorie*)[34] rather than one of reception (*Rezeptionstheorie*). Without mentioning Jauss, Iser's theoretical distinction is clearly an act of differentiation:

> . . . a theory of aesthetic response is confronted with the problem of how a hitherto unformulated situation can be processed and, indeed, understood. A theory of reception, on the other hand, always deals with existing readers, whose reactions testify to certain historically conditioned experiences of literature. A theory of response has its roots in the text; a theory of reception arises from a history of readers' judgements.[35]

The distinction, however, is not primarily between 'response' and 'reception', but rather one between actual or potential responses/receptions. Iser's interest is not in the empirical reader. His theory does not depend upon information about how previous readers might actually have responded to a text. He usefully clarifies the categories of reader that have often been invoked in literary criticism:

> In the first instance, we have the 'real' reader, known to us by his documented reactions; in the second, we have the 'hypothetical' reader, upon whom all possible actualizations of the text may be projected. The latter category is frequently subdivided into the so-called ideal reader and the contemporary reader.[36]

Iser proceeds to elaborate these subdivisions in the following way. There are, he argues, three types of 'contemporary' reader: ' . . . the one real and historical, drawn from existing documents, and the other two hypothetical: the first constructed from social and historical knowledge of the time, and the second extrapolated from the reader's role laid down in the text.'[37] By contrast, the 'oft-quoted ideal reader' is a 'structural impossibility' because

> An ideal reader would have to have an identical code to that of the author; authors, however, generally recodify prevailing codes in their texts, and so the

ideal reader would also have to share the intentions underlying this process. And if this were possible, communication would then be quite superfluous, for one only communicates that which is *not* already shared by sender and receiver.[38]

Iser expresses his dissatisfaction with all these concepts of the reader because they are all basically concerned with the 'results produced rather than with the structure of effects, which causes and is responsible for these results'.[39] Instead, Iser contends that the theory of aesthetic response entails an analysis of texts on the understanding that they presuppose potential readership without predetermining actual readers. An indeterminate reader is present in every text, and every act of reading actualises this potential being differently. 'For want of a better term', Iser calls this latent being the 'implied reader' who

> . . . embodies all those predispositions necessary for a literary work to exercise its effect – predispositions laid down, not by an empirical outside reality, but by the text itself. Consequently, the implied reader as a concept has his roots firmly planted in the structure of the text; he is a construct and in no way to be identified with any real reader.[40]

In spite of the emphasis of this last sentence, Iser is not saying, as Macherey might, that texts produce their effects. This was a variant of 'reception theory' developed at the time by East German Marxist critics who argued that texts offer a structured prefigurement (*Rezeptionsvorgabe*) of their reception. For Iser, this term ' . . . relates only to discernible textual structures and completely ignores the dynamic act which elicits the response to those structures'.[41] Concentration on the response elicited is equally an error – the 'affective fallacy'. Iser instead advocates the analysis of the encounter ('the dynamic act') between the 'textual structure' which contains the implied reader and the 'structured act' of the respondent which actualises what is implicit. The theory of aesthetic response, in other words, uses the text to generate a phenomenology of affectivity or intersubjectivity which, after the manner of Husserl, brackets both the referentiality of the text and the psychology of the reader. Significantly, Iser himself sums up his position by saying that the concept of the implied reader 'is a transcendental model'[42] and by quoting in his support from a 1960 text on the phenomenology and psychology of perspective in which the author – C.F. Graumann – claimed:

> The observing subject and the represented object have a particular relationship one to the other; the 'subject–object relationship' merges into the perspective way of representation. It also merges into the observer's way of seeing; for just as the artist organizes his representation according to the standpoint of an observer, the observer – because of this very technique of representation – finds himself directed toward a particular view which more or less obliges him to search for the one and only standpoint that will correspond to that view.[43]

Iser used this passage as evidence that his conception of textual structure followed 'a basic rule of human perception, as our views of the world are always of a perspective nature.'[44] Iser's theory tended towards a transcendental phenomenology of consciousness, identifying the function of literature in the universal, 'overall make-up of man'[45] – a tendency confirmed by his most recent *Prospecting: From Reader Response to Literary Anthropology* (1989).[46] We have seen that Bourdieu's philosophical 'fieldwork' in Algeria had been motivated by an attempt to offer a phenomenology of 'affective life'. During the 1960s, Bourdieu was coming to realise that the meanings of myths and rituals were socially constructed by the participating actors and that linguistic meaning generally was performative. Away from his empirical ethnography, the problem of understanding the meanings of cultural actions was not just one of observation. It was also one of transhistorical interpretation. When Bourdieu started to reflect on our current understanding of past culture, he was forced to consider both the ways in which meanings were intersubjectively created *in* history and the nature of our current intersubjective relations with those historical meanings. Since he was hostile to the kind of transcendental phenomenology to which Iser's work was tending, Bourdieu explored simultaneously both a descriptive phenomenology of the process of production and reception by which historical literature or art was established and a descriptive phenomenology of the process by which we currently understand past texts or pictures.

Production/Reception as Reproduction

Bourdieu first discussed the relationship between production and reception in history in 'Champ intellectuel et projet créateur' which appeared in a number of *Les Temps modernes* of 1966 devoted to 'Problems of structuralism'. Bourdieu argued his case concretely:

> It is possible to see, from the history of Western intellectual and artistic life, how the intellectual field (and at the same time the intellectual, as distinct from the scholar, for instance) gradually came into being in a particular type of historical society. As the areas of human activity became more clearly differentiated, an intellectual order in the true sense, dominated by a particular type of legitimacy, began to define itself in opposition to the economic, political and religious powers, that is, all the authorities who could claim the right to legislate on cultural matters in the name of a power or authority which was not properly speaking intellectual.[47]

Drawing extensively on L.L. Schucking's *The Sociology of Literary Taste* for detailed information,[48] Bourdieu argues that

> There began to appear *specific authorities of selection and consecration* that were intellectual in the proper sense (even if, like publishers and theatre managers,

they were still subjected to economic and social restrictions which therefore continued to influence intellectual life), and which were placed in a situation of *competition for cultural legitimacy.*[49]

Although no precise date or period is given, the argument is that at some point towards the end of the seventeenth century, writers and thinkers succeeded in establishing a market for their works and ideas which was independent of the influences – whether religious, aristocratic or economic – which had hitherto prevailed in controlling value judgements and in making or breaking reputations. At a particular point in western European history, an autonomous intellectual or cultural field established itself in competition with other fields in a society that had become structurally differentiated. This occurrence within a broad historical period was, for Bourdieu, comparable with the competition that he had already empirically exposed between the consecrated field of art gallery art and the emergent field of photographic art. It was also comparable *in* history with his own experience in seeking to construct the self-regulating and self-legitimating field of sociology in intellectual competition with the 'external' control exercised by consecrated Philosophy.

Much of the remainder of this article was devoted to a consideration of the nature of the conditions that made possible different degrees of emphasis of intellectual and cultural autonomy – especially the extreme case of the emergence of an ideology of 'art for art's sake'. The main point here, however, is that Bourdieu articulated clearly by reference to the nineteenth century his view that the production and reception of intellectual and cultural artifacts is to be seen as a strategy whereby distinct social groups have sustained their distinction and reproduced themselves. The analysis of the historical development of secular culture is, therefore, no different in kind from the analysis of, for instance, the aristocracy or the clergy.

In the year of the May events, Bourdieu published 'Outline of a sociological theory of art perception'. The article was an attempt to understand sociologically the ways in which we respond in the present to works of art of the past which, as Bourdieu had already argued, were themselves the products of a reciprocal process of production and reception in history. As in *La Reproduction* which was to follow in 1970, Bourdieu here advances his argument by a set of propositions, beginning with the statement that 'Any art perception involves a conscious or unconscious deciphering operation . . . '[50] followed immediately by a characterisation of the situation which Iser had regarded as a 'structural impossibility' and which Bourdieu labels later as an 'unrecognized special case':

1.1. An act of deciphering unrecognized as such, immediate and adequate 'comprehension' is possible and effective only in the special case in which the cultural code which makes the act of deciphering possible is immediately and completely mastered by the observer (in the form of cultivated ability or inclination) and merges with the cultural code which has rendered the work perceived possible.[51]

Bourdieu posits first of all the hypothetical extreme case of a communicative process in which the meaning received is identical with the meaning offered. He does this in order to assert that this (impossible) harmony would be the consequence of the identity of codes of production and reception rather than any intuitive empathy between a producer and a receiver. This extreme case shows that Bourdieu applies to the process of perception the same two-tiered approach as he does to the process of production. Socioeconomically conditioned receivers have to 'log on' to the codes to which authors were 'logged on' in producing their works. Since, however, as Iser recognised, the perfect matching of codes of production and reception negates communication, the actual situation is always one of partial misunderstanding. As Bourdieu puts it:

> . . . the illusion of immediate comprehension leads to an illusory comprehension based on a mistaken code. In the absence of perception that the works are coded, and coded in another code, one unconsciously applies the code which is good for everyday perception, for the deciphering of familiar objects, to works in a foreign tradition . . . [52]

Alien codes can be learnt, and Bourdieu's second set of propositions in 'Outline of a sociological theory of art perception' relate to the gradations of perception within codes rather than to the categoral misapplication of codes. He writes: 'Any deciphering operation requires a more or less complex code which has been more or less completely mastered.'[53] And he claims that here, again, sociological observation is useful because, through it,

> . . . it is possible to reveal, effectively realized, forms of perception corresponding to the different levels which theoretical analysis frames by an abstract distinction. Any cultural asset, from cookery to dodecaphonic music by way of the Wild West film, can be a subject for apprehension ranging from the simple, actual sensation to scholarly appreciation.[54]

The spectrum of apprehension ranges from one which deploys 'art competence' to one which deploys 'artistic competence'. Art competence, Bourdieu says, ' . . . can be provisionally defined as the preliminary knowledge of the possible divisions into complementary classes of a universe of representations . . .'[55] Art objects can be classified in accordance with the dominant classification systems of the day (Impressionist, post-Impressionist, Cubist, Surrealist or whatever) or by reference to everyday classification systems whereby objects *in* pictures are apprehended by reference to the dominant classification system of 'real' objects that they are taken to represent. The first approach displays specific 'artistic' competence. Bourdieu gives the following example of the distinction he is making:

> In the first case the beholder is paying attention to the *manner of treating* the leaves or the clouds, that is to say to the stylistic indications, *locating* the possibility realized, characteristic of one class of works, by reference to the universe of stylistic

possibilities; in the other case, he is treating the leaves or the clouds as indications or signals associated, according to the logic set forth above, with significations transcendent to the representation itself ('that's a poplar', 'that's a storm').[56]

The degree of art competence of a person is, therefore, to be measured by that person's capacity to appreciate the artificiality of artifacts so as to be able to demonstrate artistic competence. The highest level of art competence involves the recognition that the object of apprehension, whether a Cézanne painting or a U2 concert, is a self-referential system which demands to be appreciated in its own terms. It is possible to differentiate sociologically between the codes which people deploy and, according to Bourdieu, equally possible to differentiate sociologically within codes. The degree of mastery of any code is measurable independent of the supposed hierarchical status of that code.

'Outline of a sociological theory of art perception' offered an abstracted summary of the findings of the cultural analysis undertaken by Bourdieu earlier in the 1960s. It provides a theoretical framework for understanding the tendency of *Les Héritiers, Un art moyen* and *L'Amour de l'art*. The questionnaires given to students at the University of Lille and at other French universities at the beginning of the decade had provided information from which Bourdieu could correlate the artistic competence of the students with their socioeconomic condition. Questions were posed in respect of a range of cultural forms and each separate form was represented by a complete spectrum of practitioners. In effect, students were being asked to show their capacity to distinguish between cultural codes and to make classifications within them. The conclusion of *Les Héritiers* was that those with low art competence or, to use the significantly different expression coined there, low 'cultural capital', should be enabled to acquire higher competence. It should be the function of the educational system to initiate the uninitiated into the dominant scholarly culture. This, too, was the conclusion of *L'Amour de l'art* – it should be the function of schools to inculcate the codes which would thus enable all people to achieve some mastery of the codes deployed by the producers of the artifacts exhibited in museums and art galleries.

The conclusion of 'Outline of a sociological theory of art perception' makes the case for the function of the school:

> Only an institution like the school, the specific function of which is methodically to develop or create the inclinations which produce an educated man and which lay the foundations, quantitatively and consequently qualitatively, of a constant and intense pursuit of culture, could offset (at least partially) the initial disadvantage of those who do not receive from their family circle the encouragement to undertake cultural activities and the competence presupposed in any dissertation on works . . .[57]

Whereas the approach of the Konstanz School required the initiation of students of literature into the historical field of literature in order that they could become valid readers, Bourdieu still saw it to be the function of schools in society to initiate *all* students into *all* the artificially constructed cultural codes in operation in that society. Shortly after the publication of 'Outline of a sociological theory of art perception' Bourdieu was to embark on a revision of *Les Héritiers* which was to be published in 1970 as *La Reproduction*. The subtitle of the French text was *Éléments pour une théorie du système d'enseignement*, but the English translation of 1977 more accurately captured its spirit by making the full title: *Reproduction in Education, Society and Culture*. It had become clear that although schools might improve the artistic competence of pupils, they did so from a perspective which assumed the supremacy of some cultural codes over others. Schools were not involved in improving competence which might be transferable between codes but in sustaining the hierarchy of codes. Whilst apparently raising the competence and consciousness of all pupils, the pedagogic process of communication within the dominant cultural code was reproducing the social differences which were manifest in different codes. As codes of perception came to be seen as institutionalised 'fields', schooling itself represented one mechanism of codification within a society conceived as the location of competing 'fields'.

The initial proposition of *La Reproduction* in respect of 'the twofold arbitrariness of pedagogic action' is well known. Bourdieu states: 'All *pedagogic action* (PA) is, objectively, symbolic violence insofar as it is the imposition of a cultural arbitrary by an arbitary power.'[58] The 'gloss' which follows is highly significant in clarifying that the education system is now seen only as a particular manifestation of general social behaviour:

> The propositions which follow (up to and including those of the third degree) refer to all PAs, whether exerted by all the educated members of a social formation or group (diffuse education), by the family-group members to whom the culture of a group or class allots this task (family education) or by the system of agents explicitly mandated for this purpose by an institution directly or indirectly, exclusively or partially educative in function (institutionalized education), and unless otherwise stated, whether that PA seeks to reproduce the cultural arbitrary of the dominant or of the dominated classes. In other words, the range of these propositions is defined by the fact that they apply to any social formation, understood as a system of power relations and sense relations between groups or classes. It follows that in the first three sections, we have refrained from extensive use of examples drawn from the case of a dominant, school PA, to avoid even implicitly suggesting any restrictions on the validity of the propositions concerning all PAs.[59]

This contention that reproduction occurs within all autonomous fields or structures allows Bourdieu to specify the characteristics of the educational system:

> *Every* institutionalized educational system (ES) *owes the specific characteristics of its structure and functioning to the fact that, by the means proper to the institution, it has to produce and reproduce the institutional conditions whose existence*

and persistence (self-reproduction of the system) are necessary both to the exercise of its essential function of inculcation and to the fulfilment of its function of reproducing a cultural arbitrary which it does not produce (cultural reproduction), the reproduction of which contributes to the reproduction of the relations between the groups or classes (social reproduction).[60]

What followed from Bourdieu's 'placing' of schooling was that he elevated sociological awareness into a substitute for the traditional effect of schooling. The task of the sociologist is to understand the mechanisms of production and reception, to understand that they conceal social reproduction, and, by that understanding, to be more effective than schooling in making all cultural competences accessible to everyone. The task of the practising sociologist (who is explicitly not in the business of reproducing the science which he does not produce) is to produce a scientific analysis of all the various strategies of reproduction within society – just one of which would be the educational reproduction of social scientific knowledge which the practitioner might repudiate. As Bourdieu put the situation at the beginning of 'Cultural reproduction and social reproduction': 'The specific role of the sociology of education is assumed once it has established itself as the science of the relations between cultural reproduction and social reproduction.'[61] Or, as he might more clearly have stated, once the sociology of education has established that it is not exclusively concerned with the analysis of the subset of social operations which is labelled 'educational'. This brief for the sociologist entails the generation of 'The science of the reproduction of structures, understood as a system of objective relations which impart their relational properties to individuals whom they pre-exist and survive . . .'[62]

Although Bourdieu's thinking has some affinity with that of Jauss and Iser, his emphasis on the production of such a science of the reproduction of structures subsumes both his own interpretation of Marxist 'production' and 'reception' theories. Bourdieu argues that cultural fields are produced by human agents. They do not have a necessary existence. They are constructed or generated in history. Within these fields, a reciprocal process of production and reception develops. Artists internalise an 'implied reader' in order to secure recognition within their field of production. Whereas, however, for Iser, the process of current engagement with past texts can disclose transcendence, Bourdieu simply sees the historical communication between authors and their implied readers as the mechanism by which they established the value of their texts, and, by doing so, perpetuated a field which would historically reproduce itself in such a way that future participants in the field would regard those texts as canonical. After being concerned with the point at which any cultural field is historically generated, Bourdieu's interest then transfers to the present status of that field in its sedimented form. The effect of Jauss's approach was to make the study of the internal self-reproduction of the field of literary criticism one which would become constitutive of legitimate textual interpretation in the present. For Bourdieu, this would have been an ultimately sophisticated form of cultural reproduction. Rather than use cultural reproduction as the basis for current cultural criticism, Bourdieu, instead, has tried to expose the extent to which such forms of literary critical incestuousness perpetuate a social reproduction which is socially exclusive in the present.

Summary

I have suggested that Bourdieu's notion of 'production' derived from the amalgamation of his observations of the behaviour of Algerian tribes with his interpretation of Marx. Using Marx's representation of precapitalist society, Bourdieu was able to argue that the economic structures of 'primitive' societies, as much as their symbolic, legislative, political or religious structures, owed their existence to their function in sustaining social coherence. Emanating from social being, their over-riding role was to maintain a primary social organisation. Combating both those structuralists who sought to analyse structures formally as free-standing entities, and those 'Marxist' structuralists who sought to explain superstructures as the direct functions of material modes of production, Bourdieu argued that individuals in society are productive agents who produce the structures they need to safeguard the originating social condition. These individual agents receive and biologically internalise structures which are inherited from the production of previous generations, and, in turn, they take steps to conserve these inherited structures by reproducing them in future generations. There is, therefore, a process of reproduction which occurs intergenerationally *within* structures, but it must not be forgotten that these structures themselves are not absolute. They are the constantly modifying objective mechanisms by which individuals in society renew themselves and preserve the fabric of their society. Social reproduction is the hidden agenda of all forms of cultural reproduction.

Throughout the 1960s, Bourdieu articulated this position by reference to his understanding of the 'undifferentiated' social organisation of Algerian tribes – a societal organisation which extended outwards in concentric circles from a basic, domestic unit without the disruptive intervention of rival seats of power and authority. Customs which were handed down in the family were expressed without mediation in the customary practices of the whole society. The *habitus* was the mechanism by which the values of one generation were embodied in those of the next. In undifferentiated societies there was very little need for these transmitted values to be objectified or articulated at all. There is always the possibility that objective structures become self-fulfilling and, by a process of continuous intergenerational reproduction, historically become alienated from the social needs which they first satisfied, but it is a characteristic of undifferentiated society that structures are not necessary. Bourdieu attempted to transpose insights derived from his Algerian experience to analyse the 'differentiated' organisation of mainland France. At first, the French educational system assisted theoretically in this transposition because Bourdieu regarded it as an institutionalised *habitus*. The school system was seen as a catalyst in the process of social reproduction. It was a functional substitute for the family unit of undifferentiated societies. By compulsorily receiving all children, the modern state schooling system accommodated all the domestic *habitus* in play in society – all the attitudes and values transmitted intersubjectively and intergenerationally between parents and children at home. At the same time, the schooling system – through its curriculum and the associated educational qualifications – represented the range of different, objective structures in differentiated society which now were abstracted from the domestic context. It represented intellectual divisions of knowledge and the distinctions amongst professional and occupational structures. The schooling system was seen to mediate between the subjective and the objective where, in undifferentiated society, no mediation had been thought necessary. As a national, state-controlled system, the school system mediated between the totality of society and the totality of all individual social agents. As a state-financed system, it appeared to fulfil the function of precapitalist reproduction by operating as an autonomous system mediating between the primary social sphere and the secondary structures which society had historically generated to preserve itself.

To use the terms employed by Bourdieu in 'Outline of a sociological theory of art perception', the schooling system would render itself obsolete in the 'unrecognised special case' where immediate comprehension existed as a result of the identity between the codes of production and reception. In this hypothetical instance, differentiated society would have reverted to an undifferentiated state. The real situation in differentiated society is, however, that all members of society display varying degrees of mastery over the codes in which their social heritage is expressed. From the moment when codes first become objectified, communication ceases to be natural and becomes acquired. From that same moment, there is room for misunderstanding and misinterpretation but, equally, there is scope for learning what is not known naturally.

Cultural production is one social phenomenon amongst many which suffers the consequences of the transition from undifferentiated to differentiated social organisation. In the undifferentiated situation, the production of 'art' is inseparable from the production of ritual or the production of crops and, indeed, these and other forms of productivity are inextricably linked. There is not a discrete 'cultural' sphere. From the moment when this functional coherence of forms collapses, individual agents are forced no longer to act as simply social agents but as social agents who need to produce in conformity with the norms of the objectified structures which have acquired status in their society. The complete actions of individuals are no longer simply expressions of their domestic *habitus*. Actions in differentiated society become more complicated. Individuals act within the prescribed framework of pre-existing structures. To produce culturally now involves the recognition of the existence of a cultural field of production. The primary social condition of individuals no longer disposes them to be productive absolutely for the benefit of an automatically coherent whole society but, instead, it predisposes them to be productive only within those fields of production which are accessible to them.

The mechanisms which enable individuals to become culturally productive are mirrored by those which enable them to become culturally receptive. In an undifferentiated state, the codes of production and reception are identical and communication occurs without the interference of articulated structural meaning. The transition to differentiation introduces codal disparities and it also introduces the possibility of historical change. At the primary social level, individuals biogenetically reproduce the dispositions which they inherit. Varying original dispositions at first caused the generation of differentiated structures and codes. These reflected the differences within the population. From that initiating point onwards, however, structures acquired a reproductive life of their own precisely so as to consolidate their distinction from other structures and to construct a cumulatively artificial detachment from those capacities which are genetically transmitted. History became possible when social beings constructed the possibility of intergenerational cultural change that was separate from genetic mutation. The biological and the cultural interact. It is not that biological and cultural evolution proceed independently. The reproduction of social beings constantly activates the interaction of the biological and the cultural, but, at any historical moment, there is a tension for individuals to choose whether to position themselves socially by accentuating their 'natural' capacities and, therefore, by constructing original cultural forms expressive of those capacities, or by sustaining commitment to those 'consecrated' forms of culture which they already possess and which offer a ready-made social distinction.

Bourdieu has moved towards a form of productivity which amalgamates sociological craftsmanship with artistic creativity. He has himself chosen to express the 'natural' rather than sustain the 'consecrated', to be engaged with social change rather than reflectively to apprehend it. Rejecting the notion of the artist or intellectual as the privileged producer of social change, he has opted to place his understanding of the reciprocity of production and reception within a process of continuous reproduction. His sociological studies of cultural practitioners have informed the process by which he has now come to present his sociology as art.

Notes

1. P. Bourdieu (1968) 'Structuralism and theory of sociological knowledge', *Social Research*, 35, 682.
2. P. Bourdieu, 'Fieldwork in Philosophy' in *In Other Words op cit* 3.
3. D. McLellan (ed.) (1977) *Karl Marx, Selected Writings*, Oxford, Oxford University Press, 388.
4. *Ibid.*, 389.

5. L. Baxandall and S. Morawski (1973) *Marx and Engels on Literature and Art. A Selection of Writings* (with an introduction by S. Morawski), St Louis, MI, Milwaukee, WI, Telos Press, 51.
6. See Chapter 4.
7. P. Bourdieu with J.D. Reynaud (1966) 'Une sociologie de l'action est-elle possible?', *Revue française de sociologie*, VII, 4, 508–17, translated as 1974, 'Is a sociology of action possible?', in A. Giddens ed. *Positivism and Sociology*, London, Heinemann Educational Books, 101–13.
8. A. Touraine (1965) *Sociologie de l'action*, Paris, Éditions du Seuil.
9. Bourdieu, 'Une sociologie', 511; 'Is a sociology', 105. The quotation is from Touraine, *Sociologie*, 120.
10. Bourdieu, 'Une sociologie', 511; 'Is a sociology', 104.
11. Bourdieu, 'Une sociologie', 511; 'Is a sociology', 105. The quotation is from Touraine, *Sociologie*, 121.
12. Bourdieu, 'Une sociologie', 517; 'Is a sociology', 112.
13. P. Macherey (1965) 'À propos du processus d'exposition du "Capital",' in L. Althusser ed. *Lire le Capital*. Vol. I, Paris, François Maspero, 215.
14. *Ibid.*
15. *Ibid.*
16. *Ibid.*, 216.
17. Expressed in P. Bourdieu (1976) 'La lecture de Marx, ou quelques remarques critiques à propos de "quelques critiques à propos de "Lire le Capital"' ', *Actes de la recherche en sciences sociales*, 5–6, 65–79. Bourdieu writes (p. 69):

   . . . it isn't just a question of understanding Marx better than Marx himself, of superceding Marx (the young) in the name of Marx (the old), of correcting the 'pre-Marxist' Marx which survives in Marx in the name of the really Marxist Marx that the more Marxist than Marx 'reading' produces . . . By constituting the theoretical reading of theoretical texts within scientific practice, philosophy is relieved, by appropriation or by negation, of the competition from the 'so-called social sciences' and the philosophers, guardians or guarantors of the store-room, are restored to the function (to which they have always laid claim) of judges 'of the last resort' of scientific practice (which, by the same token, they render dispensable).

18. P. Macherey (1978) *A Theory of Literary Production*, London, Routledge & Kegan Paul (trans. of P. Macherey (1966) *Pour une théorie de la production littéraire*, Paris, Librairie François Maspero, 3).
19. See the discussion of P. Bourdieu *et al.* (1965) *Un art moyen. Essai sur les usages sociaux de la photographie*, Paris, Éditions de Minuit, 17–28; *Les Règles de l'art. Genèse et structure du champ littéraire*, Paris, Éditions du Seuil, 9–14.
20. Macherey, *A Theory*, 6–7.
21. *Ibid.*, 40.
22. *Ibid.*, 52.
23. *Ibid.*, 53.
24. *Ibid.*
25. See, for instance, the constant presence of the influence of Bachelard and Canguilhem in P. Bourdieu *et al.* (1968) *Le Métier de sociologue*, Paris, Mouton-Bordas, and compare with P. Macherey (1964) 'La philosophie de la science de Georges Canguilhem. Epistémologie et histoire des sciences (presented by L. Althusser)', *La Pensée*, 113, 50–74. For another indication of the influence of Canguilhem, see Foucault's introduction to G. Canguilhem, *On the Normal and the Pathological*, 1978.
26. D. Lecourt (1975) *Marxism and Epistemology. Bachelard, Canguilhem and Foucault* (trans. B. Brewster, Introduction to the English edition), London, New Left Books, 8.

27. J. Jurt (1989) 'De l'analyse immanente à l'histoire sociale de la littérature. À propos des recherches littéraires en Allemagne depuis 1945', *Actes de la recherche en sciences sociales*, 78, 94–101.
28. W. Iser (1985) *L'Acte de lecture. Théorie de l'effet esthétique* (ed. P. Mardaga), Brussels, Mardaga, 6.
29. *Ibid.*
30. H.R. Jauss (1978) 'L'histoire de la littérature: un défi au théorie littéraire', in H.R. Jauss *Pour une esthétique de la réception* (trans. from the German by C. Maillard), Paris, Gallimard, 21.
31. *Ibid.*, 24.
32. *Ibid.*, 47.
33. *Ibid.*
34. A footnote to the Preface of the English translation comments:

> The German '*Wirkung*' comprises both effect and response, without the psychological connotations of the English word 'response'. 'Effect' is at times too weak a term to convey what is meant by '*Wirkung*', and 're-sponse' is a little confusing. Confronted by Scylla and Charybdis I have finally opted for 'response'.

See W. Iser (1978) *The Act of Reading. A Theory of Aesthetic Response*, Baltimore, MD, and London, Johns Hopkins University Press, ix.
35. *Ibid.*, x.
36. *Ibid.*, 27.
37. *Ibid.*, 28.
38. *Ibid.*, 28–9.
39. *Ibid.*, 30.
40. *Ibid.*, 34. For Iser's exemplification of the use of 'the implied reader' in crit-icism, see W. Iser, *The Implied Reader: Patterns of Communications in Prose Fiction from Bunyan to Beckett*, Baltimore and London, Johns Hopkins University Press.
41. Iser, *The Act*, 36. Iser refers specifically to Manfred Naumann *et al.* (1975) *Gesellschaft – Literatur – Lesen. Literaturrezeption in theoretischer Sicht*, Berlin and Weimar, and he refers to his own critique of this book, 'Im Lichte der Kritik', in R. Warning ed. (1975) *Rezeptionsästhetik. Theorie und Praxis*, Munich, 335–41, and also to Jauss's critique also in R. Warning (pp. 343ff). For a discussion of the differences between the development of 'reception theory' in West and East Germany, see A. Billaz (1981) 'La problématique de la "réception" dans les deux Allemagnes', *Revue d'histoire de la littérature française*, 81, 109–20.
42. Iser, *The Act*, 38.
43. C.F. Graumann (1960) *Grundlagen einer Phänomenologie und Psychologie der Perspektivität*, Berlin, 14, quoted in Iser, *The Act*, 38.
44. Iser, *The Act*, 38.
45. *Ibid.*, xi.
46. W. Iser (1989) *Prospecting. From Reader Response to Literary Anthropology*, Baltimore, MD, and London, Johns Hopkins University Press.
47. P. Bourdieu (1971) 'Intellectual field and creative project', in M.F.D. Young ed. *Knowledge and Control: New Directions for the Sociology of Education*, London, Collier-Macmillan, 162.
48. L.L. Schucking (1966) *The Sociology of Literary Taste* (trans. B. Battershaw), London, Routledge. Schucking's work relates to the sociology of literature and art developing in the late 1920s and early 1930s at the Frankfurt Institute of Social Research.
49. P. Bourdieu, 'Intellectual field and creative project', op. cit., 162.
50. P. Bourdieu (1968) 'Outline of a sociological theory of art perception', *International Social Science Journal*, XX, 4, 589; republished in P. Bourdieu (1993)

The Field of Cultural Production. Essays on Art and Literature (ed. and intro. by R. Johnson), Oxford, Polity Press, 215.
51. Bourdieu, 'Outline', 589.
52. Bourdieu, 'Outline', 590; *The Field*, 216.
53. *Ibid*.
54. Bourdieu, 'Outline', 593; *The Field*, 220.
55. Bourdieu, 'Outline', 595; *The Field*, 221.
56. *Ibid*.
57. Bourdieu, 'Outline', 607; *The Field*, 233.
58. P. Bourdieu and J.-C. Passeron (1977) *Reproduction in Education, Society and Culture* (trans. R. Nice), London and Beverly Hills, CA, Sage, 5.
59. *Ibid*., 5–6.
60. *Ibid*., 54.
61. P. Bourdieu (1973) 'Cultural reproduction and social reproduction', in R. Brown ed. *Knowledge, Education and Cultural Change*, London, Tavistock, 71.
62. *Ibid*.

Part III

THE CASE STUDIES

---

4 Flaubert and the social ambivalence of literary invention

In one of the earliest works on Flaubert – first published in 1899 only 19 years after the novelist's death – Émile Faguet began his study in the following way:

> Gustave Flaubert was born at Rouen on the 12th December 1821.
>
> His father, the son of a veterinary surgeon of Nogent-sur-Seine, after studying medicine in Paris, had settled down at Rouen, where he had become the highly esteemed and even celebrated Dr. Flaubert, surgeon-in-chief of the Hôtel-Dieu Hospital, where he lived.
>
> His mother, Anne Justine Caroline Fleuriot, was born at Pont l'Évêque in Calvados, and was, through her mother, connected with the oldest families in Lower Normandy. Gustave Flaubert was therefore a Champenois through his father, and a Norman on his mother's side. Thus there is no special induction to be drawn from his descent concerning his disposition and the turn of his mind.[1]

The ghost of Taine can be glimpsed behind these opening remarks. Faguet feels obliged to itemise Flaubert's ethnic pedigree whilst, in his use of the word 'induction', simultaneously disowning both the attempt to make literary analysis scientific and the substantive effort to explain the creativity of an individual by reference to ethnicity. Instead, Faguet developed a different explanatory account. He represented literary history as a continuing oscillation between periods of 'romanticism' and periods of 'realism' in much the same way as, in England, Matthew Arnold had argued that there were always alternating periods of 'creativity' and 'criticism'.[2] Flaubert's situation within this historical dialectic was offered as an explanation of the duality of his personality. The constructed categories of literary and social history were transposed into psychological categories which explained the characteristics of Flaubert's literary production.

Faguet described the secondary properties of 'romanticism' in the following way: 'A taste for sadness and mystery, for the lugubrious and the gruesome, for exotism, for the East and for dazzling light – such are indeed the elements which make up the soul of a Romanticist.'[3] But the primary, defining property of 'romanticism' is only defined antithetically: 'The basis of Romanticism is a horror of Realism and an ardent desire to escape from it. Romanticism is essentially romantic; it does away with Observation, which means submission to the real object, and with Reason, which merely starts from reality . . .'[4] According to Faguet, Flaubert internalised the objective moment of transition from romanticism to realism:

> It is sufficiently known that Flaubert was at one and the same time a Romanticist and a Realist, as if, coming into literary life in the middle of the nineteenth century, he had wished to present in himself an epitome of the forty years which preceded him and of the forty years which were to follow.[5]

Flaubert, so Faguet's argument continues, possessed all the secondary properties of romanticism but not its primary opposition to the real. Thus, concludes Faguet, there

> . . . developed and grew that singular realistic Romanticist who was Flaubert. Which was the real man? Truly I do not know; does one ever know, in a complex nature, what constitutes its real basis? Diverse tendencies either strive with each other, neutralise each other, succeed in combining harmoniously, or else give way to each other in turn.[6]

In Flaubert's case, it was alternation which maintained the balance of personality. 'Invariably, a romantic work comes after a realistic one and *vice versa*'[7] and, hence, Faguet proceeded to discuss *Salammbô* and *La Tentation de Saint Antoine* as 'romantic' novels and *Madame Bovary*, *L'Éducation sentimentale* and *Bouvard et Pécuchet* as 'realist' ones.

Faguet's study represented one of the earliest attempts to comprehend the diversity of Flaubert's work. From 1865 until his death Flaubert had been celebrated as 'a marvellous, unrivalled realist'[8] who had dabbled aberrantly with works of imagination, but it was the first publication of his *Correspondance*, beginning, in 1884, with his *Lettres à George Sand*, which had imposed the need to come to terms with the whole personality of the novelist. Lanson, however, resisted the temptations of psychological explanation. In the sixth part of his *Histoire de la littérature française* (1894), devoted to the contemporary period, and in a section treating 'Le naturalisme, 1850–1890', Lanson offered the following summary of Flaubert's significance:

> Between the two schools – of romanticism and naturalism – is situated Gustave Flaubert who follows on from the one and establishes the other, correcting the one by the other and combining in himself the qualities of both – from which is derived exactly the perfection of his work. At the unique moment when romanticism becomes naturalism, Flaubert writes two or three novels which are the most substantial that have been produced this century.[9]

This summary is supported in a footnote by the barest of biographical details: 'Biography: G. Flaubert (1821–1880), born at Rouen, the son of a surgeon, passed most of his life at his property at Croisset, near to Rouen. He was a great worker: very bourgeois in his way of life with a romantic hatred of the bourgeois.'[10] The ingredients of Faguet's analysis are here deployed differently. The supposed transition from romanticism to what Lanson calls 'naturalism' is one which was effected by Flaubert as he 'corrected' and 'combined' the opposing tendencies. In Lanson's view, Flaubert inserted himself into the unique moment of historical transition. His work was the consequence of his sensitivity to his social position rather than the expression of a personality deduced retrospectively by critics from a retrospectively constructed historical dialectic between romanticism and realism. Eschewing psychologism, Lanson simply draws attention to Flaubert's social ambivalence *vis-à-vis* the 'bourgeoisie' but, in his short discussions of the major novels, he confines himself to an *explication de textes* without extraneous reference either to Flaubert's psychological traits or his social position. Of *L'Éducation sentimentale*, for instance, Lanson concluded: 'The profundity and the sorrow of the work lies in this flow of a life *where nothing happens*, and, *without anything happening*, the final sinking of all the hopes of youth in the silly, crass and monotonous existence of the small town bourgeois.'[11]

It was because Lanson treated texts as the constructs of authors rather than as the expressions of their personalities that he was able to perceive the difference of intention between the 'realist' and 'naturalist' novels of the second half of the nineteenth century. In an article of 1895 entitled 'La littérature et la science', Lanson offered a historical sketch in which he outlined the changing relations between science and literature. These were not, however, inevitable oscillations but fluctuations arising from the competition between intellectuals. In the late seventeenth century and for most of the eighteenth 'the scientific spirit made itself master of literature to the detriment of art'[12] or, to clarify, a scientific paradigm dominated thought such that literature was reduced to mere embellishment and ceased to be regarded as itself a medium for legitimate thinking. Romanticism reversed this domination but, according to Lanson, the scientific paradigm had regained control by the second half of the nineteenth century. Whereas the dominant scientific influence in the seventeenth century had been mathematics, it was now the physical and natural sciences, giving rise to the term 'naturalism'. As Lanson succinctly puts it: '. . . just as the mathematician Descartes supplied to Boileau the principle of his literary theory so now the physiologist Claude Bernard supplies his to Monsieur Zola.'[13]

For Lanson, it was the adoption of a scientific paradigm that differentiated naturalism from realism and made the new term necessary. He defended his use of the new term, in opposition to Faguet, in a footnote:

> It is important to distinguish the novel with a scientific intention from the picturesque realism which preceded it. We must reserve the word realism for that small school which, following painting in particular, aimed less to give scientific form to the real than to offer an aesthetic imitation of it. The 'naturalists' have at least had pretensions which realism has never claimed for itself.[14]

It followed that Lanson was able to claim that Flaubert had 'expounded the case of Madame Bovary like a lecture in a dissecting theatre'[15] and that *Madame Bovary* altogether was a masterpiece of 'exact, subtle and penetrating psychology'.[16] Lanson's understanding of the 'naturalist' intention, applied to the work of Flaubert, was, therefore, that the novels should not be regarded either as expressive of the personality of the author or as imitative of the reality which he had observed. On the contrary, Lanson quoted Zola in confirmation of his interpretation of the naturalist intention. A novel, said Zola, '. . . is not an *observation*: it is an *experiment*. I set up my experiment through conceiving an action which moves my characters; I study the modifications which the initial temperament undergoes in given milieux and conditions. That's what Claude Bernard does in his laboratory'.[17]

There is a sense in which the literary critical method which Lanson institutionalised at the Sorbonne was itself an extension of the programme of the naturalists. Certainly it was the general view that Lanson's method destroyed the 'soul' of literature by its meticulous textual dissection. The ideological opposition to the Nouvelle Sorbonne had its influence on the interpretation of Flaubert. Albert Thibaudet published a book in defence of Bergsonism in 1923 just one year after publishing his influential study of Flaubert entitled *Gustave Flaubert 1821–1880. Sa vie – ses romans – son style*. The form and the content of Thibaudet's criticism was Bergsonian. Thibaudet's biographer (and ex-student) – Alfred Glauser – deliberately echoed Bergson's *L'Évolution créatrice* in calling his study *Albert Thibaudet et la critique créatrice* and the biography follows Thibaudet's creative career with almost no reference to the factual circumstances of his life, representing his criticism as an extension of his youthful poetic inclinations. Thibaudet had the capacity to animate and be animated by those authors whom he studied and, as such, was the only critic since Sainte-Beuve to realise the potential of the critical vocation. Glauser claimed that Thibaudet was the only critic '. . . who has lived with others in such a continuous way, and whose genius has been precisely to let others speak, but to let them speak with originality as a result of his being present in his discussion with others with the whole force of his own originality'.[18]

There was, in other words, a subterranean creative force underlying his 'critical' engagement with the work of others, a force which released new creative energies. The metaphor is apt here because, faced with the dualities of Flaubert's personality and of his literary production posited by the critical tradition, Thibaudet remarked of *La Tentation de Saint Antoine* and *Madame Bovary*: 'If there is no continuity between the two books . . . there remains the continuity of the life of Flaubert, the intelligible transition beneath the appearances of fracture, the deep folds which explain the geological unity of two separate massifs.'[19]

Rejecting the historical dialectic imposed by Faguet on Flaubert's life, Thibaudet identified an unconscious continuity, or duration, through time. Having asserted that 'The psychology of Flaubert during the composition of *Madame Bovary* is one of the most interesting literary problems which can be posed'[20] Thibaudet presented the popular view that in *Madame Bovary* there was 'less of Flaubert than of counter-Flaubert'[21] and cited in evidence Descharmes's argument in *Flaubert avant 1857* that Flaubert had '. . . forged artificially a nature opposed to the one which perhaps heredity and certainly his earliest education . . . had fashioned . . .'[22] For Thibaudet, however, this explanation makes no sense. His specific reaction broadened out into a general critique of the application of psychological explanation which did not acknowledge the dynamic evolution of the personality:

> So long as it has not reached the automatism of old age, the nature of a man modifies constantly and nothing is psychologically more arbitrary nor more false than to cut off in this nature a morsel which is called natural nature and a morsel which is called artificial nature. We live in duration, and to live in duration is to have a present, that is to say a nature which modifies, which we modify from within or which is modified from outside, and a past, that is to say a fixed nature.[23]

Unlike Lanson, Thibaudet was not disposed to see novels as constructs or as laboratories for experimentation. Unlike Lanson again, Thibaudet did not cultivate a scientific detachment from the texts which he interpreted. In the introduction to his book on Flaubert which originated in lectures given at the universities of Uppsala and Geneva, for instance, Thibaudet apologised that these contexts had caused his text to be rather more 'scholarly'[24] than he would have liked. From 1920 until his death in 1936 Thibaudet was the principal literary critic of the *Nouvelle revue française* such that Fowlie has described him as 'practically the official French critic'[25] during this period. He was, therefore, a 'professional critic' which meant that he was neither an 'academic' critic, like Lanson, nor, to use Fowlie's category, a practising 'creative' critic, that is to say a poet or novelist – like Valéry or Gide – whose criticisms were integral parts of their creative activities.

Thibaudet was most certainly not an 'existentialist' critic either but, after his death, it was, nevertheless, Sartre who most pre-eminently sustained the psychological orientation in Flaubert criticism. Simultaneously, as novelist, a 'creative' critic and, as editor of *Les Temps modernes* from 1945, a 'professional' critic, Sartre was, as an existentialist intellectual, least of all an 'academic' critic. Without specific reference to literary production, Sartre had made clear in *L'Imagination* (1936) that, in his view, Bergson's philosophy was just the most recent, plausible manifestation of the varying classical accounts of a representational relationship between the real and the imaginary. The phenomenological psychology which Sartre proposed would dispense with the notion that there is an underlying, autonomously continuous 'personality' that occasionally erupts in apparently contradictory forms. Instead, individuals construct their personalities existentially without reference to any prescribed, unconscious pattern.

It was in *What is Literature?* that Sartre first directly reflected on the relationship between the philosophy he had advanced in *L'Être et le néant* and the practice of writing literature. As a result of asking 'What is writing?' and 'Why write?', Sartre concluded that 'To write is thus both to disclose the world and to offer it as a task to the generosity of the reader'[26] or, in other words, that the process of reading written texts is one which intersubjectively and phenomenologically brings the transcendent into being. It followed, therefore, that in discussing 'For whom does one write?', Sartre should comment:

> And since the freedoms of the author and reader seek and affect each other through a world, it can just as well be said that the author's choice of a certain aspect of the world determines the reader and, vice versa, that it is by choosing his reader that the author decides upon his subject.[27]

Sartre then proceeded to explore the implications of this constituting reciprocity in history. With the emergence in the eighteenth century of the bourgeoisie, those writers who were themselves bourgeois in origin were trapped between class contexts: they still benefited from the patronage of the aristocracy but increasingly it was the socially and politically oppressed bourgeoisie that was 'presenting itself to the writer as a real public'.[28] To cope with this ambivalence, writers, in Sartre's view, 'unclassed' themselves and sought to communicate universal values to all classes. Their unclassed ideology involved the denial of class distinction and, as a result, bourgeois writers were ill-equipped to deal with the nineteenth-century emergence of the proletariat. Literature continued to 'set itself up as being, in principle, independent of any sort of ideology'[29] and it 'had not yet understood that it *was itself* ideology'.[30] The consequence was that writers believed that they could, independently, write about anything. Here we approach Sartre's explanation of the apparent discontinuity of Flaubert's writing. Referring to *Madame Bovary* and *Salammbô*, Sartre illustrated his general point by reference to Flaubert:

> There was no doubt about the fact that one might write felicitously about the condition of the working class; but the choice of this subject depended upon circumstances, upon a free decision of the artist. One day one might talk about a provincial bourgeoisie, another day, about Carthaginian mercenaries.[31]

Flaubert was able to shift readily between 'romantic' and 'realist' writing because, for all his rejection of bourgeois values, he was, nevertheless, resisting the inevitable rise of the proletariat. Flaubert's romanticism and his realism were both equally inauthentic.

It is clear that Sartre was hostile to Flaubert in 1947. In a footnote to *What is Literature?*, Sartre offered eleven quotations from Flaubert's correspondance to argue that he had not been unfair to Flaubert in suggesting that Flaubert had been contemptuous of the working classes.[32] Sartre wrote with such feeling because he was conscious of himself being trapped within the same class ambivalence that was the legacy of the late nineteenth century. As a bourgeois writer he had himself already produced novels which showed contempt for bourgeois values, but, still like Flaubert, Sartre had in practice resisted the relentless progression of class struggle. The question, therefore, which he posed for himself in the final chapter of *What is Literature?* – 'Situation of the writer in 1947' – was: 'How can one make onself a man in, by, and for history?'[33] and, as a writer, he was acutely aware that the techniques of novel-writing which seemed to be at his disposal possessed characteristics which 'are rigorously opposed to our designs'.[34] Sartre was, therefore, a man in search of new forms of expression. Of the question posed and of other problems, he wrote: 'We can rigorously attack these problems in the abstract by philosophical reflection. But if we want to live them . . .'[35] and the *Critique of Dialectical Reason* demonstrated this tension between Sartre's desire to reflect about the relationship between existentialism and Marxism and his desire to do and be what he was writing about. Consideration of the life and work of Flaubert began to fulfil a new function in Sartre's thinking.

Questions de méthode was published as a separate text in 1960 although it had originally been intended that it should be published with the *Critique de la raison dialectique*. Although in *What is Literature?* Sartre had posited existentially that writing sets up an encounter between writer and readers, he had then proceeded to offer a history of French literature which supposed that the nature of these writer/reader encounters and, hence, the nature of literature itself, varied as a consequence of changing class relations. An existentialist account of writing was added to an essentially 'vulgar' Marxist interpretation of historical change. *Questions de méthode* sought, instead, to insert the writer within the process of historical change so that it is the encounter between writer and readers which *actualises* historical change. Taking our understanding of Flaubert as an example, Sartre writes: 'Contemporary Marxism shows, for example, that the realism of Flaubert is in reciprocal symbolic relation with the social and political evolution of the petite bourgeoisie of the Second Empire. But it *never* shows the genesis of this perspectival reciprocity.'[36] Marxism is content to say that Flaubert had to live and write he did because he 'belonged to the bourgeoisie',[37] but Sartre's main concern is now to ask what 'belonging to' and 'bourgeoisie' might mean in the particular circumstances of Flaubert's life. Vulgar Marxism can be redeemed with the assistance of psychoanalytical study because it is psychoanalysis which allows us '. . . to study in depth the process by which a child, groping about blindly in the dark, comes to try to play out, uncomprehendingly, the social person that adults impose upon it'.[38]

It follows for Sartre that it is no longer possible to attempt to explain works by reference to a preconstructed social 'structure', but only to understand them immanently as elements in the process by which writers restructure the reality which they experience. In Sartre's own words:

From now onwards it becomes impossible to link *Madame Bovary* directly to the socio-political structure and to the evolution of the petite bourgeoisie; it will become necessary to relate the work to the present reality as it was lived by Flaubert as a consequence of his childhood [*à travers son enfance*].[39]

Having already published biographies of Genet and Baudelaire, it is no surprise, therefore, that, in 1966, Sartre published in *Les Temps modernes* two extracts[40] from what was to become his biographical study of Flaubert entitled *L'Idiot de la famille* in which, in laborious detail, he sought to analyse the psychological influences in Flaubert's youth which caused him to live always in 'bad faith' – always to condemn the bourgeoisie without ever ceasing to be bourgeois.

In writing about Flaubert, Sartre was not simply illustrating his new analytical method in practice. His work on Flaubert became a substantive part of his own work. In an interview given in 1970, Sartre said:

> A writer is always a man who has more or less chosen the imaginary: he needs a certain dosage of fiction. For my part, I find it in my work on Flaubert, which one can, moreover, consider a novel. I even wish people to say that it is a *true* novel.[41]

Sartre's analysis of Flaubert's project lost its 'objective' status and, in an Hegelian manner, became incorporated in his own endeavour to become a significant participant in dialectical historical progression. By comprehending Flaubert, Sartre considered that he was able to transcend the past and contribute, as a totalising agent, to a future in which previous conditions would become superceded.

Bourdieu's analyses of Flaubert also operate simultaneously on these two levels: Bourdieu wishes to oppose Sartre's account of what was happening in history and, as part of the same movement, to oppose Sartre's view of what he was himself doing in history by formulating that account.[42] It was in 'Intellectual field and creative project' – published in *Les Temps modernes* less than six months after Sartre's essays on Flaubert – that Bourdieu first brought the case of Flaubert into his argument. Bourdieu quotes a passage from *What is Literature?* in which Sartre contended that 'There are some qualities that come to us entirely from the judgements of other people'[43] and suggests simply that Flaubert was, perhaps, excessively amenable to the influence of his readers and critics. Bourdieu's discussion of the 'Birds of Psaphon' effect is not significantly un-Sartrean. It was, however, in 'Champ du pouvoir, champ intellectuel et habitus de classe' (1971) that Bourdieu's thinking about Flaubert shows signs of the general trend in his ideas which was occurring at the end of the 1960s. Emanating from a seminar on the sociology of texts and of culture that Bourdieu had been leading at the École Normale Supérieure since 1968, this article relates in particular to 'Sociology and philosophy in France since 1945; death and resurrection of a philosophy without subject' (1967) in which Bourdieu had briefly outlined the changing social conditions in postwar France which gave a perspective on the rise and fall of existentialism. Bourdieu begins 'Champ du pouvoir, champ intellectuel et habitus de classe' with the comment that the analysis of literature is particularly resistant to a sociological approach because the romantic view of the artist as creator has become so accepted as natural or true. The sociologist has to indicate successfully that this ideology of creativity is the product of particular social conditions before having the opportunity to subject 'creative' works to sociological scrutiny. Bourdieu continued:

> Thus, the theory of biography as the retrospective integration of the whole personal history of the artist in a purely aesthetic project or the representation of 'creation' as the expression of the person of the artist in his singularity, are only able to be completely understood if they are relocated within the ideological field of which they are part and which expresses, in a more or less transformed fashion, the position of a particular category of writers within the structure of the intellectual field which is itself included in a specific type of political field that assigns a determined position to the intellectual and artistic sector.[44]

In short, the field in which biographical criticism is practised is a reproduction of the field generated by the romantics. In order not simply to reproduce a romantic ideology of art, criticism must, therefore, generate a field which is capable of understanding the conditions in which fields have been, and still are, in competition. Following the methodological procedure outlined in *Le Métier de sociologue*, Bourdieu argues, therefore, that criticism of literature has to make an epistemological break from the prenotions of existing literary criticism. Turning specifically to Sartre's analysis of Flaubert (as presented in the two 1966 articles), Bourdieu argues that Sartre '. . . breaks only apparently with the dominant tradition in the history of art and literature . . .'[45] The factors used by Sartre to explore the individual process of Flaubert's production are, according to Bourdieu, those factors which correspond with Sartre's general viewpoint as adopted in relation to the productivity of all writers at any time or place. Sartre's exploration of Flaubert's particularity is prescribed by his disposition to advance a formula about the relations between consciousness and the material conditions of existence. In effect, Bourdieu claims, Sartre's apparent investigation of the social context in which Flaubert wrote enabled him to reaffirm his subjective idealism. The consciousness which, for Sartre, is operative in history is exposed as an a-historical consciousness, and Bourdieu quotes from Marx to emphasise, by contrast, just how far Sartre's position causes him to see mind as the determinant of matter rather than the reverse.

It is not surprising, Bourdieu contends, that biographical information does not adequately disclose an author's social situation because it can only disclose that author's perception of his situation. Remembering that Bourdieu's *Esquisse d'une théorie de la pratique* was to be published in 1972, we can say that biographical data, such as letters and diaries, offer the author's primary, unreflecting knowledge of his situation, whereas sociological criticism sees the primary knowledge of individuals in the context of an understanding of the whole structure of relationships in society. Bourdieu's refutation of Sartre's mentalism does not lead him into vulgar sociology. The structural portrait of society that is required by Bourdieu does not explain the particularity of authors – how such or such an author 'came to be what he is'[46] – but rather lays out the range of social, intellectual, aesthetic and political positions available to writers at any time. Bourdieu asks for analysis which outlines the structure of possibility for writers rather than one which outlines a structure which is thought to condition actuality.

Bourdieu could, however, be said to be vulnerable to the same charge that he had levelled against Sartre in that Bourdieu was seeing authors in the context of his own sociological structuralism just as much as Sartre had seen them in the context of his own idealist Marxism. Bourdieu's subsequent interpretation of Flaubert in the early 1970s was integrally associated with the development of his general ideas in relation to the structure/agency debate. 'Les fractions de la classe dominante et les modes d'appropriation de l'oeuvre d'art' (1974) explores the different strategies in making 'choices' of tastes adopted by different categories of the dominant classes. Bourdieu used material derived from his museum research, but the article was clearly preparatory to the analysis which was to be offered in 'Anatomie du goût' (1975) and, then, supremely, in *La Distinction* (1979). Bourdieu was preparing to lay out the contemporary structure of possible tastes at the disposal of contemporary social agents. At the same time and particularly arising from the research on 'le patronat' which was then under weigh, Bourdieu confronted the issue of 'choice', especially 'career choice', in 'Avenir de classe et causalité du probable' (1974). Attempts to understand economic behaviour have oscillated between what Bourdieu calls, on the one hand, mechanism, and, on the other, finalism. It is assumed, in other words, that rational action is either the mechanical enactment of preformulated deliberation or is guided by constant reference to a rationally calculated forward projection. By contrast, Bourdieu tries to argue that strategic or pragmatic action is rational. It is this kind of action which enables agents to find their ways through their social structures without either being obliged in advance by those structures to behave in predetermined ways or being constrained to fit in with the perception of the structures that is offered to them.

Bourdieu had already, in September 1973, produced a mimeographed paper entitled *Gustave, Flaubert et Frédéric. Essai sur la genèse sociale de l'intellectuel* which was to be published in the second number of the *Actes de la recherche en sciences sociales* as 'L'invention de la vie d'artiste'. The change in title is significant. It indicates a shift of emphasis away from the structural observation of the social genesis of the generic 'intellectual' towards an appreciation of the act of choosing a life-style within the range of available structural opportunities. Concentrating exclusively on *L'Éducation sentimentale* and writing, now, in the knowledge of the first volume of Sartre's biography of Flaubert, Bourdieu is concerned to clarify in what sense the character of Frédéric Moreau is autobiographical. The error, for Bourdieu, is to suppose that this means that Frédéric is a 'sort of imaginary portrait painted by Flaubert in the likeness of Gustave'.[47] Bourdieu quotes passages both from Flaubert's letters and from the text of his novel which suggest in similar terms that Flaubert and Frédéric were young men who were confused in their attempt to make a choice of career. Flaubert actually and Frédéric fictionally were aware of the structure of possible careers within which they had to make a choice but, in Bourdieu's view, Flaubert does not use Frédéric to represent himself as conditioned by these structures. Rather, Flaubert uses his characters to act out some of the range of possible trajectories available to him. Flaubert does not express himself or constitute himself through Frédéric. Instead, by locating Frédéric as an impersonal agent rather than a self, Flaubert carries out a proactive sociological experiment from which findings can be derived which may assist himself and his readers in making their life choices.

In short, Bourdieu treats *L'Éducation sentimentale* as a naturalist rather than realist novel, but insists that the experimentation is sociological rather than psychological. Like an experiment, the world of the novel is a closed system. As Bourdieu significantly puts it: 'In this Leibnizian universe, every conduct states precisely the system of the differences which oppose each of the characters to all the other members of the group, without really ever adding anything to the initial formula.'[48] Nevertheless, *L'Éducation sentimentale* is a novel and Flaubert, not Frédéric, was the novelist. In an important post-script, Bourdieu comments that 'By writing, Flaubert bestowed on himself the gift of social ubiquity . . .'[49] Bourdieu goes on to argue that by reproducing the system of relations within which he was himself living 'under the form'[50] of the relations within which Frédéric was living, and by characterising his own disposition 'under the form' of the impossibility of Frédéric's life chances, Flaubert was in fact distancing himself from a social self-understanding. He was transposing a social self-awareness into formal art, aestheticising sociology. In the formal context of the novel, Bourdieu argues, Flaubert's sociological insights were subordinated to the rules of autonomous literature which were the product of the society within which he lived. As a consequence, Flaubert's novels were, formally, denials of their content. In so far as Bourdieu was experiencing an affinity with Flaubert in the process of writing about him – in so far, in other words, as *La Distinction* was to offer a sociological account of contemporary cultural possibilities comparable to *L'Éducation sentimentale*'s sociological account of possible social trajectories in mid-nineteenth-century France – the challenge for Bourdieu was whether he would remain a possible person within a world of social possibilities or would trans*form* his sociological practice into a detached vision of the world.

Notes

1. É. Faguet (1914) *Flaubert* (first published 1899; trans. R.L. Devonshire), London, Constable, 1.
2. See, for instance, in 'The function of criticism at the present time', first published in November 1864 in M. Arnold, (1964) *Essays in Criticism*, London, Everyman's Library, Dent, 9–34.
3. Faguet, *Flaubert*, 31.
4. *Ibid.*
5. *Ibid.*, 29.
6. *Ibid.*, 37.
7. *Ibid.*, 38.
8. *Ibid.*, 212.
9. G. Lanson (1896) *Histoire de la littérature française* (4th edn), Paris, 1055.
10. *Ibid.*
11. *Ibid.*, 1057.
12. G. Lanson (1965) *Essais de méthode, de critique et d'histoire littéraire*, Paris, Librairie Hachette, 100.
13. *Ibid.*, 101.
14. *Ibid.*, footnote 1.
15. 'comme une leçon d'ampithéatre . . .', *ibid.*
16. *Ibid.*, 105.
17. Quoted in Lanson, *Essais de méthode*, 109.
18. A. Glauser (1952) *Albert Thibaudet et la critique créatrice*, Paris, Éditions Contemporains, Boivin & Cie, 279.
19. A. Thibaudet (1922) *Gustave Flaubert 1821–1880. Sa vie – ses romans – son style*, Paris, Librarie Plon, 63.
20. *Ibid.*, 69.
21. *Ibid.*
22. R. Descharmes, *Flaubert Sa vie, son caractère et ses idées, avant 1857*, Paris 1909, 546, quoted in Thibaudet, *Gustave Flaubert*, 69.
23. Thibaudet, *Gustave Flaubert*, 71.
24. Glauser, *Albert Thibaudet*, 198, quotes here from the Preface to Thibaudet, *Gustave Flaubert*.
25. W. Fowlie (1968) *The French Critic, 1549–1967*, Carbondale, IL, Southern Illinois University Press, 37.
26. J.-P. Sartre (1967) *What is Literature?* (trans. B. Frechtman), London, Methuen, 43.
27. *Ibid.*, 52.
28. *Ibid.*, 74.
29. *Ibid.*, 90.
30. *Ibid.*
31. *Ibid.*, 90–1.
32. *Ibid.*, 120, footnote 6.
33. *Ibid.*, 165.
34. *Ibid.*
35. *Ibid.*
36. J.-P. Sartre (1960) *Questions de méthode*, Paris, Gallimard, 82.
37. *Ibid.*
38. *Ibid.*, 85.
39. *Ibid.*, 90.
40. 'La conscience de classe chez Flaubert', in *Les Temps modernes* (1966), 240, 1921–51 ('I. De la bourgeoisie considérée comme une espèce'), and in *Les Temps modernes* (1966), 241, 2113–53 ('II. Bêtise et bourgeoisie').
41. J.-P. Sartre, interview of 1970 (*Situations IX*) quoted in D. LaCapra (1979) *A Preface to Sartre. A Critical Introduction to Sartre's Literary and Philosophical Writings*, London, Methuen, 169.

42. See Bourdieu's obituary of Sartre: 'Sartre' (trans. R. Nice), *London Review of Books* (1980), 2, 20 November–3 December, 11–12.
43. P. Bourdieu (1971) 'Intellectual field and creative project', in M.F.D. Young, ed. *Knowledge and Control. New Directions for the Sociology of Education*, London, Collier-Macmillan, 166. Footnote 13 (p. 186) gives the reference to J.-P. Sartre (1948) *Qu'est-ce que la littérature*, Paris, Gallimard, 98, which is p. 56 of *What is Literature?*
44. P. Bourdieu (1971) 'Champ du pouvoir, champ intellectuel et habitus de classe', *Scolies* (Cahiers de recherches de l'École Normale Supérieure), 1, 8.
45. *Ibid.*, 12.
46. *Ibid.*, 15.
47. P. Bourdieu (1975) 'L'invention de la vie d'artiste', *Actes de la recherche en sciences sociales*, 2, 67.
48. *Ibid.*, 78.
49. *Ibid.*, 91.
50. *Ibid.*, 92.

5 Courrèges, the fashion system and anti-semiology

The conclusion of Bourdieu's account of Flaubert's social situation was that Flaubert had taken refuge in constructing an 'artist's life' and had transposed his social perceptions into 'art'. It was important for Bourdieu that we should not fall into the same trap in responding to Flaubert. Formalist responses to Flaubert's formalism had to be doubly sociologised – by recognising both the social circumstances in which the formalism was produced and also the social circumstances of the formalist mode of reception. Without this double sociological recognition, the literary formalism which was in origin pathological would be socially reproduced and the pathology sustained.[1] Bourdieu admired so much, and quoted so often, A. Cassagne's *La Théorie de l'art pour l'art en France chez les derniers romantiques et les premiers réalistes* (1906)[2] because the author – a disciple of Lanson[3] – had refused to take Flaubert's views at face value and had, instead, attempted to use the methods of scientific literary and social history to understand the emergent aesthetic of aestheticism.

Bourdieu's work on Flaubert of the early 1970s was at the same time an explicit rejection of Sartre's psychological explanation of Flaubert's production and a redeployment of the data of Sartre's social history of the nineteenth-century bourgeoisie so as to offer a defence of Flaubert as someone who had been capable of using 'fiction' as an experimental device for objectifying his social position. It was essential for Bourdieu to oppose Sartre in order to articulate what it was in Flaubert's achievement that was worthy of emulation. Flaubert's use of 'art' for its own sake and as an end in itself rather than as a discardable instrument of sociological inquiry (the *ars inveniendi* of *Le Métier de sociologue*[4]) was a mistaken extension of an otherwise correct approach. The mistake was to attempt to attain a position of social detachment and transcendence and to acquire the permanence secured by a-temporal artifacts. In spite of Bourdieu's preference for Flaubert's sociology over Sartre's psychology, Flaubert's final refuge in formalism pandered to the subsequent social reproduction of totalising literary intellectuals. Bourdieu needed to show, therefore, that it was possible to remain a sociological practitioner without 'restless yearnings after' or final capitulation to, formalist or idealist 'absolutes'.[5]

Quite apart from outlining his position directly in *Esquisse d'une théorie de la pratique* (1972), there were two main elements in Bourdieu's campaign. First, he sought to support or undertake work which attempted to discredit claims of 'purity' or independence of social circumstances advanced for themselves by poets, artists or philosophers – whether those claims were advanced in the name of 'idealism' or of 'realism'. It was in this perspective that Bourdieu had engaged with the work of Flaubert and it was to be the concealed agenda of his interpretation of Manet. It was this orientation that caused Bourdieu to publish posthumously Peter Szondi's *Poésie et poétique de l'idéalisme allemand* in 1974 in the *Le Sens commun* series produced under his general editorship by Éditions de Minuit. It was Szondi's view in that book that Schiller's text on Demetrius represents 'a tragedy on the very idea of idealism'[6] – a view which suited Bourdieu's purposes well. At the same time, Bourdieu was himself producing his article – 'L'ontologie politique de Martin Heidegger'[7] – in which he argued that it was the formalist pretensions of Heidegger's ontology as 'academic philosophy' at a time when academicism had been deprived of its autonomy, and not its content which rendered it socially and politically dangerous.

In tandem with this critical strategy, Bourdieu launched, secondly, his positive effort to generate ongoing, untotalising sociological practice: he founded the *Actes de la recherche en sciences sociales*. Immediately after the manifesto – 'Méthode scientifique et hiérarchie sociale des objets'[8] – in which Bourdieu argued that it was the task of social science to analyse scientifically all aspects of culture rather than simply those which have traditionally been 'consecrated' as suitable for sociological treatment, such as religion or suicide,[9] he published, with Yvette Delsaut, 'Le couturier et sa griffe. Contribution à une théorie de la magie'[10] by way of immediate demonstration of his intentions. Bourdieu had already given a lecture in November 1974 entitled 'Haute couture et haute culture'[11] and these two pieces represent an engagement with the world of 'fashion' that is indicative of his approach to the analysis of other social practices such as, actually, sport[12] or the law,[13] and, potentially, an infinity of practices, however trivial or 'significant'.

The world of fashion as an object of inquiry was not, however, quite as unconsecrated as Bourdieu wished, perhaps, to imply. Roland Barthes had published *Système de la mode* in 1967, and had commented, in a footnote, that: 'As early as Herbert Spencer, Fashion became a privileged sociological object . . .'[14] Barthes gave several reasons for this, the first of which was that '. . . it constitutes "a collective phenomenon which shows us with particular immediacy . . . what is social about our own behaviour" [J. Stoetzel (1963) *La Psychologie sociale*, Paris, Flammarion, 245] . . .'[15] Barthes was concerned to clarify that his intentions were not at all sociological. He characterised the province of the 'sociology of fashion' in the following way. It starts, in his view,

> . . . from a *model* of imagined origin (the garment conceived of by the *fashion group*) and follows (or should follow) its actualization through a series of real garments (this is the problem of the circulation of models); it therefore seeks to

systematize certain actions and to relate them to social conditions, standards of living, and roles.[16]

Barthes also assumed that, methodologically, sociology had to be interested in factors, particularly statistical factors, which were of no relevance to his kind of inquiry. He commented, for instance, that 'Structurally, a rare feature of Fashion is as important as a common one, a gardenia as important as a long skirt; the objective here is to *distinguish* units, not to count them'.[17] And he added in a footnote to this passage that 'Disparity of frequencies is of sociologic but not of systematic importance; it informs us about the "tastes" (the obsessions) of a magazine (and thus of a readership), not about the general structure of the object . . .'[18] Barthes assumed, in other words, that the sociological approach from which he was distinguishing his own semiological method was that of a form of positivist social psychology evident in another book to which he refers – P. Lazarsfeld and E. Katz (1955) *Personal Influence. The Part Played by People in the Flow of Mass-Communications*.[19]

It was, however, the growing influence of American positivist sociology in France that Bourdieu resolutely attacked in 'Sociology and philosophy in France since 1945: death and resurrection of a philosophy without subject' (1967).[20] He had presented an anti-positivist case for the use of statistics in sociology in a section of *Travail et travailleurs en Algérie* (1963)[21]; was hostile to the notion of any 'collective phenomenon' at all, arguing, instead, that 'collective' norms are the result of competition between interest groups in a plural society; and regarded the concept of 'role' as analoguous to that of 'rule'-dominated behaviour to which he was opposing the idea of strategic action on the part of social agents.

Barthes' semiology was unashamedly formalist. In *Système de la mode*, he attempted to apply to the world of fashion an approach derived from structuralist linguistics and, in particular, derived from Saussure. Bourdieu had himself read and lectured on Saussure at the end of the 1950s.[22] In the 1970s, however, he was in the process of adapting Saussure's insights to suit his different interests. In *Esquisse d'une théorie de la pratique* (1972) he explicitly rejected Saussure's linguistic theory as 'objectivist'[23] and, by *Ce que parler veut dire* (1982), was advocating socio-logical[24] analysis in place of arid sociolinguistic study. In writing about fashion after Barthes, Bourdieu was, therefore, maintaining his campaign on both fronts at the same time: he was offering a paradigmatic analysis of an aspect of common culture whilst tacitly undermining the formalist threat posed by the work of Barthes which was all the more dangerous for Bourdieu because of the common origin of the opposing positions in the work of Saussure.

In the Foreword to *Système de la mode*, Barthes at once makes it clear that 'The object of the inquiry is the structural analysis of women's clothing as currently described by Fashion magazines . . .'[25] It is crucial to understand that the analysis is of the descriptions and not, directly, of the clothing itself. Barthes quickly points out that this represented a change from his original intention:

> ... whereas initially my project was to reconstitute the semantics of actual Fashion (apprehended in clothing as worn or at least as photographed), I very soon realized that a choice had to be made between the analysis of the real (or visual) system and that of the written system. The second course was chosen ... The analysis which follows deals only with the written system of Fashion.[26]

Barthes was driven to this apparent limitation by his increasing awareness that it was no limitation at all – that, in other words, it was inevitable that he should 'invert' Saussure's view that linguistics would become a part of an over-riding semiology. For Barthes, any science of signs is subordinate to the science of language and, in relation to fashion, this means that

> ... as soon as we observe Fashion, we discover that writing appears constitutive ... the system of actual clothing is always the natural horizon which Fashion assumes in order to constitute its significations: without discourse there is no total Fashion, no essential Fashion. It thus seemed unreasonable to place the reality of clothing *before* the discourse of Fashion: true reason would in fact have us proceed from the instituting discourse to the reality which it constitutes.[27]

If the field of fashion had remained the field of real garments, clothes would have been worn until they were worn out. Instead, economic forces caused the creation of a field of fantasy fashion discourse which would ensure that still functional clothing would prematurely be considered re-dundant or *démodé*. As Barthes eloquently puts it:

> In order to blunt the buyer's calculating consciousness, a veil must be drawn around the object – a veil of images, of reasons, of meanings; a mediate sub-stance of an aperitive order must be elaborated; in short, a simulacrum of the real object must be created, substituting for the slow time of wear a sovereign time free to destroy itself by an act of annual potlatch.[28]

In order to justify his concentration on fashion discourse, Barthes here suggests the conditions which had generated its autonomy. The explana-tion given is one with which Bourdieu would agree: socioeconomic condi-tions do not affect fashion styles directly but affect the emergence of the distinct field of fashion within which stylistic distinctions can then be gener-ated. Barthes, however, chose to bracket these field-generating conditions with a view to concentrating exclusively on discourse within the field of fashion. The introductory section of *Système de la mode* – on 'Method' – demonstrates, however, the difficulty of this task.

Barthes distinguishes first between three garments, that is to say, be-tween three ways of describing the same garment: 'image-clothing', 'writ-ten clothing' and 'real clothing'. The first operates with a visual language, the second with a verbal, and the third offers a technical language. The first two are languages of representation whereas the third 'is constituted at the level of substance and its transformations . . .'[29] This is another terminological way by which Barthes can say that he is confining himself to verbal language and he makes it clear that his analysis is to be synchronic (by treating one fashion year as a synchronic unit) and to be based only on the exhaustive reading of two fashion magazines. He is not interested in variation over time nor in the degree of representativeness of his sample of magazines. This is because his preliminary rule is to '. . . *retain no other raw material for study than the language provided by the Fashion magazines* . . .'[30] but this reduction of the garment to its oral or verbal version poses a key problem which Barthes first formulates specifically and then widens so as explicitly to encompass the nature of literary as much as fashion discourse:

> *What happens when an object, whether real or imaginary, is converted into language?* or rather, *when an object encounters language?* If the garment of Fashion appears to be a paltry thing, we would do well to keep in mind that the same relation is established between literature and the world: isn't literature the institution which seems to convert the real into language and place its being in that conversion, just like our written garment? Moreover, isn't written Fashion a literature?[31]

Barthes specifically uses Saussure to help him with a solution to this problem of conversion or what he calls 'commutation'. Clothing language operates in two contexts – as *langue* in the context of institutionalised, self-referential fashion discourse and as *parole* when 'actualised, individualised' as *dress*. All written clothing operates on two levels at the same time – with reference to Fashion and to the 'World'. By this dual reference, the language of 'clothing' is actualised, but Barthes insists importantly that '. . . commutation always takes place either between clothing and the world or between clothing and Fashion, but never directly between the world and Fashion . . .'[32]

Having identified these two types of signifying relation in the 'vestimentary' sign, Barthes sought to 'disengage the signifying elements from the Fashion utterance they form'[33] or to ignore the fact that the language which he was analysing, taken from fashion magazines, was, by definition, already contextualised within the discourse of fashion.

Culler has suggested that the vestimentary code is 'not especially interesting to read about' and that Barthes' account of the rhetorical system is 'far more interesting'.[34] In offering this latter account, Barthes accepted that the vestimentary code that he had derived from the language of the magazines could not be divorced from the rhetorical strategies of those magazines in the fashion world. Before commencing detailed study of the rhetorical system, Barthes quotes an 'utterance' from one of the magazines: '*She likes studying and surprise parties, Pascal, Mozart, and cool jazz. She wears flat heels, collects little scarves, and adores her big brother's plain sweaters and those bouffant, rustling petticoats.*'[35] Maintaining his analytical commitment to the three dimensions of reference already outlined – clothing, world and fashion – Barthes suggests that these sentences demonstrate all three. The phrases such as 'flat heels' and 'little scarves' relate to the clothing itself whereas 'She likes studying and surprise parties, Pascal, Mozart, and cool jazz' contains, in Barthes' expression, 'an utterance of the worldly signified', or a reference to non-fashion taste correlates. Out of these two separate systems of reference, Barthes argues, magazines construct a discourse of 'fashion' without there ever being any direct correspondence between the clothing and the worldly components, between, for instance, liking Mozart and collecting little scarves. As Barthes puts it:

> Finally, . . . the ensemble of the utterance (or the utterance of signification) is provided with a certain form (use of the present tense, parataxis of verbs: *likes, wears, collects, adores*), which functions as the rhetorical signifier of a final, total signified, namely the entirely consequential way in which the magazine represents itself and represents the equivalence between clothing and the world, i.e. Fashion.[36]

Barthes clustered together descriptions of tastes in the same way as Bourdieu was to cluster together, in *La Distinction*, sets of taste behaviours or allegiances. Barthes insisted that the meanings of these clusters were entirely constituted by the fashion magazines. In considering the rhetorical system, Barthes was especially aware that the discourse of fashion constituted by magazines was related to the audiences of those magazines, but he continued to insist that this awareness did not subvert his formal, semiological intention. Late in *Système de la mode*, Barthes wrote: '. . . since Fashion is entirely a system of signs, variations in the rhetorical signified no doubt correspond to variations in audience.'[37] But he added as a footnote to this remark: 'Since we are not here concerned to establish a sociology of Fashion, these indications are purely approximate: however, there would be no methodological difficulty in defining sociologically the level of each Fashion magazine.'[38]

This passage is one of those seized upon critically by Bourdieu in 'Le couturier et sa griffe'. Typically, Bourdieu's attack of Barthes is buried in small print in his text, but it is nevertheless an unequivocal attack. It comes at the point in Bourdieu's discussion in which he argues that value judgements in the field of fashion do not depend on the 'charisma' of designers so much as on their capacity to 'mobilise . . . the energy of symbolic transmutation . . . which is immanent in the field in its totality . . .'[39] The autonomous field of fashion produces and reproduces itself as a field and individual designers manage their self-presentations in accordance with their perceptions of the field. Bourdieu uses his critique of Barthes here to indicate the way in which the formal analysis of fashion as a formal 'language' *participates in* the construction of the discourse of the field of fashion. Barthes' work explains neither the operation of the field of fashion nor the structure of fashion language. Instead, it is part of the field's celebration of itself. It makes itself part of the structure of the field which designers, as agents, then manipulate strategically. Bourdieu makes his point abstractly in the following way:

> Roland Barthes is perfectly right to recall that the 'metalanguage' of the analyst is itself worthy of analysis and so on ad infinitum: for having failed to constitute his object in its truth, that is to say in its celebratory function, the analyst of the discourse of fashion does nothing other than supply a supplementary contribution to that celebratory discourse, just as the literary critic – from whom he is separated only by the lesser legitimacy of his object – participates in the cult of luxury goods and, hence, in the production of their value – a value which is *interconnectedly* economic and symbolic.[40]

Barthes' failure was a failure of what one might call scientification – a failure, in Bachelard's terms, to construct the scientificity of his object. Bourdieu illustrates this failure by reproducing, in a box, an extract from an article by Barthes published in *Marie Claire*, 181, September, 1967, entitled: 'Le match Chanel Courrèges arbitré par un philosophe'. Barthes offers an opposition between Chanel and Courrèges as one between 'classicism' and 'futurism' and, of course, Bourdieu's point is here graphically established: Barthes' analysis provides no 'arbitration' at all precisely because he allows his thought to be appropriated by a journalistic medium. Barthes' failure – that of the 'spontaneous sociology of the semiologist'[41] – is of the same kind as Heidegger's: both men used the label of 'philosophy' and its associated connotations of objective detachment to conceal the extent to which their philosophy participated in common discourse.

Without reference to this internal critique of Barthes' analytical position, Bourdieu offers, in 'Le couturier et sa griffe', a demonstration of his own sociological practice – practice which avoids the mere repetition of social phenomena that, for Bourdieu, is the characteristic function of both 'spontaneous' and positivist sociology. The complicating factor here, however, is that Bourdieu 'constructs the object' of his social inquiry by adapting Saussure's linguistic theory. Bourdieu rejected Saussure's distinction between *langue* and *parole* and, influenced by J.L. Austin, developed the view that our use of language is social and strategic rather than rule governed – that we use *parole* in relation to how other people use *parole* rather than by reference, mechanistically, to a predetermining structure of *langue*. Nevertheless, Bourdieu borrowed the distinction between *langue* and *parole* from Saussure to help him counteract the anthropological structuralism of Lévi-Strauss. This meant that, for Bourdieu, social agents are sociologically what *parole* is linguistically in his version of Saussure. The meanings of social actions are constructed relationally and immanently in the same way as are the meanings of words. Bourdieu differs from Barthes, therefore, in that, first, he rejects the 'objectivist' use of the *langue/parole* model and, secondly, he analyses society by analogy with language whereas Barthes sought to analyse society as language. Barthes' project collapsed because he sought to interpret society as language by interpreting its language whereas Bourdieu claims that he can analyse society and the function of language within society because he only deploys a linguistic *model* as an instrument of his sociological *method*.

Bourdieu's sociology works with the same three dimensions as Barthes' linguistic theory. If we substitute 'fields' for 'discourses', we can say that individuals (equivalent to 'clothing') define themselves at any time by reference to the particular field within which they situate themselves at that time (for instance, the 'Fashion' system) and to the field of their *habitus* (the 'World') which is, initially, their inherited social condition but is also the accumulating position-taking in fields other than the particular field of activity currently in play. Individuals are not governed by rules, but they act strategically with rules. Individuals opt to participate in many social fields simultaneously and, in doing so, they act in relation to the rules in force in each field, but this means that behaviour in relation to the internal rules of one field always occurs alongside behaviour in other fields which is external to that field. There is no direct, defining relationship between the World and the particular system such as 'Fashion'. At any time the relationship between these two dimensions is defined uniquely by the ways in which individuals balance internal and external forces to establish positions for themselves. The choices made by individuals both within and between fields modify the perception of the parameters of choice acting as a constraint on others.

'Le couturier et sa griffe' tries to illustrate the mechanisms of this dynamic and relational social system by reference to the workings of the field of fashion. Bourdieu begins with this general statement:

> The field of haute couture owes its structure to the unequal distribution between the different 'houses' of the particular kind of capital which is at once the stake in the competition within this field and the condition of entry into the competition. The distinctive characteristics of the different institutions for production and diffusion and the strategies which they adopt in the struggle in which they are opposed to each other is dependent on the positions which they occupy within this structure.[42]

At any time, the capacity of institutions (or individuals) to improve their positions within the field derives from their ability to deploy in that field the capital or power acquired in fields external to it. Without this exchange between fields, every field would exist in static equilibrium, and Bourdieu proceeds to analyse the opposition between what he calls, in 'Haute couture and haute culture', the 'conservation strategies' of the 'dominant' and the 'subversion strategies' of the 'dominated' 'parvenus'.[43] Bourdieu first contends that the field of fashion defines itself in binary terms – in an opposition between 'right' and 'left' which is embodied tangibly in the Parisian spatial demarcation between 'rive droite' and 'rive gauche' but which is also reinforced symbolically by corresponding differences of style. These stylistic differences are illustrated in a double page showing, to use Barthes' terms, both visual and written images of the interiors belonging to five designers, and offering, additionally, a column which glosses these images sociologically. At one extreme, the style of Balmain is represented as the style of the dominant incumbant whereas that of Hechter is represented as that of the aspirant. The design of the apartment of Courrèges also symbolically reinforces his position as an external challenger to the dominant style:

> As for Courrèges, his apartment shows – even down to his bedroom, his bathroom or his kitchen, all of which, in his eyes, equally deserve to be seen by a visitor – his revolutionary will to make a clean slate ('he clears away everything'), and to rethink everything in its own terms *ex nihilo* – the spatial distribution of functions and forms, materials, and colours, all in relation to the sole imperatives of comfort and effectiveness . . .[44]

The distinctions between fashion designers which are manifested in distinctions between their choices of interior design are also manifested in their distinctive uses of language in their catalogues. So far from identifying a general discourse of fashion, therefore, Bourdieu relates the written language of fashion to the positions and strategies of different designers within the social field of fashion. Whereas, for instance, the dominant designers emphasise elegance and refinement, the language of Courrèges – taking him again as an indicative type and quoting from the prospectus of his 1970 collection – is of the avant-garde which, in opposition, emphasises '. . . austerity or audacity, but always freedom, youth, and fantasy'.[45] Having described some of the mechanisms by which the binary structure of the fashion field is sustained, Bourdieu next explores some of the dynamic issues involved in perpetuating this structure. The age of a fashion house becomes one aspect of its stylistic self-representation and aspirant designers strategically acquire their capital *within* the field by appropriating some of the legitimacy possessed by established houses. In a passage in which Bourdieu sketches some of the internal trajectories of designers in relation to a diagram that represents the rise and fall of French fashion houses this century, he comments: '. . . even Courrèges and Ungaro left Balenciaga together to found the house of Courrèges, which Ungaro left in 1965.'[46] This movement within the field that is dependent on the prior acquisition of status within the field assures 'change within continuity' and, as Bourdieu comments: '. . . in effect everything happens as if the possession of a capital which can only be acquired in relation to established houses constitutes the very condition for successful breaches.'[47] Historical changes in the structure of the field are not only dependent on such breaches or ruptures. Succession is a constant problem and source of change. Just at the time that Bourdieu was investigating the reproduction strategies of industrialists in the work leading up to the publication of 'Le patronat', so, here, he investigates the succession strategies of the established fashion houses. These strategies depend on the balance between the individual or institutional character of the house. There is a spectrum – which mirrors the spectrum identified in respect of artists and intellectuals in 'Intellectual field and creative project' – between those designers who position themselves on the basis of their personal creativity and those who position themselves through a socially constructed label (*griffe*). This latter strategy is most often adopted by innovators and it is this strategy which involves managing the industry in such a way as to impose the value of the product. It involves creating a 'name' and using public relations to 'sell' it. According to Bourdieu's analysis, the strategy adopted by Courrèges is an exception which proves the rule. Courrèges is quoted as saying that he had 'become a manager to be master of my own product'.[48] He had sought to institutionalise his own identity and to maintain personal control over the marketing of that identity. The consequence, Bourdieu suggests, is that the house of Courrèges was bedevilled with financial difficulties, booming in 1965, suffering four difficult years subseqently until the launching of a new line in 1970 restored it to its earlier position.

The dynamic of the field of fashion is, however, a consequence as much of influences from outside the field as of internal mechanisms. In a final section, Bourdieu anticipates much of the discussion of both *La Distinction* and *Homo Academicus*. He writes: 'What is described as a crisis of haute couture is perhaps only one sign amongst many of a restructuration of this apparatus linked to the appearance of new signs of distinction (such as leisure sports, foreign travel, second houses, etc.) . . .'[49] The aspirant designers respond to these new developments in the 'World' and, in the case of Courrèges, for instance, respond particularly to the new, liberated expectations of women. The capacity of designers to respond to these external developments – to modify the field of fashion by assimilating influences from outside the field – relates to the total trajectories of those designers. Crucially, Bourdieu is suggesting, the *habitus* of some designers equips them better than others to absorb features in the 'World' precisely because, by background, they are in tune with the movement of that 'World'. Courrèges again provides the example. He, who '. . . distinguishes himself from older and more classical couturiers like Balmain or Givenchy, at the same time by his social origin (popular) and by his studies (scientific), is the first to have broken with the traditional definition of the role that "society" imparted to the couturier, especially before the war'.[50]

Bourdieu contends, therefore, that the world of fashion can be understood sociologically as long as society is conceived, by analogy with linguistic theory, as a network of meaning-creating actions and contexts. The sociologist does not construct static representations of social structures. Unlike Flaubert, the sociologist does not construct a representation of society that acquires the status of a fiction within which he is not prepared to articulate a personal presence. Bourdieu was analogously present in the field of fashion that he describes just as he was actually to insert himself into his representation of his own academic field in *Homo Academicus*. The fact that Bourdieu is analogically present in 'Le couturier et sa griffe' – by constant analogy with Courrèges – is made clear when Bourdieu illustrates the *habitus* of Courrèges by quoting from an interview between J. Chancel and Courrèges, published in *Radioscopie*. Chancel begins: 'You were born in the Béarn, and you have kept your accent . . . Isn't there a bit of snobbery there . . .'[51] In reply, Courrèges explains that he spent ten years working with Balenciaga who suggested that he should take lessons in diction but that, in spite of all his attempts, he cannot change it – 'I can't do it, it's not possible'.[52]

Bourdieu perceived himself to be an aspirant in the academic field and to be in tune with social movements better than the dominant academics as a result of his social background. He perceived himself to be a creative intellectual and, like Courrèges, sought to retain control over the way in which his intellectual *griffe* was marketed. If Bourdieu's analysis of Flaubert helped him to crystalise his thinking about the constant danger that artistic creativity might become a formal device to evade social engagement, his consideration of the field of fashion and of the place of Courrèges within it enabled him to reflect upon the strategies at his disposal in reconciling his creative individuality with the label attached to his institutional position. His published work on Manet tangentially offers a *post hoc* reflection on the consequences for his position in culture of his acceptance, in 1980, of the institutional meaning attaching to his post as Professor at the Collège de France.

Notes

1. The homology between formalism in literature and in literary criticism is clearly exemplified in Culler's work of this period – J. Culler (1974) *Flaubert. The Uses of Uncertainty*, London, Paul Elek, and J. Culler (1975) *Structuralist Poetics. Structuralism, Linguistics and the Study of Literature*, London, Routledge & Kegan Paul.
2. A. Cassagne (1906) *La Théorie de l'art pour l'art en France chez les derniers romantiques et les premiers réalistes*, Paris, Hachette. Bourdieu describes this as an 'admirable work' in 'Champ du pouvoir, champ intellectuel et habitus de classe', *Scolies* (1971), 1, 23, footnote 1.
3. He is listed by H. Peyre as one of the Normaliens inspired by Lanson in G. Lanson (1965) *Essais de méthode, de critique et d'histoire littéraire*, Paris, Librairie Hachette, 17, footnote.
4. P. Bourdieu with J.C. Chamboredon and J.-C. Passeron (1968) *Le Métier de sociologue*, Paris, Mouton-Bordas, 12; P. Bourdieu with J.C. Chamboredon and J.-C. Passeron (1991) *The Craft of Sociology*, Berlin and New York, de Gruyter, 5.
5. These are the phrases used by Keats of Coleridge in elaborating the idea of 'negative capability'.
6. These are the words used by Szondi in a letter of 1 July 1969 to Bourdieu which is quoted in the Preface to P. Szondi (1974) *Poésie et poétique de l'idéalisme allemand*, Paris, Éditions de Minuit.
7. P. Bourdieu (1975) 'L'ontologie politique de Martin Heidegger', *Actes de la recherche en sciences sociales*, 5–6, 109–56, subsequently published in modified form as (1988) *L'Ontologie politique de Martin Heidegger*, Paris, Éditions de Minuit, and in translation as (1991) *The Political Ontology of Martin Heidegger*, Oxford, Polity Press.
8. P. Bourdieu (1975) 'Méthode scientifique et hiérarchie sociale des objets', *Actes de la recherche en science sociales*, 4–6.

9. See p. 16 of this book.
10. P. Bourdieu and Y. Delsaut (1975) 'Le couturier et sa griffe. Contribution à une théorie de la magie', *Actes de la recherche en sciences sociales*, 1, 7–36.
11. P. Bourdieu, 'Haute couture et haute culture', conference *Noroit*, 192, November 1974, pp. 1–2, 7–17; also in P. Bourdieu (1980) *Questions de sociologie*, Paris, Éditions de Minuit, 196–206, translated in P. Bourdieu (1993) *Sociology in Question*, London, Sage, 132–8.
12. See, for instance, 'Comment peut-on être sportif?', in Bourdieu, *Questions de sociologie*, 173–95, and translated as 'How can one be a sportsman?' in Bourdieu, *Sociology in Question*, 117–31.
13. See, for instance, P. Bourdieu (1986) 'La force du droit. Éléments pour une sociologie du champ juridique', *Actes de la recherche en sciences sociales*, 64, 5–19, translated as (1987) 'The force of law: toward a sociology of the juridical field', *Hastings Law Journal*, 38, 5, 814–53.
14. R. Barthes (1985) *The Fashion System*, London, Jonathan Cape, 9, footnote 13. (Originally published as *Système de la mode*, Paris, Éditions du Seuil, 1967.)
15. *Ibid.*
16. *Ibid.*, 9.
17. *Ibid.*, 11.
18. *Ibid.*, footnote 20.
19. Cited in Barthes, *The Fashion System*, 9, footnote 13.
20. P. Bourdieu and J.-C. Passeron (1967) 'Sociology and philosoophy in France since 1945: death and resurrection of a philosophy without subject', *Social Research*, 34, 162–212.
21. P. Bourdieu (1963) *Travail et travailleurs en Algérie*, Paris and The Hague, Mouton, 9–12. See my translation: P. Bourdieu (1994) *Statistics and Sociology*, (trans. and intro. by D.M. Robbins), London, Group for Research into Access and Student Programmes, Working Paper no. 10, University of East London.
22. See P. Bourdieu (1990) *In Other Words. Essays Towards a Reflexive Sociology* (trans. M. Adamson), Oxford, Polity Press, 6.
23. See P. Bourdieu (1972) *Esquisse d'une théorie de la pratique, précédé de trois études d'ethnologie Kabyle*, Geneva, Droz, 164–70; P. Bourdieu (1977) *Outline of a Theory of Practice*, Cambridge, Cambridge University Press, 23–6.
24. For this hyphenation, see P. Bourdieu (1982) *Ce que parler veut dire. L'Économie des échanges linguistiques*, Paris, Fayard, 71; P. Bourdieu (ed. and intro. by J.B. Thompson) (1991) *Language and Symbolic Power*, Oxford, Polity Press, 74.
25. Barthes, *The Fashion System*, ix.
26. *Ibid.*
27. *Ibid.*, xi.
28. *Ibid.*, xi–xii.
29. *Ibid.*, 5.
30. *Ibid.*, 12.
31. *Ibid.*
32. *Ibid.*, 22–3.
33. *Ibid.*, 26.
34. J. Culler (1990) *Barthes*, London, Fontana Press, 75.
35. Barthes, *The Fashion System*, 226.
36. *Ibid.*, 227.
37. *Ibid.*, 244.
38. *Ibid.*, footnote 14.
39. Bourdieu and Delsaut, 'Le couturier et sa griffe', 21.
40. *Ibid.*, 23.
41. *Ibid.*, 27.

42. *Ibid.*, 7.
43. Bourdieu, 'Haute couture', 133.
44. Bourdieu and Delsaut, 'Le couturier et sa griffe', 11.
45. *Ibid.*, 12.
46. *Ibid.*, 16.
47. *Ibid.*
48. *Ibid.*, 19, footnote 11.
49. *Ibid.*, 29–30.
50. *Ibid.*, 32.
51. *Ibid.*
52. *Ibid.*

6   Manet, the Musée d'Orsay, and the installation of art

If you climb the steps of the National Gallery in London, erected in 1832–38 by William Wilkins, to 'provide the crowning visual effect for the newly made Trafalgar Square'[1] at the top of the government offices of Whitehall extending northwards from the Houses of Parliament, and if you pass, free of charge, through the vestibule designed by Sir John Taylor in 1885–87,[2] and then mount the stairs to the right, you reach the galleries exhibiting 'Painting from 1700 to 1920', the third of which contains three paintings by Édouard Manet (1832–83). You approach Room 43 (which contains the Manets) through Room 45 ('Nineteenth to Twentieth Century. Cézanne. Monet.') and through Room 44 ('Nineteenth Century. Seurat. Van Gogh. Cézanne.'). As you enter Room 43 through the open doorway leading from Room 44, you can see, on the opposite side of the room, the pictures on either side of the doorway which leads beyond to the next room. To the left, you can see Manet's *The Execution of Maximilian* and, to the right, an English suburban landscape painted by Pissarro entitled *The Avenue, Sydenham*. Through the open doorway between these two pictures you can see a portrait by Ingres: *Monsieur de Norvins* on the far wall of Room 41 ('Nineteenth Century. Goya. Ingres. Delacroix.'). Coming back into Room 43 from Room 41, you can see, framed in the same way by the open door, Henri Rousseau's *Tropical Storm with a Tiger* on the far side of Room 45 – situated visually between Cézanne's *Landscape with Poplars* and Monet's *The Thames below Westminster* which you can see opposite on the wall of Room 43. Entering from Room 44, the other two Manets hang on the right-hand wall: *Eva Gonzales* is in the centre flanked by Degas' *Ballet Dancers* on one side and by Renoir's *At the Theatre (La Première Sortie)* on the other. In the corner beyond the Renoir is Manet's *Corner of a Café Concert* which is hung at right angles from Monet's *The Beach at Trouville* which is below Berthe Morisot's *Summer's Day*.

  Viewing pictures is a physical experience. Meanings are imposed spatially both by the organised juxtaposition of hung pictures and by the unexpected juxtapositions of lines of vision. The interpretation of a picture involves the same factors as the interpretation of a novel: it involves a comprehension of the artist's field of production as well as a capacity to receive the visual or verbal messages conveyed by a canvas or text. Unlike novels, however, pictures in art galleries are staged and their language is performative and relational. Bourdieu had analysed the accessibility of art galleries in *L'Amour de l'art* and had discussed philosophically the nature of the perception of pictures in 'Outline of a sociological theory of art perception' but, in those discussions, he had not developed the idea that art galleries, as 'official' art institutions, might perform a key role in the production and reception of art and in ensuring that these two activities combine to safeguard social reproduction.

Bourdieu published two articles on Manet in 1987 – 'L'institutionnalisation de l'anomie' and 'La révolution impressioniste'. The former was described in a footnote as a chapter in a 'forthcoming book on Manet and Impressionism', but no such full text has yet materialised. It is clear, however, that Manet has constituted a reference point in Bourdieu's thinking and the two articles of 1987 pull together arguments which relate to the issues raised in the mid-1970s in respect of Flaubert and Courrèges and to the post-1980 interest in the social function of institutions. Whereas Bourdieu's analysis of Flaubert of the 1970s suggested that the novelist's production was only constrained by the formal rules of that genre after he had failed to give form to his sociological imagination, Bourdieu's analysis of the work of Manet supposes that the artist, like Courrèges, generated his distinctive style in opposition to the dominant cultural tradition within which he had been apprenticed. Bourdieu was anxious to demonstrate that it was possible to make a revolutionary change in the ways in which we see the world, either visually or ideologically, from a base within the world that was to be reversed. Not only was it and is it possible, but, rather, it was and is inescapable. The challenge, however, is to ensure that revolutionary changes are not subsequently neutralised by the appropriative actions of those self-reproducing institutions against which the changes were effected in the first place.

The occasion that provoked Bourdieu's two articles of 1987 was the opening by President Mitterand, in December 1986, of the Musée d'Orsay. The Gare d'Orsay had been opened in May 1900 at the time of the opening of the World Fair. Conceived by the architect, Victor Laloux, around metal structures, it was a celebration of modern engineering design and *fin-de-siècle* decoration. For forty years it was the terminal of the main railway line servicing the southwest of France but, by the end of 1939, electrification was reducing the viability of the station's short platforms and it was reduced only to servicing the suburbs. In 1961, SNCF decided to sell and it was only saved from demolition by the Ministry of Cultural Affairs which decided, in 1973, to place it on a list of protected buildings. The directors of the Musées de France conceived the idea of a new museum and defined its specific features to be: 'multi-disciplinary, presenting all the forms of artistic creation from the second half of the 19th to the early years of the 20th centuries.' In 1977, a Cabinet meeting took the decision, at the initiative of President Giscard d'Estaing, to build the new museum.[3]

Quite apart from the opposition to his paintings which Manet experienced in his lifetime – an opposition which Bourdieu discusses in his articles – the subsequent public display of all impressionist paintings was problematic certainly until about 1930. In 1924, Gaston Brière produced a catalogue of all the paintings displayed in the galleries of the Louvre. There were only twelve Manets. Of these, four were part of a donation made in 1906 by M. Moreau-Nélaton, and seven were part of another donation made in 1911 by M. Camondo. The terms of the Moreau-Nélaton donation also meant that these four paintings (notably including *Le Déjeuner sur l'herbe*) had to be displayed separately in a different art gallery.[4] Six years later, Brière wrote a history of the collections of paintings in the Louvre in which he summarised the scandalous history of the official acceptance of impressionist paintings in the following way:

> Finally, the 'Impressionists', so often excluded from the Salons and scorned by the members of the Académie des Beaux-Arts, made their way, not without lively polemics and formidable opposition, into our public galleries. In 1890, the famous *Olympia* by Manet was offered by a group of amateur collectors and was displayed at the Luxembourg . . . Thanks to L. Bénédite, keeper of the Musée du Luxembourg, a financial arrangement was made and two Manets . . . were hung on the walls of a modest room of the Musée devoted to living artists. In 1929, these canvases, disdained for such a long time, at times the objects of derision, were brought triumphantly to the Louvre and placed alongside *Olympia* which had been in a place of honour since 1908.[5]

It is quite clear that Brière thought that the representation of impressionist painting in the Louvre was outrageously at odds with the recognised importance of the movement and its painters. He complained about the incoherence of the Louvre's modern collection as well as about its poverty. French paintings from the fifteenth century until the end of the eighteenth century were grouped and were displayed in rooms which followed on from each other normally, but '. . . after the school of David, the continuity is broken. The 19th Century which is already so rich . . . is dispersed in rooms which are distant from each other . . . '[6] Brière's suggestion is that the authorities of the Louvre were reluctant to give physical recognition to the paintings which were being celebrated by the dominant art critics and historians. Henri Focillon was one such influential intellectual. Born in 1881 – two years before Manet's death – Focillon's life roughly coincided with that of the Third Republic. He saw himself as a successor to the artistic and intellectual tradition launched by the 'Group of 1863' of which he considered Manet to have been the leader. That group was itself, in Focillon's view, fulfilling the revolutionary aspirations of the men of 'Quarante-Huit' (1848) – aspirations which had only been temporarily suppressed during the reign of Emperor Napoleon III. Writing in 1928 in *La Peinture aux XIXe et XXe siècles. Du réalisme à nos jours*, Focillon analysed developments in this period by reference back to the ideological polarity of the 1840s:

> In the 1840s France saw the clash between two groups of men, and the opposition between these groups gave the century its colour contrast, its light-dark of

ideas. One group, disappointed by the world, sought refuge in nature and the past, drunk on solitude, ruins, storms, antiquities, and only having confidence in the individual. The other group was made up of men who were exhiliarated by the spectacle of urban growth, by the power of association, by the benefits of exchanges between peoples, and by the dignity of work. The groups confronted each other in '48; the social utopians were only apparently defeated. The future of the modern world belongs to them. Romanticism was hit more enduringly.[7]

In arguing that the painters of 1863 associated themselves with the work of the men of '48, Focillon was not simply setting up the sort of antithesis between romanticism and realism used by Faguet to analyse Flaubert. Rather, Focillon was establishing an antithesis between conservatism and modernism. The 'social utopians' of '48 were on the side of social, economic, technological and democratic progress. They were striving to bring into being 'a sort of enlarged humanism'[8] which went beyond the traditional humanism of classicism. Their social engagement was physical and energetic rather than spiritual. In relation to the artistic movements of the mid-nineteenth century, Focillon made his working distinction most explicit in his damning dismissal of the English pre-Raphaelites:

> Pre-raphaelitism and its English friends do not count amongst the active forces which we study. Pre-raphaelitism was a return to nature and to fidelity, but through archaism . . . It belongs to the history of high culture more than to that of painting and, more than every other art form born of the European movement in the middle of the century, it was obsessed with content and tended, not to life but to eternity. It expressed the desires and dreams of an elite of superior men rather than the sensibility of the time.[9]

Only those artists who were 'painters' rather than conservers of culture were of interest to Focillon. Only those painters who were artistic technologists could be said to be in tune with the vital forces of modernity and the new humanism. Of the 'realists', in contrast with Chenavard whose project for the decoration of the Panthéon was accepted in 1848, Focillon commented: 'They were men, they were painters: Chenavard was only mind [*esprit*], and that very laboriously.'[10] Similarly, Focillon quoted approvingly Courbet's remark that he wished '. . . not only to be a painter, but even more a man, in a word to make living art, that is my ambition'.[11] And, in assessing the work of the realists, he said of Courbet, Millet and Daumier: 'They had the audacity to turn to life more than to the past – they looked at the face of man and not at his time-honoured, old-fashioned image in museums. They cherished the old masters, not as the professors of tradition but as living people of earlier times.'[12] With this kind of understanding of the history of the nineteenth century – as a conflict between moribund, institutionalised conservatism and energetic, liberated progressivism – it is not surprising that Focillon accentuated the struggles for official recognition experienced by the early impressionists. Manet's *Le Déjeuner sur l'herbe* was one of three of his entries for the Salon of 1863 which were all rejected by the jury. The Emperor Napoleon decreed that all the rejected pictures should be displayed in what was to become known as the Salon des Refusés. Focillon says of this Salon that '. . . for a few moments it brought to light the deep and hidden efforts of the independent painters, opposed at the same time to the academic tradition, . . . and to the facile triumphs of fashion'.[13] It is equally unsurprising that Focillon should see the continuing resistance to the exhibiting of the impressionists highlighted by Brière as an indication that the opposition experienced by Manet in 1863 still persisted. After the realists, Focillon argued, there was still a need for someone who could '. . . give to painting a technique in conformity with the genius of modern life, and, above all to the particular quality of its sensibility'.[14] That someone was Manet. For Focillon, Manet was the emblem of the painter of modernity. In arguing for the institutional recognition of Manet in the late 1920s, therefore, art critics and historians were fighting to uphold the values of the men of 1848 and fighting to safeguard the socialist ideals of the Third Republic.

Attitudes towards Manet were less politically charged after the Manet Exhibition in Paris in 1932 which Valéry described as 'le triomphe de Manet'.[15] Writing about Manet, originally in 1959, Pierre Courthion asserted somewhat blandly: 'Our eyes are so accustomed to his luminous canvases that we can scarcely believe the intrigues that tormented him each year at the time of the Salon. The public no longer even contests the painter's right to a free choice of subject matter. Today *Olympia* is in the Louvre.'[16] Courthion casually depoliticises both the production and the reception of Manet's paintings: the fuss about the Salons is now faintly incredible; we are now 'accustomed' to Manet's novelty without reflecting on how we have become accustomed to it; the 'free choice' of subject matter is, superficially, unquestioned; and the presence of Manet's most outrageous picture in the Louvre is thought to be indicative of our liberal tolerance. What Courthion offers is Manet's art: 'His work was already . . . what is now called *peinture-peinture*, or pure painting. There is no psychology and nothing to allow us to glimpse the secrets of mind or heart . . . The value of his art lies in the brush stroke, the color, and the creative light with which it sparkles.'[17] Academic art criticism had already transformed Manet into a formalist artist for art's sake whose work should be appreciated 'aesthetically'.

Had it not been for the opening of the Musée d'Orsay, Bourdieu's discussion of Manet might not have been significantly different from his discussion of Flaubert. He might, perhaps, have been content to analyse the social context within which Manet developed his style and to substantiate in detail his general contention that the consideration of art as an autonomous field of study is a way of reproducing formalistically – and without responding to contemporary conditions – formalisms which were once historically constructed. It was, however, the resurgence of an academic criticism that saw itself explicitly as the contemporary inheritor or defender of academic traditionalism which provoked a different reaction from Bourdieu.

That different reaction makes it clear that Bourdieu was no longer prepared to present himself as an impartial observer of cultural relativity.
Inert formalism, that is to say, formalism which is reproduced and reproduces itself, is to be fought by activity which necessarily involves the
imposition of form. In the tradition of Focillon, Bourdieu uses an analysis
of Manet as an oblique way of defending the social and intellectual project
of modernism.

It was a colleague at the Collège de France – Jacques Thuillier – who
threw down the gauntlet. In 1983, he wrote 'L'artiste et l'institution: l'École
des Beaux-Arts et le Prix de Rome' as the first part of a booklet published
by the École des Beaux-Arts entitled *Le Grand Prix de Peinture. Les
concours des Prix de Rome de 1797 à 1863*. In his introduction, Thuillier
discussed the nature of the booklet to which he was contributing. It was not
the catalogue of a museum nor was it a study in the history of art. Instead,
he suggests, '. . . it constitutes the inventory of an inheritance, or rather of a
fragment of the venerable inheritance accumulated by that great French
institution: the Ecole des Beaux-Arts'.[18] In France, Thuillier immediately
argues, the word 'institution' is detested and seems to represent the complete opposite of 'inspiration'. The École des Beaux-Arts has been vilified
as the sponsor of institutional and official art, encouraging 'uniform education, the gradual substitution of repetition for invention, and the subjection
of genius to competition'.[19] This has been so much the dominant view for a
century that, in Thuillier's view, there has been a 'sort of intellectual terror-
ism in play'[20] which has outlawed any questioning of it. The taboos have,
however, gradually disappeared in the fields of politics, economics and
history and should now disappear in the field of art history. A revision,
Thuillier concludes, is now 'essential' (*Une révision s'impose . . .*).

Thuillier proceeds to defend the École des Beaux-Arts and to celebrate
the extent to which the system by which students prepare for entry (the
'classes préparatoires') functions as a way of disseminating the values of
the *école* much more effectively than simply through the education of
successful applicants. Thuillier explicitly draws attention here to the comparable mechanisms of value formation imposed by the other Grandes
Écoles, including the École Normale Supérieure. He argues that this is a
benign social influence, especially since the *école* has always offered an
education which is free and egalitarian. Although 'one may scarcely dare
say it these days',[21] the competitiveness introduced by the *École* was '. . . a
victory for democracy, the mechanism consciously chosen to substitute
merit for wealth or birth'.[22] Some people are ashamed of this today, arguing that meritocratic competition 'eliminates the notion of class'.[23]
Thuillier accepts that the system of competitions did not generate the
greatest art for the simple reason that the annual prize-winning exhibits
were produced in accordance with a standardised stylistic brief and were
always the products of artists in their mid-20s. By implication, however, the
esteem in which individual artists have been held has been over-rated at
the expense of respect for a long-sustained consistency of taste.

Thuillier's article highlights a dilemma for Bourdieu's thinking. He had already published, in 1981, 'Epreuve scolaire et consécration sociale. Les classes préparatoires aux Grandes Écoles' in which he argued that the 'meritocratic' admissions procedures for the Grandes Écoles constituted a closed system that was only accessible to those possessing the appropriate social and cultural characteristics. This is a position which goes back to *Les Héritiers* and was to be pushed further in *La Noblesse d'état* (1989) where Bourdieu was to argue that the socially determined educational conveyor belt continues on into positions of power and authority in politics and state administration. At the same time, however, Bourdieu had always argued against individual 'charisma', insisting that value judgements in art take place within fields of discourse which are embodied in institutions. Much of Bourdieu's work from the early 1980s had already involved an exploration of the relationship between the power of individuals and the power of the institutions with which they allow their names to be associated. As we have seen, Bourdieu drew attention, as early as 1975, to the difficulty experienced by Courrèges in sustaining his personal, individual control over his institutionalised *griffe*. Bourdieu's work on Manet exposes his own irresolution in relation to institutions. He is reluctant to relinquish the legacy of his earlier thinking in which he opposed the discrimination effected by state-controlled educational institutions, but he increasingly accepts that opposition to the exclusive mechanisms of institutions of state can only be mounted by mobilising institutional power to support subversive individuals. It is apparent, therefore, that Bourdieu does not reject institutionalisation as such. Instead, he conceals a value judgement about what is institutionalised behind an attack which is largely directed against the process. Given that the Collège de France was thought by Bourdieu to be an institution that was sufficiently independent of state control to enable him within it to institutionalise his own anomie, it was particularly important that he should oppose a fellow professor in the same institution who might be queering his pitch by seeking to associate the Collège with an opposed institutional image.

Bourdieu begins 'Manet et l'institutionnalisation de l'anomie' by outlining the two essential prerequisites for understanding the emergence of the modern movement in painting. It can only be understood '. . . if one analyses the situation in and against which it developed, that is, the academic institution and the conventional style which is a direct expression of it, and also if one resolutely avoids the alternatives of depreciation or rehabilitation governing most current debates'.[24] In short, the need to make value judgements between the work of Manet and the work sponsored by the École des Beaux-Arts is removed by concentrating both on the social situations underlying the production of the opposed works and on the social situations underlying contemporary debates. The article spends most time on the former. Bourdieu is very clear about the nature of the educational experience offered in the Grandes Écoles. He characterises the consequences of the logic of competitiveness as being:

... the incredible docility that it assumes and reinforces in students who are maintained in an infantile dependency by the logic of competition and the frantic expectations it creates ... , and the normalization brought by collective training in the
ateliers, with their initiation rites, their hierarchies linked as much to seniority as to
competence, and their curricula with strictly defined stages and programmes.[25]

He complains that Thuillier's analysis is defective because it is unreflexive:
'The unanalysed relation to the object of analysis (I refer here to the homology of position between the analyser and the analysed, the academic master)
is at the origin of an essentially anachronistic comprehension of this object
... '[26] Thuillier's 'analysis' is made from within the institutional and aesthetic field which it analyses and, therefore, contributes to its reproduction.
Bourdieu does not, however, satisfactorily justify his claim that such reproduction is intellectually 'anachronistic'. Thuillier might certainly respond that
Bourdieu's mode of analysis was an anachronistic legacy of the founding
fathers of social science. The question here is whether Bourdieu is prepared
to articulate sociologically the contrary positions represented by himself and
by Thuillier or whether the sociological argument is only being used to
discredit an analysis which Bourdieu wishes to oppose on other grounds – by
reference to tacit criteria of value.

Bourdieu proceeds to distinguish between artisans, artists and masters.
The system of the École des Beaux-Arts produces masters of technique
and works of art which are 'readable' and 'finished'. These traits are precisely those that the early critics found lacking in the work of Manet and, as
Bourdieu summarises, 'By imposing on his work a construction whose
intention is not to help in the "reading" of a meaning, Manet dooms the
academic eye, used to seeing a painting as a narrative, as a dramatic representation of a "story", to ... disappointment'.[27] It is Manet's opposition
to the academic tradition that explains the deliberate unreadability of his
canvasses, the lack of explicit or deducible emotion in the figures in, for
instance, *L'Exécution de Maximilien* or *Le Balcon*.

Bourdieu is clearer about what Manet negated than about the means by
which he institutionalised his alternative. The academic tradition was, in
effect, a state-controlled aesthetic regulator:

> Through the Academy and its masters, the state imposes the principle of vision
> and legitimate division in questions of the figurative representation of the world.
> This principle is itself a dimension of the fundamental principle of vision and
> legitimate division that the state ... has the power to impose universally within
> the limits of its jurisdiction.[28]

There is here a latent research agenda in respect of all the consequences of
the decline of the nation-state.[29] Bourdieu suggests that it was the expansion
of the *école* – the 'ever-increasing numbers of candidates'[30] – which brought
about the decline of its state-sponsored monopoly. It was numerical pressure
which generated a critical situation within the institution and then to 'the
successful institutionalisation of this break'.[31] Bourdieu describes briefly the

process that he had registered in moving from the analysis of *Les Héritiers* to that of *La Reproduction* – the movement from state control to the open competition between fields struggling for social domination:

> As it ceases to operate as a hierarchical *apparatus* controlled by a professional body, the universe of the producers of art-works slowly becomes a *field* of competition for the monopoly of artistic legitimation. From now on no one can claim to be an absolute holder of the *nomos*, even if everyone has claims to the title. The constitution of a field is, in the true sense of the word, an *institutionalization of anomie*. This is a truly far-reaching revolution which, at least in the realm of the new art in the making, abolishes all references to an ultimate authority capable of acting as a court of appeal: the monotheism of the central *nomothete* gives way to a plurality of competing cults with multiple uncertain gods.[32]

The new factor, however, is that Bourdieu is no longer primarily the observer of the deregulated society which he describes. Instead, he is a competitor within it who sees himself to be in opposition to those who attempt to reintroduce state regulation.

Presented originally as a talk, 'La révolution impressioniste' clearly summarises all the issues which concerned Bourdieu in his consideration of Manet. In particular, he states explicitly that the opening of the Musée d'Orsay – the fact that *Les Romains de la décadence* by Manet's early master, Couture, against whom he rebelled, was receiving pride of place in its display – was one factor in causing him to turn his attention to Manet. Bourdieu also felt the need to oppose the related tendency to disparage the achievement of the impressionists – to insinuate that they effected no revolution at all but, simply, a transformation of bourgeois taste. Bourdieu spends time illustrating the homology between the contemporary academic defence of academic art and its historical production, and in criticising Thuillier specifically, but more time is spent in explaining how the institutional crisis of this historical academicism had been '. . . exploited by people like Manet'.[33] In particular, Bourdieu asks why '. . . when there had been heaps of earlier attempts to subvert the academic regime (Delacroix, Courbet etc.) Manet's attempt succeeded whilst the others failed or only partially succeeded'.[34] Bourdieu insists that Manet's achievement was revolutionary. The critical overproduction of painters coincided with the establishment of a field of critical discourse involving position-taking in relation to the paintings displayed at the Salons. By introducing criticism which was no longer exclusively concerned to interpret the messages contained in the favoured historical paintings but was, instead, concerned to interpret paintings as such, the critics performed a function that they had not for earlier artists. As Bourdieu puts it, the critic '. . . accomplished in his sphere the equivalent of the formal revolution accomplished by the painter in transforming the definition of what could be represented (the hierarchy of significance and insignificance) and the manner of representing it'.[35] It was this conjunction of creativity and the field of criticism that ensured that the changes of style adopted by the painters became dominant after 1863 in ways which had not been possible earlier in the century. Manet's artistic innovation became revolutionary precisely because he was able to mobilise a new field which, in turn, could exercise the power to modify the visual perception of the population and of subsequent generations. In other words, the art of Manet was not intrinsically 'revolutionary' but his innovations acquired revolutionary status because they were successfully diffused. The success also has to be attributed to the fact that his innovation was one of form rather than content. Revolution is, in effect, the introduction of a new form backed by a mobilised social support. Changes in content are predefined in terms of the content which they are changing. The breakthrough effected by Manet was that he undermined the academic expectations of readability. He achieved for painting exactly what Flaubert achieved for the novel. Bourdieu quotes a phrase of Flaubert – 'to write well about the mediocre' (*'écrire bien le médiocre'*) – and claims that it exactly fits Manet's endeavour. Bourdieu elaborates: 'To fulfil the exigences of form to their limits is, effectively, to transgress the hierarchies of the significant and the insignificant and to defy the hierarchy by constituting aesthetically things that the traditional hierarchy refuses to allow to be constituted aesthetically.'[36] The scandal of *L'Exécution de Maximilien* was precisely that it was not emotionally *about* the execution but was, instead, a formal arrangement on a canvas of figures adopting poses associated with the actions of a firing squad. Bourdieu drives home the comparison with Flaubert in the following way: 'The tension is extreme between the formalist distancing and the tragedy of the situation. *The execution of Maximilien* is a typically Flaubertian situation – with an operatic emperor who even so finishes up by being shot.'[37] In seeking to establish an identity of situation between Flaubert and Manet, Bourdieu revises the attitude towards formalism which he had adopted at the end of 'L'invention de la vie d'artiste'. Whereas Flaubert had stood condemned as a proto-sociologist who had taken refuge in artistic creation, he is now, alongside Manet, praised as the paradigmatic artist who shook off the yoke of social realism and representation in art. Bourdieu continues:

> The Barbizon painters, amongst whom we can see the precursors of Manet or even Courbet, had something which reassured observers – notably the fact that they conveyed a message. The 'realists' satisfied Proudhon, whom Flaubert detested because of his insistence that art should have a meaning, that it should say something. With Courbet, you could say: that's human suffering, the sorrow of peasant life, etc. You could write things about the work of Delacroix, but there was nothing more to say about the emperor Maximilien . . .[38]

It is now Proudhon who stands condemned, and the inadequacy of Courbet's representationalism is expressed in a phrase which resonates retrospectively in the present: Bourdieu was to strive to create a form in *La Misère du monde* (1993) in which suffering (*souffrance*) might speak rather than be sociologically represented.

As promised, Bourdieu finally asks why it should have been the person Manet who made this revolutionary breakthrough. Drawing upon Weber's

Ancient Judaism, Bourdieu argues that revolutionaries, like heresiarchs and prophets, emanate from the caste of priests. They are not self-taught. They have '. . . been taught by the learned but have gone out to say in the streets what they have been told in consecrated places'.[39] Manet was initiated into the values of the École des Beaux-Arts and was therefore in a position to mobilise those values to effect a transvaluation and transformation. It was, Bourdieu concludes, a life-and-death struggle in which Manet was engaged. There could be no quarter. The reformist art of a Corot could coexist with academic art, but, with Manet, this was impossible. Manet had so attacked the heart of academic art that it was bound to be a case of either 'him or them':

> What Manet was in the process of inventing and imposing was the autonomous artist, that is to say one capable of legislating about himself. Artistic legitimacy was no longer in the hands of a State which conferred certificates, or by the certificated masters of the academic institution. It was in the hands of a group of artists who affirmed their recognition of legitimacy by their struggle to retain the monopoly of it for themselves.[40]

For Bourdieu, equally, there could be no quarter for those who wished to reduce Manet to a Corot, to suppose that Manet's work could be displayed in the new Musée d'Orsay alongside the 'rehabilitated' products of those academic masters whom Manet had discredited. Like Focillon, Bourdieu believes in a 'life of forms'[41] which is constantly renewed by human agency. Bourdieu's final sentence above makes it clear that new fields, possessing their internal rules of legitimacy, are constantly emerging and battling for dominance. Like Focillon, Bourdieu believes that the 'life' of forms lies precisely in the fact that forms are constantly being re-formed. True re-formation is revolutionary. It is distinguished from the rearrangement of previous forms as much as from the mere reproduction of those forms. Bourdieu is a man of 1848 and of 1863, but he argued for the exhibiting of Manet with prominence in the Musée d'Orsay not as a way of 'consecrating' Manet, and thereby constituting an alternative academic tradition, but as a way of making public the *process* by which Manet secured legitimacy – so as to contribute to the legitimation of that *process* of continuous re-formation.

Notes

1. N. Pevsner, revised by B. Cherry (1989) *The Buildings of England. London. I. The Cities of London and Westminster*, London, Penguin Books, 326.
2. *Ibid.*, 327.
3. For this information, I am grateful to the Service de Presse et Communication of the Musée d'Orsay, Paris.
4. For this information, see G. Brière (1924) *Musée National du Louvre. Catalogue des peintures exposés dans les galeries. I. École française*, Paris, Musées Nationaux, 172–3 and xi.
5. G. Brière (1930) *Histoire des collections de peinture au Musée du Louvre. I. L'École française*, Paris, Musée National du Louvre, 38.

6. *Ibid.*, 43.
7. H. Focillon (1928) *La peinture aux XIXe et XXe siècles. Du réalisme à nos jours*, Paris, Librairie Renouard, 2–3.
8. *Ibid.*, 4.
9. *Ibid.*, 150.
10. *Ibid.*, 7.
11. *Ibid.*, 8.
12. *Ibid.*, 32–3.
13. *Ibid.*, 75.
14. *Ibid.*, 172.
15. P. Valéry (1932) *Triomphe de Manet*, quoted in F. Cachin (1994) *Manet 'J'ai fait ce que j'ai vu'*, Paris, Découvertes Gallimard, Réunion des Musées Nationaux, Peinture, 153–7.
16. P. Courthion (1988) *Edouard Manet*, London, Thames & Hudson, 7 (this is a concise edition of Courthion's *Manet*, originally published in 1959).
17. *Ibid.*
18. J. Thuillier (1983) 'L'artiste et l'institution; l'École des Beaux-Arts et le Prix de Rome', in *Le Grand Prix de Peinture. Les concours des Prix de Rome de 1797 à 1863*, Paris, École des Beaux-Arts, 55.
19. *Ibid.*
20. *Ibid.*
21. *Ibid.*, 75.
22. *Ibid.*
23. *Ibid.*
24. P. Bourdieu (1993) 'Manet and the institutionalization of anomie', in P. Bourdieu (ed. and intro. by R. Johnson) *The Field of Cultural Production*, Oxford, Polity Press, 238.
25. *Ibid.*, 241.
26. *Ibid.*
27. *Ibid.*, 248.
28. *Ibid.*, 250.
29. This maps out the ground covered in many of the articles collected in P. Bourdieu (ed. J.B. Thompson) (1991) *Language and Symbolic Power*, Oxford, Polity Press.
30. Bourdieu, 'Manet', 252.
31. *Ibid.*
32. *Ibid.*, 252–3. The use of the word *apparatus* is a reminder that Bourdieu is opposing the Althusserians here as much as the conservatives. See P. Bourdieu (1980) 'Le mort saisit le vif. Les relations entre l'histoire réifiée et l'histoire incorporée', *Actes de la recherche en sciences sociales*, 32–3, 3–14, for an open critique of Althusser.
33. P. Bourdieu (1987) 'La révolution impressionniste', *Noroit*, 303, 6.
34. *Ibid.*
35. *Ibid.*, 15.
36. *Ibid.*, 15–16.
37. *Ibid.*, 16.
38. *Ibid.*
39. Bourdieu, 'La révolution', 16.
40. *Ibid.*, 18.
41. See H. Focillon (1989) *The Life of Forms in Art*, New York, Zone Books, originally published in 1934 as *La Vie des formes*. As far as I am aware, Bourdieu does not refer to Focillon at all, but I suggest that Focillon stands in relation to Bourdieu for art criticism rather as Lanson stands for literary criticism. Bourdieu uses the work of Panofsky, but Focillon represents the tradition of art history and criticism within which Bourdieu's thought is situated.

Part IV

THE CRITICISMS

---

7 Evaluating fragmented responses

Reviewing *Choses dites*, Brubaker made the point that: 'Since Bourdieu's texts are products – and instruments – of particular intellectual strategies and struggles, their emphases vary considerably from text to text, depending on the particular intellectual field in which a text is situated and the structure of that field at the time the text was written.'[1] What Brubaker says here about the production of Bourdieu's texts could equally well be said of their consumption. In the corporate conclusion to *An Introduction to the Work of Pierre Bourdieu. The Practice of Theory*, the authors comment:

> A study of the secondary literature . . . reveals many specific criticisms. Some of these criticisms, however, are less substantial than they appear; others are telling and enduring. For example most arise from reviews of single texts, or reviews of single themes in his work. While it is wholly understandable, given the limited translation of other materials into English, we hope to have displayed enough of Bourdieu's wide interests to put these views to rest.[2]

Lest these should be thought to be the views solely of apologists, even Richard Jenkins has been prepared to admit that

> . . . much of the discussion of Bourdieu concentrates on a fairly narrow spectrum of his work. Very few critiques span the full range – from Algerian ethnology to the sociology of education to methodology – or even a substantial slice of it . . . It does Bourdieu a considerable injustice, for example, to regard him as primarily a sociologist of education or culture.[3]

Without going into detail, as had Wacquant in his 'Bourdieu in America: notes on the transatlantic importation of social theory'[4] about the 'blurred visions' and the 'fragmented readings' of his work, Bourdieu's response to the situation was to announce that he would like, '. . . rather than taking up each point of disagreement one by one, to try to unearth the factors that seem to me to constitute their roots'.[5] This chapter will not try to take up every point of disagreement with Bourdieu that has been made in the secondary literature, but it will try to summarise, and comment on, a selection of significant points. The intention is to defer consideration until the following chapter of the meta-critical assumptions hidden in the comments, already quoted, made by Brubaker, Harker *et al.*, and Jenkins. Is there, it will be asked, a hidden totality of Bourdieu's work by reference to which, in Leibnizian fashion, all local errors will be seen to be parts of a greater good? How should we know when we have displayed 'enough' of the 'wide interests' that disclose this totality to lay criticisms 'to rest'? Does it do Bourdieu 'a considerable injustice' to be found wanting, perhaps, in individual intellectual fields because it is assumed that he should be viewed in a meta-perspective in which justice would be done? Is such a perspective attainable and, whether or not it is, do we not have to take seriously the objections made in specific fields? If, as Bourdieu suggests, we understand the 'roots' of the objections without responding to their content, do we not simply endorse his practice and bracket the objections? Is it possible to understand relationally the conditions which generated criticisms and still preserve the substance of the objections?

These questions get right to the heart of Bourdieu's work as well as to the possibility of criticising it and consideration of them leads naturally to the concluding remarks of the book. To revert to the concern of this chapter, however, Brubaker's comment above aptly leads into the first of the local disagreements with Bourdieu which has pervaded the secondary literature. The phenomenon that Brubaker was prepared to view positively – the strategic status of Bourdieu's conceptual activity or the polysemic nature of his concepts – has been regarded negatively since the first readings of Bourdieu's texts.

In one of the earliest articles to review Bourdieu's educational work to that date, Swartz wrote of his method and style in 1977 that '. . . all too often he creates categories and concepts without carefully specifying their corresponding empirical referents'.[6] Bredo and Feinberg made the same point in 1979: 'One of the major theoretical weaknesses with the book is the key concepts that remain unclearly specified.'[7] The main reservation has often been that Bourdieu's imprecise formulation of concepts has meant that they are empirically untestable. Swartz's phrase – 'their corresponding empirical referents' – displays a positivist disquiet about Bourdieu's procedures.

Specific concepts have variously been targeted for this criticism – for example, the concepts of 'habitus', 'cultural capital' and 'educational system'. It was Swartz again, in a later article, who commented:

> The theoretical construct 'habitus' presents a number of conceptual and empirical ambiguities that will need clarification in future work. The concept permits Bourdieu to make conceptually appealing transitions from micro- to macro-levels of analysis and to generalize through quite different domains of human activity. But this very appealing conceptual versatility frequently renders ambiguous just what the concept actually designates empirically.[8]

What the concept 'actually designates empirically' is here the ultimate criterion of worth. Much of the literature about the 'habitus' has been equally concerned about the looseness of Bourdieu's use of it but, unlike Swartz, other authors have wanted to articulate more clearly its conceptual meaning or function without reference to any empirical value. Without reference to Bourdieu at all, Granovetter (1985) argues the need for a concept fulfilling all the functions of the 'habitus' to explain the relations between economic action and social structure, and Camic (1986) charts the social history of the use of 'habit' in American sociology and welcomes its revival in Bourdieu's work. Conversely, although again without regard to the empirical utility of the concept, Schatzki expresses philosophical reservations about Bourdieu's use of 'habitus'. He writes: 'Bourdieu, therefore, assigns two very different functions to one and the same "mechanism": production of action and the specification of intelligibility. As implied, I believe that this is a mistake. The production of action is a matter of bodily mechanism. The determination of intelligibility is a separate affair.'[9] Jenkins has linked the confusion he experiences about 'habitus' to a more general confusion that he finds in Bourdieu's use of the concept 'culture'. Culture, he argues,

> . . . appears in his work as either an assemblage of consumable, material artifacts – everything from pop records to children's clothes to paintings – or as an abstract, rhetorical concept, which occupies the realm of the unconscious. Either way it does not do much explanatory work. The concept of the habitus – *embodied* dispositions – functions as an analogue for culture when it comes to explaining behaviour. But what does embodiment *mean* in this context, other than a gesture of faith in the direction of materiality (as in 'biological individuals')? What exactly *is* the habitus? How does it relate to the notion of 'culture'?[10]

More inclined than Jenkins to search for empirical utility than for conceptual meaning, Lamont and Lareau are similarly confused by Bourdieu's use of 'cultural capital':

> . . . in Bourdieu's global theoretical framework, cultural capital is alternatively an informal academic standard, a class attribute, a basis for social selection, and a resource for power which is salient as an indicator/basis of class position. Subtle shifts across these analytical levels are found throughout the work. The polysemy makes for the richness of Bourdieu's writings . . . However, the absence of explicit statements makes systematic comparison and assessment of the work extremely difficult.[11]

Lamont and Lareau tacitly admit that Bourdieu's practice conforms to his theory of polysemy but they seem able to use that theory to explain the actions of others without being prepared to use it in explanation of Bourdieu's behaviour. Certainly from *Outline of a Theory of Practice* onwards, Bourdieu was willing to see logical 'fuzziness' in the practice of others as well as of himself. Before that, however, he had cultivated a different kind of logic. In an article on the work of Bourdieu and Bernstein, Archer accused Bourdieu (and Passeron) of using the concept of 'educational system' with 'negligence'. Her contention was not that the concept was too imprecise to generate empirically testable hypotheses so much as that it was a concept which did not do justice to empirical reality. Both Bernstein and Bourdieu attached '. . . primacy to cultural universals which override comparative differences in educational structure . . .'[12] She took Bourdieu and Passeron to be offering sociological explanations deduced from their empirical findings whereas *La Reproduction* represented a deliberate abstraction from the findings that had already been reported in *Les Héritiers*, an abstraction that sought to offer conceptual propositions which might have universal inductive value. Bourdieu and Passeron were not finding 'cultural universals' in social reality and, in doing so, neglecting other variables. They were positing propositions which might have different degrees of explanatory value in different situations. Even if, by 1986, Passeron thought that Bourdieu's work subsequent to *La Reproduction* had confused the logical with the real, he was clear that the sociological conceptualisation offered in that text provided a 'model' rather than an account of social or educational change. He wrote:

> Models that bring into play the concept of 'cultural reproduction' or 'social reproduction' are often objected to on the grounds that the very way they are constructed prevents them from taking account of 'historical change' which, in effect, is what history most clearly exhibits to the observer. It is this objection that I should like to answer here, by showing that it bears not on the use of reproduction models in sociological analysis, but on the association of a theory of reproduction with the Marxist (or, to be more precise, Hegelian) idea that historical change can come about only through an 'internal contradiction' that is logically rooted in the core of any reproduction model.[13]

These various responses to Bourdieu's supposed conceptual looseness have not, of course, only amounted to criticisms of his conceptual style or of his methodology. They have entailed further, more specific and more substantive criticisms which now need scrutiny.

One corollary of the predominantly American positivist critique of Bourdieu has been the constant refrain that his methods or his findings do not transfer cross-culturally. Behind this apparently simple criticism of Bourdieu's 'Frenchness' or recognition of his cultural difference has lain an intellectualist nationalism given legitimacy by deference to a tacit hegemony of international social scientists operating with technically correct, standard empirical procedures. In their specific remarks on *Reproduction in Education, Society and Culture*, Bredo and Feinberg confirmed their general antipathy to Bourdieu's approach with the following comment:

> The essays in the second part are generally more accessible than the theoretical part of the book, although they have considerable theoretical content themselves. However, they actually use rather less in the way of systematic data than

is claimed and are empirical primarily in that they consider a particular historic case, France, in an interpretative fashion.[14]

Writing a year later in 1980, Gorder introduced her critical appraisal of Bernstein and Bourdieu with the comment that '. . . the lack of understanding of the French school system by most Americans as well as the density of his writing style impede complete comprehension of his theories and limit their direct applicability to U.S. institutions'.[15] How was it supposed that 'complete comprehension' of any theories is possible or how might 'direct applicability' be achievable across cultures for any theory? Unknown, apparently, to Gorder, Bourdieu himself had already discussed these questions both in relation to pedagogic communication in his 'Langage et rapport au langage dans la situation pédagogique'[16] and in relation to the transnational comparison of educational systems in 'La comparabilité des systèmes d'enseignement'.[17] More importantly, however, Gorder interestingly attributes the poor transference of Bourdieu's theories about education to the facts, first, that the American receivers of his messages are insufficiently informed about the object of his researches – the French educational system – and, secondly, that Bourdieu's communicative transmission of his theories is poor.

Other critics have supposed that Bourdieu's work is not easily transferable either because the conditions of its production make it foreign or because the object of his research imposes a specificity on his findings. These are different points. Lemert has consistently taken the positive view, largely derived from a sympathetic understanding of Bourdieu's theoretical position, that the work can be received and applied cross-culturally if the social and intellectual conditions of its production are fully understood:

> . . . competent reading of French sociology (as of other French writings) can go quite smoothly if one first bothers to understand the total field in which a given text is situated. To isolate Bourdieu and Touraine from their field is to court readerly confusion. Bourdieu's sociology of education by the standards of American or British sociology of education will make only partial sense.[18]

Others, however, have been less inclined to regard sociological texts as predominantly authorial productions analoguous to works of fiction or 'other . . . writings'. Going beyond Gorder's claim that ignorance of the French system inhibits American understanding, the positivist or realist position has suggested that the cultural specificity of the phenomena studied by Bourdieu has so constituted his theories that they cannot relate to other cultures. Reviewing *Reproduction in Education, Society and Culture* and *Outline of a Theory of Practice*, diMaggio was sceptical of the claims that he took Bourdieu to be making:

> While Bourdieu writes of the French educational system, which is more intricately stratified than that of the United States, his theoretical statements suggest that his conclusions may apply more generally. The absence of any explicit

comparison between France and either the United States or the socialist countries is a source of ambiguity in his work.[19]

Archer's exposure of the probable effects of the character of the French
system on Bourdieu's theorising about it was more sophisticated. It was
likely, she argued, that the phenomenon of cultural arbitrariness could be
explained by the distinctive, highly centralised character of the French
system, and it followed, therefore, that '. . . if the existence of a dominant
"cultural arbitrary" were contingent upon the low level of educational
diversity in a centralized system then the possibility of theorizing in this
way varies with the structure of the educational system and could only be
generalized to other systems of the same type'.[20] The corollary here, based
on a Weberian stance, seems to be that social theories only explain the
societies of which they are the product or, at most, societies which are of
the 'same type', but it is not clear from what a-social perspective the
sameness of 'types' is to be established.

Just as a form of realism has caused criticism to suggest that Bourdieu
only explains what he explains (or that what he explains causes him to
explain it in the way in which he does) and that, therefore, his explanations
are not transferable, so it has led criticism to suppose that his published
findings are invalidated as a consequence of the time gap between research
and publication. In his 1986 review of *Distinction*, Jenkins offers graphic
instances of how 'passé' are some of the popular cultural figures discussed
in the text and makes the general point that '. . . the time lag between data
collection and publication (in the case of the English edition, up to 21
years) renders much of the detail of the book incomprehensible to all but
the dedicated cultural archaeologist . . .'[21] Bourdieu has himself responded to this criticism – or anticipated it – early in the text of *La
Noblesse d'état* (1989),[22] just as he has on several occasions since the late
1980s outlined his position concerning the cultural transferability of his
texts[23] but there is one example in the secondary literature of both criticisms pushed interestingly to their logical extreme. In 1985, Robinson and
Garnier – of the Department of Sociology at Indiana University –
published an article entitled 'Class reproduction among men and women in
France. Reproduction theory on its home ground'. They claimed that 'An
analysis of class reproduction in France at approximately the time that
reproduction theory was developed (1970) affords a test of some of these
arguments on their home ground, where they should be most consistent
with the *actual situation*'[24] (my italics). They used statistics supplied by the
Institut National de la Statistique et des Études Économiques (INSEE) for
1970 on the grounds that this was the date of publication of *La Reproduction* (even though the statistical information used by Bourdieu and Passeron was acquired from INSEE for the writing of *Les Héritiers* (1964)
rather than for the later reconceptualisation of their findings). Robinson
and Garnier found by this means that '. . . French reproduction theory has
overstated the role of education in reproducing class advantage from

generation to generation'[25] and that this is related to the failure of reproduction theory to '. . . consider gender difference in the reproduction of classes'.[26] They proceeded to make two specific comments on the methodology adopted by Bourdieu in the educational research of the 1960s. First: 'Bourdieu generally uses father's class or occupation as an indicator of father's educational or cultural capital. This is consistent with his assumption that father's class and education are very highly associated . . . '[27] and, secondly,

> The most serious limitation of Bourdieu's empirical work is that it has been confined to samples of students. Because students have not as yet assumed the class positions they will occupy in their work lives one cannot assess the effects of their class and educational background and own educational capital on their class placement.[28]

In relation to the second point, Bourdieu and Passeron had themselves explicitly discussed, in *Les Étudiants et leurs études*, the validity of generalising to the whole of society from the experiences of a subgroup possessing particular characteristics such as the student subgroup. The text of *Les Héritiers* considers the unique social position of students both in relation to the trajectories of their parents and in relation to their condition of potentiality *vis-à-vis* the labour market, but, mainly, these texts move towards the view that was to be stated more overtly later that, in effect, the condition of students is the norm for all agents within society. That is to say that Bourdieu was moving away from any attempted objective correlation between occupations and class, mediated by education, towards an attempted understanding of the position-taking of individuals, of how individuals strategically deploy 'class' identity, educational 'capital' and occupational status to make their way through the social system. In relation to the first point, Bourdieu's response might well be that he had already indicated in a methodological section of *Travail et travailleurs en Algérie* that he advocated a continuous reciprocity in inquiry between quantitative and qualitative data. The insights derived from interviews with particular subjects and the generalised statistical information derived from large samples are different kinds of objectification that are both functions of the questions posed by inquirers. Refinement of findings can be obtained by shifting between the quantitative and the qualitative, but neither procedure gives access to any objective truth lying behind their instrumentality. Robinson and Garnier's 1985 perspective on the data of 1970 might correctly have deduced a gender difference that Bourdieu did not observe because his research instruments made it structurally unobservable, but the relativist's response would be that the uses of the evidence made by Bourdieu and by Robinson and Garnier are both explicable sociohistorically such that neither falsifies the other.

The question raised by this second substantive argument against Bourdieu – in relation to time – is how far specific shortcomings of his work which sometimes manifest the changing social conditions of the last forty years should detract from his 'total' achievement. It is bizarre that Robinson and Garnier's attempt to replicate the empirical situation of 1970 so as to launch a critique of Bourdieu's methodology in that historical period should, in 1985, conclude that Bourdieu's procedures had caused him to overstate the role of education in class reproduction without acknowledging that all Bourdieu's work after 1970, whether in respect of employment in the work leading to the publication of 'Le Patronat' in 1978 or in respect of the diversity of cultural forms analysed in *Distinction* (available in English translation in 1984) had itself been undertaken to explore the nature of that overstatement. There have been several variants of this time-related critique of Bourdieu's work.

Robinson and Garnier chose to imply that Bourdieu's educational analyses were out of date when in fact it was they who were out of date in respect of the development of Bourdieu's thinking. The implications of comparable criticisms, however, are less clear. Garnham has, on occasions, implied with sadness that Bourdieu's failure to analyse the media constitutes a critical weakness, suggesting that Bourdieu's theory of communication – derived from thinking about primary, one-to-one human contact – is ill-equipped to deal with the phenomenon of contemporary communication industries. The 'total' Bourdieu response can now point to his recently delivered, on television, talks entitled 'Sur la télévision' and 'Le champ journalistique et la télévision'[29] or a wider counterargument might be that other researchers in the Centre de Sociologie Européenne, Paris, have pursued the implications of Bourdieu's work in this field. In this case, for instance, it could be argued that the work of Patrick Champagne demonstrates the kind of detailed analysis that Bourdieu might be expected to make of the relations between politics and the media. Similarly, Berger asked rhetorically, in 1986, 'How did it become possible – and reasonable – to ignore the aristocracy?'[30] The practical answer here has to be that one of the culminations of the long collaboration between Bourdieu and Monique de Saint Martin going back to the 1960s has been her publication, in 1993, of *L'Espace de la noblesse*[31] – a text which can be seen to date back to her 'Une grande famille' of 1980[32] and to run in parallel with the research on the French episcopacy which was undertaken in collaboration with Bourdieu at the same time.[33]

Bourdieu's work seems to arouse expectations of comprehensiveness, and his failure to provide this personally has, at times, generated criticism which can legitimately be countered by reference to the work of his colleagues. But one variant of this criticism raises more difficult issues. Moving beyond Garnham's charge that Bourdieu '. . . neglects the effect of the growth of the so-called "cultural industries"' and his elaboration of the charge with the question: 'What may be the effect on the operation of symbolic power of the increased intervention of economic capital directly into the field of the production of symbolic goods?'[34] Lash has gone as far as to suggest that '. . . Bourdieu's work is so central now because the real world has changed to a point at which it has come to agree with Bourdieu's world'.[35] On this reading, in other words, Bourdieu's descriptions have prescribed[36] so effectively that the temporal dimension in criticism potentially generates a new argument against his achievement – that, in his own terms, his analyses currently appear to endorse social reality and no longer to criticise it. This is not, however, precisely the criticism that Lash makes from his observation. He argues, instead, that Bourdieu's theory cannot explain the process of social change which has caused that theory now to be thought to be an accurate explanation of reality. As Lash puts it: 'My claim is that the real world has become increasingly like Bourdieu's theoretical world; that Bourdieu is right in terms of how things are, but wrong in *his* implicit claim that they have always been like this.'[37] Lash seems here to be struggling to express his disquiet at the sense that Bourdieu's theories have been shown to be a priori true, that they have acquired a truthfulness without being able to account for the conditions that have brought this about. He struggles with the paradox that Bourdieu appears to have been able to explain changing conditions without being able to explain the conditions of change.

This hesitant anxiety about Bourdieu's achievement is just one of the more recent articulations of the third substantive criticism of Bourdieu's work that has been advanced right from the earliest reviews and articles. The last criticism to be considered here – but the most fundamental – is that Bourdieu's theory has not been able to account for social change. This position has been adopted with different emphases which need to be distinguished. Some critics have attacked Bourdieu's 'determinism'; some have focused on his political 'quietism'; some have argued that his work condones the dominance of dominant culture; whilst others have been especially hostile to what they take to be his disrespect for the creative potential of the working class. In many cases these arguments have been mixed and the motivation for the attacks has often been as much political as social scientific. They can best be exemplified in relation to the last emphasis – Bourdieu's supposed antipathy to what has been labelled 'cultural Marxism'.

In spite of the fact that the 'gloss' of proposition (1) of *Reproduction: In Education, Society and Culture* (that 'All *pedagogic action* (PA) is, objectively, symbolic violence insofar as it is the imposition of a cultural arbitrary by an arbitrary power') makes the following clear statement: 'The propositions which follow . . . refer to all PAs, . . . , and, unless otherwise stated, whether that PA seeks to reproduce the cultural arbitrary of the dominant or of the dominated classes . . .'[38] critics have refused to accept this assertion at face value. Bredo and Feinberg, for instance, wrote of Bourdieu and Passeron:

> Their inability to find any convincing method for changing the relations of dominance that are found in the educational system highlights a much more serious problem with their system – it is the inability to account for any significant social change at all. In part this failure can be accounted for by one key assumption that seems to pervade their book. This is the notion that the habitus

that is reproduced in the lower classes by the school must inevitably be a carbon copy, albeit one fainter than the original, of the mentality that is found in the dominant group.[39]

The same interpretation is repeated by Gorder: 'Thus, the power of the educational system derives from the structure of class relations but adds to it its own symbolic force. It does this through the imposition of the "cultural arbitrary" which is not arbitrary at all, but based upon the culture of the dominant class.'[40] This is a Marxist reading of Bourdieu which paraphrases, but appears not to understand, the function performed by 'symbolic force' in Bourdieu's system – that of distorting any supposed direct correspondence between education and 'class'. In suggesting that the cultural 'arbitrary' is not arbitrary at all, Gorder correctly identifies a tension in the presentation between the logical and the historical – the tension about which, *ex post facto*, Passeron has clarified *his* position – but she assumes that the idea that arbitrariness should be understood as historical rather than philosophical contingency conceals, for Bourdieu, an acquiescence in the structural relations of a determined class hierarchy. Working herself with a fixed view of historical necessity in terms of dialectical materialism, Gorder does not realise that the historical process to which Bourdieu's cultural arbitrary contingently relates is itself contingent on factors other than simply the changing modes of economic production. The combination of Bourdieu's relativism with his acceptance of Realpolitik means that he seeks to analyse dominated cultures in relation to the dominant *only because* this is the relationship which, *de facto*, is tautologuously the case.

There are two further problems associated with this response to Gorder's criticism. The first – that Bourdieu shifts too readily backwards and forwards between what must logically be the case and what is really the case, that dominated people do not necessarily experience themselves in relation to the dominant even though the one might logically entail the other – will be discussed in the next chapter. The second – that, for Bourdieu, a relativistic form of stratification seems to be unidirectional, assuming that relatively dominated cultures define themselves exclusively in relation to the cultures by which they are dominated rather than those which they themselves dominate – will be considered shortly by reference to Honneth's criticisms. For the moment, it is important to register that Gorder's crude Marxist critique expressed itself in a form of special, political pleading on behalf of working-class culture.

Gorder's final sentence outlined the direction that 'we on the left'[41] should take in research and it is clear that Willis's *Learning to Labour*, rather than *Reproduction*, was her model. She argued that 'By further defining the value of any cultural capital by its approximation to the culture of the dominant class, Bourdieu seems to deny the value and by extension the very existence of working class culture'.[42] Jenkins has been much more outspoken on this point. Reviewing *Distinction*, he wrote that

. . . the superficiality of Bourdieu's discussion of the working class is matched only by its arrogance and condescension. In this . . . he betrays the influence of his membership of French bourgeois cultural networks. Despite his good intentions, this perspective taints the entire analysis with a sense of the author's own distinction, and that of his intended audience.[43]

In passing, it should be noted that this passage also exemplifies a common form of criticism of Bourdieu, that of attempting to condemn the man in terms of his own theory. Taking *Distinction* alongside *Homo Academicus*, as Jenkins can very well do, given that he has reviewed both texts, it should be possible to see that Bourdieu sought to insert himself within the objective structure that he presented. Just as he was able to situate himself within his objectified version of the field of Parisian higher education, so his representation of the relations between dominant and dominated cultures in *Distinction* is self-consciously a representation which is a function of his position within the dominated fraction of the dominant class. Bourdieu's analysis does not 'betray the influence of his membership'. Rather, the objective analysis overtly accommodates the grounds for self-criticism within itself. In constructing a model of relations, Bourdieu relativises the model, making it a function of itself.

On behalf of the working class, Jenkins takes offence at the following passage from *Distinction*: '. . . nothing is more alien to working-class women than the typically bourgeois idea of making each object in the home the occasion for an aesthetic choice . . .'[44] This passage elicits a sarcastic 'Oh yeah?' What Jenkins too readily fails to understand is that Bourdieu is not denigrating working-class women for their lack of 'culture' but, instead, arguing that a working-class aesthetic is functional rather than aestheticist. The complexity of Bourdieu's position would have become obvious if Jenkins had continued the above quotation from *Distinction* thus:

> . . . of extending the intention of harmony or beauty even into the bathroom or kitchen, places strictly defined by their function, or of involving specifically aesthetic criteria in the choice of a saucepan or cupboard . . .
>
> This conventionalism, which is also that of popular photography, concerned to fix conventional poses in the conventional compositions, is the opposite of bourgeois formalism and of all the forms of art for art's sake recommended by manuals of graceful living and women's magazines, the art of entertaining, the art of the table, the art of motherhood.[45]

Bourdieu is not denigrating working-class taste. If there is any non-scientific denigration here, it is of the taste of bourgeois women. If anything, Bourdieu is idealising the working class in the fashion of Hoggart's *The Uses of Literacy*. Bourdieu argues that the aristocracy has generated an exclusive concept of the 'aesthetic'. Everything therefore conspires to impose the dominant view that the non-aestheticism of the working class is non-aesthetic, but, for Bourdieu, practical, functional choices can be as aesthetic as aestheticist ones. Bourdieu's position is clear from his introduction to *Un art moyen* (1965) which should be taken alongside the gloss of proposition (1) of *La Reproduction* (1970) but which, unhappily, was not available in English translation until 1990. Bourdieu wrote:

> The most banal tasks always include actions which owe nothing to the pure and simple quest for efficiency, and the actions most directly geared towards practical ends may elicit aesthetic judgements, inasmuch as the means of attaining desired ends can always be the object of a specific valuation: there are beautiful ways of ploughing or trimming a hedge, just as there are beautiful mathematical solutions or beautiful rugby manoeuvres. Thus, most of society can be excluded from the universe of legitimate culture without being excluded from the universe of aesthetics.[46]

Bourdieu's orientation has been consistent over the years. He has analysed the dominant culture that possesses the power to make itself 'legitimate' and he has analysed the ways in which lower classes are inclined to legitimate their own cultures by adopting the formalism of the dominant culture to which they aspire. These analyses, however, have to be seen in the context of Bourdieu's disposition to favour practical behaviour regardless of 'class', to believe that all ethical behaviour has an aesthetic dimension and to contend that such ethical behaviour is preferable to any aestheticist veneer. It follows that Bourdieu's view of those of his critics who present themselves as apologists for working-class or 'popular' culture must be that they exemplify his analysis because *they* seek to justify the uniqueness of working-class culture by reference to the criteria of, or the rules of, 'high' culture rather than in its own, functional terms. In seeking to do this, they operate as if the 'legitimacy' of 'legitimate' culture is an absolute attribute, whereas he understands it sociologically.

Referring to the chapter of *Distinction* in which the passage occurred that annoyed Jenkins, Honneth has made the general point that 'These passages in which Bourdieu uses empirical evidence and sketches to try to shed light on the working class "choice of the necessary" are not among the best in the study . . .'[47] But Honneth acknowledges that Bourdieu's apparent bias is simply a function of his mode of presenting his argument:

> To be sure, Bourdieu only uses the analyses of proletarian 'mass taste' as a foil for his study of the symbolic competitive struggles of the other social strata . . . The real aim of his inquiry is to uncover those mechanisms which operate for the cultivation of competing styles of life within the world of distinguished culture.[48]

The problem, for Honneth, is not that Bourdieu denigrates the working classes but that he so treats cultural and social positions as homologuous that he cannot appreciate the range of diverse actions which all help to constitute *any* class or collective identity. As Honneth puts it:

> Bourdieu has so strictly interpreted the group-specific behavioural model from the functionalistic viewpoint of cultural adaptation to social class situations that

evidently he is unable to acknowledge all the varied tasks of ensuring collective identity (including oppositional strategies of resistance) – which everyday culture also accomplishes – which is documented in more recent writings on cultural history.[49]

In spite of Honneth's tacit side-lining of the cultural Marxist critique, the same argument against Bourdieu has been made from a different political and sociological perspective.

Lamont and Lareau are familiar with Bourdieu's texts in French and with the context of their French production, but they misinterpret his position in order to adapt his concepts in such a way that they will retain functional utility for American research. The false exegesis of the authors needs to be exposed, even if their overall aim is defensible. They say, of Bourdieu and Passeron, that 'The authors often use the term "legitimate culture" interchangeably with cultural capital'.[50] And they justify this claim with the following footnote:

> In *Reproduction* (1977 (1970), p. 46), cultural capital is defined as cultural goods and values that are transmitted through class differentiated families and whose *value* as cultural capital varies with its *cultural distance* (dissimilarity?) from the *dominant cultural culture* promoted by dominant agencies of socialization. This suggests that various types of cultural capital could have different values, and that some are even 'illegitimate', or of low value. However, most of Bourdieu's writings suggest that cultural capital refers only to highly valued signals.[51]

The passage to which Lamont and Lareau refer is on page 46 of *La Reproduction* and pages 30–1 of *Reproduction*. The relevant propositions are (2.3.2.1), (2.3.3) and (2.3.3.1). This last reads:

> *2.3.3.1. In any given social formation, the system of PAs, insofar as it is subject to the effect of domination by the dominant PA, tends to reproduce, both in the dominant and in the dominated classes, misrecognition of the truth of the legitimate culture as the dominant cultural arbitrary, whose reproduction contributes towards reproducing the power relations (by 1.3.1).*[52]

The original French for the latter half of this sentence is as follows: '. . . *la méconnaissance de la vérité objective de la culture légitime comme arbitraire culturel dominant.*'[53] Much hangs on the translation of 'méconnaissance' and it is worth pursuing this point so as to demonstrate *en passant* that there are genuine linguistic difficulties associated with the cross-cultural communication of Bourdieu's work. Nice was particularly conscious of this in respect of 'méconnaissance' when making his translation of *La Reproduction*. In using 'misrecognition' in rendering Bourdieu and Passeron's introduction to the French edition, Nice offered the following explanation:

> I.e. 'méconnaissance', the process whereby power relations are perceived not for what they objectively are but in a form which renders them legitimate in the eyes of the beholder. The (admittedly 'artificial') term 'misrecognition' has been

adopted because it preserves the link with 'recognition' (*reconnaissance*) in the sense of 'ratification', and is consistent with the usage of other translators.[54]

'Méconnaissance' might as usefully be rendered as 'lack of comprehension of' or 'misappreciation of', but, certainly, an appropriate paraphrase of 'misrecognition of the truth of the legitimate culture as the dominant cultural arbitrary' might be: 'not understanding that the objective truth of legitimate culture is that it is the dominant cultural arbitrary.' In other words, the meaning is that 'legitimate culture' is only such *by virtue of* its dominance rather than of any intrinsic quality. Bourdieu and Passeron are careful to say that 'in any given social formation', legitimacy is nothing other than a function of dominance. The 'dominant' is not an absolutely dominant 'high status' culture but only the dominant for that particular social formation. It is not, as Lamont and Lareau contend, that every rung defines itself in relation to 'high' culture but that, at every level, there are distance differentiations in respect of the dominant culture of that level. Each level's dominant culture is dominated in relation to the greater power of the 'higher' level. Bourdieu does have a horizontally stratified view of society but he does not, as Lamont suggests elsewhere, posit that '. . . intellectual life is a zero-sum game'[55] in which all subcultures define themselves relatively only in relation to one non-relative, 'legitimate' or 'high status' culture.

Lamont and Lareau's position explicitly has affinity with that adopted by Willis and others but, interestingly, their work brings together some of the strands of disagreement with Bourdieu's work that have been surveyed in this chapter. They set themselves the task of rescuing the concept of 'cultural capital' from misuse or abuse. They misrepresent Bourdieu's view of cultural capital but imply an exoneration of Bourdieu from his supposed position by arguing that it was the consequence of the particular characteristics of Parisian society which made possible a 'zero-sum' game of cultural position-taking. Their misrepresentation seems to endorse the cultural Marxist critique but, in fact, their argument is advanced so as to use Bourdieu's work to come to terms analytically with a society which is politically decentralised and without a strong tradition of 'high culture'. The focus of the next chapter is on whether their 'criticism' constitutes a positive and valid response to Bourdieu's work.

Notes

1. R. Brubaker (1989) 'Review of *Choses dites*', *Contemporary Sociology*, 18, 5, 783.
2. R. Harker, C. Mahar and C. Wilkes (1990) *An Introduction to the Work of Pierre Bourdieu. The Practice of Theory*, London, Macmillan, 210.
3. R. Jenkins (1992) *Pierre Bourdieu*, London, Routledge, 12.
4. In C. Calhoun, E. LiPuma and M. Postone (1993) *Bourdieu: Critical Perspectives*, Oxford, Polity Press, 235–62.
5. P. Bourdieu (1993) 'Concluding remarks: for a sociogenetic understanding of intellectual works', in C. Calhoun *et al.*, *Bourdieu: Critical Perspectives*, Oxford, Polity Press, 263.

6. D. Swartz (1977) 'Pierre Bourdieu: the cultural transmission of social inequality', *Harvard Educational Review*, 47, 4, 553.
7. E. Bredo and W. Feinberg (1979) 'Meaning, power and pedagogy: Pierre Bourdieu and Jean-Claude Passeron, Reproduction in Education, Society and Culture', *Journal of Curriculum Studies*, 11, 4, 324.
8. D. Swartz (1981) 'Classes, educational systems and labor markets. A critical evaluation of the contributions by Raymond Boudon and Pierre Bourdieu to the sociology of education', *Archives of European Sociology*, XXII, 346.
9. T. Schatzki (1987) 'Overdue analysis of Bourdieu's theory of practice', *Inquiry*, 30, 121.
10. Jenkins, *Pierre Bourdieu*, 92–3.
11. M. Lamont and A. Lareau (1988) 'Cultural capital: allusions, gaps and glissandos in recent theoretical developments', *Sociological Theory*, 6, 156.
12. M.S. Archer (1983) 'Process without system', *Archives européennes de sociologie*, 24, 1, 196.
13. J.-C. Passeron (1986) 'Theories of socio-cultural reproduction', *International Social Science Journal*, 38, 4, 619.
14. Bredo and Feinberg, 'Meaning', 317.
15. K.L. Gorder (1980) 'Understanding school knowledge: a critical appraisal of Basil Bernstein and Pierre Bourdieu', *Educational Theory*, 30, 4, 335.
16. (With J.-C. Passeron) in P. Bourdieu, J.-C. Passeron and M. de Saint Martin (eds.) (1965) *Rapport pédagogique et communication*, Paris and The Hague, Mouton (Cahiers du Centre de Sociologie Européenne, 2); translated as (1994) 'Introduction: language and relationship to language in the teaching situation', in *Academic Discourse. Linguistic Misunderstanding and Professorial Power*, Oxford, Polity Press.
17. (With J.-C. Passeron) in R. Castel and J.-C. Passeron (eds.) (1967) *Éducation, développement et démocratie*, Paris and The Hague, Mouton (Cahiers du Centre de Sociologie Européenne, 4).
18. C. Lemert (1981) 'Literary politics and the *champ* of French sociology', *Theory and Society*, 10, 651.
19. P. diMaggio (1979) 'Review of P. Bourdieu, *Reproduction in Education, Society and Culture* and *Outline of a Theory of Practice*', *American Journal of Sociology*, 84, 6, 1463, footnote 6.
20. Archer, 'Process', 216.
21. R. Jenkins (1986) 'Review of P. Bourdieu, *Distinction*', *Sociology*, 20, 1, 104.
22. See P. Bourdieu (1989) *La Noblesse d'état. Grandes Écoles et esprit de corps*, Paris, Éditions de Minuit, 20–1.
23. See, in particular, P. Bourdieu (1994) *Raisons pratiques. Sur la théorie de l'action*, Paris, Éditions du Seuil, and, for a discussion and further references, see D.M. Robbins, (1996) 'The international transmission of ideas; Pierre Bourdieu in theory and practice', *Journal of the Institute of Romance Studies*, 4, 297–306.
24. R.V. Robinson and M.A. Garnier (1985) 'Class reproduction among men and women in France: reproduction theory on its home ground', *American Journal of Sociology*, 91, 2, 256.
25. *Ibid.*, 250.
26. *Ibid.*, 255.
27. *Ibid.*, 256–7.
28. *Ibid.*, 257.
29. Delivered in May 1996 and produced by the Collège de France on cassette and available from *Le Livre qui parle*, 24550 Villefranche-du-Périgord, France.
30. B.M. Berger (1986) 'Review essay: "Taste and domination"', *American Journal of Sociology*, 91, 6, 1450.
31. M. de Saint Martin (1993) *L'Espace de la noblesse*, Paris, Éditions Métailié.
32. M. de Saint Martin (1980) 'Une grande famille', *Actes de la recherche en sciences sociales*, 31, 4–21.

33. P. Bourdieu and M. de Saint Martin (1982) 'La sainte famille. L'épiscopat français et le champ du pouvoir', *Actes de la recherche en sciences sociales*, 44–45, 2–54.
34. N. Garnham (1986) 'Extended review: Bourdieu's *Distinction*', *The Sociological Review*, 34, 2, 432.
35. S. Lash (1993) 'Pierre Bourdieu: cultural economy and social change' in Calhoun *et al.*, *Bourdieu*, 210.
36. See Bourdieu's own discussion in (1981) 'Décrire et prescrire. Note sur les conditions de possibilité et les limites de l'efficacité politique', *Actes de la recherche en sciences sociales*, 38, 69–73.
37. S. Lash (1993) 'Pierre Bourdieu: cultural economy and social change' in Calhoun *et al.*, *Bourdieu*, 210.
38. P. Bourdieu with J.-C. Passeron (1977) *Reproduction in Education, Society and Culture*, London and Beverly Hills, CA, Sage, 5.
39. Bredo and Feinberg, 'Meaning', 329.
40. Gorder, 'Understanding', 341.
41. *Ibid.*, 345.
42. *Ibid.*, 344.
43. Jenkins, 'Review', 104.
44. P. Bourdieu (1984) *Distinction, A Social Critique of the Judgement of Taste*, London, Routledge & Kegan Paul, 379; quoted in Jenkins, 'Review', 104.
45. Bourdieu, *Distinction*, 379.
46. P. Bourdieu with L. Boltanski, R. Castel and J.C. Chamboredon (1990) *Photography, a Middle-Brow Art*, Oxford, Polity Press, 7–8.
47. A. Honneth (1986) 'The fragmented world of symbolic forms: reflections on Pierre Bourdieu's sociology of culture', *Theory, Culture and Society*, 3, 3, 61.
48. *Ibid.*, 61–2.
49. *Ibid.*, 61.
50. Lamont and Lareau, 'Cultural capital', 157.
51. *Ibid.*
52. Bourdieu, *Reproduction*, 31.
53. P. Bourdieu with J.-C. Passeron (1970) *La Reproduction. Éléments pour une théorie du système d'enseignement*, Paris, Éditions de Minuit, 46.
54. Bourdieu and Passeron, *Reproduction*, xiii.
55. M. Lamont (1989) 'Slipping the world back in: Bourdieu on Heidegger', *Contemporary Sociology*, 18, 5, 782.

8 Meta-criticism: charting interminable territory

The previous chapter tried to represent critically some of the criticisms that have been made of Bourdieu's work. It showed that the main local disagreements – that the work does not transfer cross-culturally or cross-temporally and that it denigrates working-class culture – all follow from the disinclination of critics to accept the particular epistemological basis of Bourdieu's projects.

In his own brief response to his critics (published as 'Concluding remarks: for a sociogenetic understanding of intellectual works', in *Bourdieu: Critical Perspectives*) Bourdieu first emphasises those misunderstandings which relate to the international circulation of ideas. He argues that consumers of his works have found grounds for criticising them either because they have synchronised them or because they have atomised them. Scrutiny of the secondary literature certainly confirms that many critics have responded to single texts in isolation or have thematically aggregated several texts without reference to the sequence of their production. Bourdieu proposes two responses to this situation.

He first proposes that the consumers of his work should reflect systematically on the social conditions within which they receive the messages transmitted by his texts:

> Texts, as we know, circulate without their contexts, . . . It follows that the categories of perception and interpretation that readers apply to them, being themselves linked to a field of production subject to different traditions, have every chance of being more or less inadequate . . . To prevent the cultural disjunctures due to the gap between different historical traditions from introducing misunderstanding at the very heart of even the most benevolent and welcoming communication, I believe it is necessary that all researchers concerned about the progress of their respective scientific fields ask of the sociology of science weapons against the social mechanisms capable of introducing distortions into scientific exchanges. In such matters, the implementation of the principle of *reflexivity* is one of the most efficient ways to put into practice the internationalism that science presupposes and promotes.[1]

Secondly, however, Bourdieu suggests that some misunderstandings of his works can be attributed to the failure of critics to consider the field of their production. As Bourdieu puts it:

They thus uncover apparent contradictions that would vanish if they replaced each of the theses or hypotheses in question back in the movement, or even better, in the progress of my work; if, more precisely, they strove to reproduce the evolution (or the chain) of thought that led me to change progressively without for that ever effecting a resounding 'self-critique' . . .[2]

The problem with these two proposed forms of response is, of course, that both formally consolidate the model which is itself in question. By expecting his critics to attend to the field of their consumption or to the field of his production, Bourdieu is asking his critics to accept his model of cultural production and consumption, conceptualised in terms of fields, as a prerequisite for evaluating it. Critics are forced to take two tacks away from engagement with the *content* of Bourdieu's work. On the one hand, Bourdieu's deployment of his concepts within his texts discourages any assessment of their capacity to explain anything that one might call 'reality'. On the other hand, Bourdieu's embodiment of his concepts in his actions means that he asks that his texts should be read as elements in the process which is his social trajectory. Bourdieu denies referentiality within his texts and of his texts. The situation, therefore, for Bourdieu criticism is as described by MacIntyre in respect of moral discourse when he wrote that 'The most striking feature of contemporary moral utterance is that so much of it is used to express disagreements; and the most striking feature of the debates in which these disagreements are expressed is their interminable character'.[3] Or, as MacIntyre elaborates, the situation is one of 'conceptual incommensurability', by which he means that 'Every one of the arguments is logically valid or can be easily expanded so as to be made so; the conclusions do indeed follow from the premises. But the rival premises are such that we possess no rational way of weighing the claims of one as against another'.[4]

In his review of *Distinction*, Berger graphically represents this dilemma when he writes of Bourdieu: '. . . in saying that I think that he is fundamentally correct in his systematic understandings of the linkages between class and status I am aware that I am saying little more than: I like the way he thinks because he thinks as I do.'[5] What we might call 'MacIntyre's position' is also trapped within its own diagnosis and Bourdieu might retort that his sense of incommensurability arises from a mistaken elevation of the function of rationality in resolving disputes. For Bourdieu, perhaps, incommensurability can be avoided if all parties in disputes are adequately reflexive in such a way that they acknowledge that the artificially produced 'rational' discourses which they use simply conceal processes of social reproduction which have distorted an original or underlying ontological harmony.

The purpose of this chapter is to try to find a way out of the impasse of interminability and incommensurability which either does or logically should inhibit fundamental discussion of Bourdieu's work. It will explore two strategic responses to the problem. It will draw on Bourdieu's own proposed responses but will seek to do so in such a way that a solution is suggested which does not necessarily endorse Bourdieu's own concepts even though it does endorse his view of the function of conceptualisation.

Bourdieu's first response was to encourage critics to be reflexive within their fields. In making this suggestion, Bourdieu tacitly insists that consumers should see themselves as situated within a field that is external to the field of production. Reflexive external consumption takes the product as given. It rules out the kind of inquiry into the validity of a text which, in accordance with Bourdieu's theory, is competitively possible within the field of its production. Bourdieu's second response invites critics to understand the genesis of his intellectual products. Expressed in this way, the invitation seems to have a teleological impetus: the genesis has to be understood *in order to* vindicate the products and to ensure that they are not open to criticism in themselves. My first strategic response to incommensurability is to offer, in outline, a vicarious reflexivity by examining the contexts of some of the local disagreements that have already been discussed. This will have the effect of relativising Bourdieu's products by comparative reference to several fields of consumption. My second strategic response is to explore some criticisms that have been made of Bourdieu from within the French intellectual field. These will also have the effect of relativising his production because they will show that Bourdieu made conceptual choices within the field of alternative possibilities that were available to him. The intention is to argue that these strategies remove incommensurability because they disclose some of the alternative possibilities of production and consumption within which Bourdieu's work is situated. By contrast, it is argued, Bourdieu's responses – understandably – contrive to consolidate commitment to his actual choices rather than to point to the commensurability of all possible choices.

My outline for a sociology of the critical reception of Bourdieu's work highlights three clusters of response which are defined nationally, temporally and, in part, by disciplinary or emergent disciplinary discourse. The first of these clusters is associated with the 'cultural Marxism' response discussed in the previous chapter and considered *en passant* in the Introduction. By the end of the 1960s, Bourdieu had, with colleagues, carried out researches on student culture as well as on photography as an emergent cultural form and on museums as purveyors of consecrated culture. Most of this work was unknown in England in the 1970s. Until the publication of *Reproduction* in 1977, the few articles that were known were appropriated by the institutionalised discourse which derived its name – 'new directions in the sociology of education' – from the subtitle of M.F.D. Young's collection of essays called *Knowledge and Control*. Nevertheless, at the height of their collaboration at the end of the 1960s, the interests of Bourdieu and Passeron were primarily 'cultural' and only secondarily 'educational'. Hence, in 1970, Bourdieu's publication, in the collection which he edited for the Éditions de Minuit, of Passeron's translation of Hoggart's *The Uses of Literacy* with the title: *La Culture du pauvre: étude sur le style de vie des classes populaires en Angleterre.*[6] *The Uses of Literacy* – first published in

1957 – was the work of a man who had grown up in an area that was 'half-surrounded by working-class terrace houses'[7]; had gained a place at the local grammar school; then studied English literature at the local university and, after World War II, had been a tutor in English literature in the Adult Education Department of the University of Hull. The study can be said to have been ethnographic and presociological. Bourdieu and Passeron were attracted by the text of a man who, without any partisan ideology, sought to describe a working-class culture with which he was familiar but from which he was educationally separated. Hoggart established the Centre for Contemporary Cultural Studies at the University of Birmingham in 1964, but he was succeeded as Director, in 1968, by Stuart Hall. It was Hall who gave the field of Hoggart's interest an ideological orientation and it was Hall who found Bourdieu's understanding of 'ideology' theoretically useful in effecting this shift of orientation. In his 'The hinterland of science: ideology and the "Sociology of knowledge"', Hall discusses Bourdieu on the basis of two translations[8] made by Nice – a member of staff in the centre – and published internally in the year of the publication of *Reproduction*. As Foley has summarised, the centre produced, in the 1970s, '. . . a series of in-house theoretical debates on ideology . . . , culture . . . , history . . . , and several empirical critiques of the English state . . . , student sub-cultures . . . , school reforms . . . , and racism . . .'[9] and he suggests that this was the 'general context' of the thought of Paul Willis. Foley's 'Does the working class have a culture in the anthropological sense?' begins with an account of the background to Willis's *Learning to Labour* (1977) – the text to which so many cultural Marxist critics have referred in criticising Bourdieu. Foley argues that Willis followed Raymond Williams and E.P. Thompson to make the case that '. . . class cultures are lived, profane experiences rooted in working-class communities that struggle against bourgeois ideological dominance. Working-class people construct their own distinct, rewarding, honorable ways of life'.[10] There is a sense in which Willis and researchers at the Birmingham centre wanted to see their work as contributing to the struggle against bourgeois dominance. For them, perhaps, Hoggart was a *transfuge* – a deserter to his class, someone whose work was ideologically patronising because it was not informed by an understanding of the socio-economic forces constituting the conditions which he observed. It was in this situation, I suggest, that the critiques of Bourdieu acquire their significance. There was an ambiguity in the response to Bourdieu in the English cultural study community, an ambiguity that was sustained by Bourdieu's willingness to carry translations of extracts from the work of Williams, Thompson, Klingender and Willis in the *Actes de la recherche en sciences sociales* in the late 1970s.[11] There was the feeling both that Bourdieu was, like Hoggart, a socialist, intellectual *transfuge*, and also that his solutions to the theoretical difficulties posed by Marx and Weber were stimulating and satisfying. Hence the tension that often, for instance in the work of Jenkins, leads to a response which confusedly merges an affinity with Bourdieu's intellectual problem-solving with an apparent contempt for his social position. Hence the enthusiasm of the critical account of Bourdieu given collaboratively by Williams and Garnham which, nevertheless, has to be qualified by uncertainty about 'the question of Bourdieu's politics'.[12]

The key figure in the second cluster of respondents is Axel Honneth, although the *éminence grise* in the background is Habermas. In March 1983 – less than a year after Bourdieu had given his inaugural lecture as professor – Habermas delivered four lectures at the Collège de France, Paris, which were to be published as the first four chapters of his *The Philosophical Discourse of Modernity* (1987). This text was published in German in 1985 and, in an *Excursus on the Obsolescence of the Production Paradigm*, Habermas comments:

> As long as the theory of modernity takes its orientation from the basic concepts of the philosophy of reflection – from ideas of knowledge, conscious awareness, self-consciousness – the intrinsic connection with the concept of reason or of rationality is obvious. This is not as evident with the basic concepts of the philosophy of praxis, such as action, self-generation, and labor.[13]

He goes on to argue that notions of practice and reason were still linked in Marxian theory, but that two different lines of thought had developed in western Marxism since the 1920s, one influenced by Weber and the other by Husserl and Heidegger. The early Lukacs and Critical Theory, he continues, '. . . developed a critical concept of rationality on the basis of a materialistic appropriation of Hegel, but without appealing to the production paradigm *for this purpose*'.[14] Whereas the early Marcuse and later Sartre '. . . renewed the production paradigm . . . without appealing to a concept of rationality *for this purpose*'.[15] This diagnosis is the prelude to Habermas's contention that 'These two traditions start to converge only within the paradigm shift from productive activity to communicative action and the reformulation of the concept of the life-world in terms of communications theory . . .'[16] And, finally, he claims that '. . . the theory of communicative action establishes an internal relation between practice and rationality. It studies the suppositions of rationality inherent in ordinary communicative practice and conceptualizes the normative content of action oriented to mutual understanding in terms of communicative rationality'.[17]

The problem for the German response to Bourdieu was to decide whether his theory – which clearly borrowed from Marx, Weber and Sartre – retained the notion of production or could be conducive to the theory of communicative rationality. Honneth was research assistant to Habermas at this time and, in 1984, he published in German the paper which appeared in translation in 1986 as 'The fragmented world of symbolic forms: reflections on Pierre Bourdieu's sociology of culture'. In the mean time, with two Frankfurt colleagues, he had been given an interview by Bourdieu in April 1985. A version of this interview appeared in translation alongside Honneth's translated article in 1986. The interview begins with an introductory statement by the interviewers to the effect that it is Bourdieu's attempt to reconcile Marx with Weber that is of most interest. They say: 'It is the attempt to integrate class and life-world analysis, economic and culture analysis, that we find so interesting in your work.'[18] Honneth's article had tried to investigate the development of Bourdieu's thinking in order to understand how he had merged the Marxist and Weberian legacies, '. . . how both elements coalesce into a single unified theory, how Bourdieu brings the concept of class struggle and the study of symbolic forms of expression together into a theory of late-capitalist culture . . .'[19] Honneth's interpretation of *Outline of a Theory of Practice* is that Bourdieu had recourse to a form of utilitarianism to overcome structuralism – that in emphasising human agency Bourdieu adopted a view of human behaviour that supposes that individuals and groups are motivated by the desire to maximise their status or their happiness. This interpretation leads Honneth to comment that

> . . . this utilitarian transformation of anthropological structuralism was based from the outset on an unclarified problem still to be found in Bourdieu's theory today: does Bourdieu regard the symbolic struggles on which he focused as disputes over the interpretation of an intersubjectively recognized system of classification and value, or does he regard them as struggles for the establishment of group-specific ways of classification, which totally lack the common bond of a social consensus?[20]

Honneth has a shrewd idea that Bourdieu follows the second option. He regards the concept of *habitus* as a device which enables Bourdieu to present individuals as the *unconscious* implementers of the utility maximisation drives of the groups to which they belong. This leads Honneth to conclude that, in terms of the opposition posited by Habermas, Bourdieu's theory gives too much prominence to human action as a form of production rather than to human rationality. As Honneth expresses it: 'The central economic concepts upon which his cultural analysis is based, compel him to subsume all forms of social conflicts under the type of struggles which occur over social distribution – although the struggle for the social recognition of moral models clearly obeys a different logic.'[21] Or, as he decisively concludes:

> Bourdieu's study repeatedly gives rise to the erroneous idea that the social recognition of a life-style and of the values it embodies can be gained in the same way as an economic good. Only by decisively abandoning the utilitarian framework of his empirical analyses could he have avoided making this crucial misunderstanding.[22]

The reception of Bourdieu's work in the German intellectual field in the mid-1980s, therefore, was dominated by the essentially theoretical concerns of social and political philosophers. Bourdieu's work was thought to make a contribution to the debate between 'class' and 'status' which was still perceived to be a live issue.[23] This German response showed little awareness of the influence of Durkheim on Bourdieu's work, or of the tradition of French naturalism which, as manifested in the work of Flaubert and Manet, Bourdieu sought to espouse, or, importantly, of the influence of the Bachelardian tradition of historical epistemology. It received Bourdieu on its own terms and found the 'theory' which they endeavoured to extrapolate from his work wanting on those terms. Bourdieu's reissue of his *L'Ontologie politique de Martin Heidegger* in 1988 should, perhaps, be seen as a form of retaliatory critique of the highly theoreticist nature of the German academic tradition.

Elements of the German critical orientation have been transported to the USA. Ringer, Joppke and Brubaker hold American academic posts but see Bourdieu within a conceptual framework which is essentially German. Brubaker has been a significant figure in the third exemplary cluster of respondents to Bourdieu's work – a cluster that might, imprecisely, be described as the Chicago cluster. Brubaker's *The Limits of Rationality: An Essay on the Social and Moral Thought of Max Weber* (1984) sustained the influence of Weberian thinking in the USA, but it offered a perspective on Weber which would have been anathema to the Frankfurt School. Brubaker explored the paradox of Weber's thought – that 'Modern man, then, cannot escape making a criterionless and therefore non-rational choice about the very meaning of rationality'.[24] Or, spelling this out in terms reminiscent of the 'MacIntyre position', that '. . . in Weber's view there is no rational way of deciding among the plurality of conflicting possible value commitments. Every rational life, in short, is founded on a non-rational choice'.[25] Given this reading of Weber, it is not surprising that Brubaker should have been attracted to Bourdieu's work. His 'Rethinking classical theory. The sociological vision of Pierre Bourdieu' (1985) offered '. . . an analytical overview and critical appraisal of Bourdieu's work . . .'[26] but it did so in a way that acknowledged, as the positivists did not, that Bourdieu's concepts are 'metatheoretical notions' that 'are not intended to constitute a theory'.[27] This realisation led Brubaker to seek to understand Bourdieu's social theory *as* habitus rather than to understand objectively his theory *of* habitus, and hence 'Social theory as habitus' was the title of his contribution to *Bourdieu: Critical Perspectives* (1993).

Several American articles of the mid-1980s drew attention to the way in which the concept of 'habit' had been used in American sociology down to around 1918, but had been suppressed in the period between the two world wars. In the abstract of his 'The matter of habit' (1986), Camic summarised his argument to the effect that the concept had been excised from the discipline as a result of '. . . the interdisciplinary disputes that surrounded the institutionalization of sociology as an academic discipline, particularly sociology's struggles with behaviorist psychology, which had by then projected into prominence a notion of habit deriving from 19th-century biological thought'.[28] He praises Bourdieu's attempt to revive the concept. Ostrow had earlier attempted to insert Bourdieu's notion of *habitus* into a tradition of thought which he associated in part with Husserl but, equally importantly, with Dewey. Citing Dewey's *Human Nature and Conduct: An Introduction to Social Psychology* (1922), Ostrow refers his reader to a secondary text for '. . . a comprehensive analysis of Dewey's theory of habit, or, rather, of experience *founded* on habits . . .'[29] Without referring to Bourdieu, but building on the article by Camic, Baldwin sought, in 1988, to extend '. . . the research on the removal of the concept of habit from sociological theory by evaluating the treatment of habit by George Herbert Mead and symbolic interactionists'.[30] The sense that the response to Bourdieu's work in the USA is linked with an anti-positivist attempt to revive the orientation of the first Chicago School of Sociology is confirmed not just by the association of *habitus* with the use of 'habit' by Dewey and Mead, but, also, by the way in which Wacquant headed his 'Symbolic violence and the making of the French agriculturalist: an enquiry into Pierre Bourdieu's sociology' (1987) with W.I. Thomas's dictum that 'If men define situations as real, they are real in their consequences'.[31] Wacquant's article had first been given at a conference on social theory held in Chicago in April 1986. Wacquant was employed at the University of Chicago as research assistant to W.J. Wilson on the project which led to the publication of *The Truly Disadvantaged* (1987), and it was a year later that there began the sequence of encounters which formed the basis for *Réponses* (1992), translated as *An Invitation to Reflexive Sociology* (1992). What is known in that text as the 'Chicago Workshop' was the product, first of all, of Bourdieu's encounter in the spring of 1988 with a group of doctoral students at the University of Chicago '. . . who had organized, under the guidance of Loïc Wacquant, a semester-long seminar on my work'.[32] Meanwhile, during this same period, readings and discussions of Bourdieu's work had taken place within the Social Theory Group that had been established at the Center for Psychosocial Studies in Chicago in 1983. Bourdieu joined in these discussions on two occasions, including a conference held between 31 March and 2 April 1989, which led to the collection of essays published as *Bourdieu: Critical Perspectives*. Although only two of the contributors to this volume were academic staff of the University of Chicago, it was, nevertheless, the culmination of a second Chicago-based initiative in the reception of Bourdieu's work. If this conference assembled people who were sympathetic towards Bourdieu's position, a second conference held in Chicago in the same week deliberately engineered a confrontation between intellectual positions represented by Bourdieu on the one hand and Coleman – Professor of Sociology at the University of Chicago – on the other. In his Prologue to the published version of the conference proceedings – *Social Theory for a Changing Society* (1991) – Coleman argued that social theory had developed on the basis of an interpretation of 'primordial social organization' but should now concern itself 'with the problems of constructed social organization'.[33] The clear suggestion is that Bourdieu's kind of social anthropology or sociology seeks to maintain a link between the primordial and the constructed that ought now to be severed.

These Chicago encounters of the late 1980s indicate that Bourdieu's work had become a battleground for competing conceptions of contemporary society and, relatedly, of competing ways of understanding it. Typically, Bourdieu's response to Coleman was to argue not, as Coleman implies, that professional social theorists have to adapt their understandings to fit the new, constructed condition of society, but, instead, that reflexive sociological practitioners have to construct a space within society from which they can influence the course of social construction. Bourdieu asks for the formation of an international community which will reconcile the diverse primordial cultures of its members and, in doing so, constitute a challenge to the constructed social organisation that owes its dominance to its divorce from human agency.

Bourdieu's epilogue to the text – 'On the possibility of a field of world sociology' – offers a humanist vision of the role of sociology in global society. It would appear to prescribe a function for sociological thinking that transcends partisan differences within the sociological field. It is the climax of Bourdieu's attempt to make his particularity universal. But the response of the Chicago cluster to Bourdieu's work makes clear that Bourdieu's approach is in direct opposition to positivism and, as such, has been involved in a partisan struggle within the sociological field. The epilogue's virtual call for a universalisation of ethnomethodology is a direct challenge to the universalist positivism that has consistently found Bourdieu's procedures unscientific and untransferable.

In the final sentences of his 'Symbolic violence and the making of the French agriculturalist: an enquiry into Pierre Bourdieu's sociology' (1987), Wacquant concluded that 'The time may be ripe for speaking about the coming of age of a new "school" in French sociology. If this is so, then it is crucial, both for it and for a critical science of society, that it not remain exclusively French too long'.[34] He was, in other words, involved in a conscious attempt strategically to universalise Bourdieu's particularism. Although Wacquant was concerned to secure the validity of Bourdieu's theory, he also advanced the view that Bourdieu's work could best be understood by appreciating the pragmatic utility of his concepts. Many other authors have responded in this same way to Bourdieu's work, demonstrating the practical uses of *habitus* or 'cultural capital' in their empirical investigations. Articles by Schiltz; Bentley; Hanks; Sack; Gerhards and Anheier; Rupp and de Lange; and Ringer all testify to the pragmatic value of Bourdieu's work in different intellectual fields and applied in different cultural contexts.[35] These texts provide consumer testimony to the value of Bourdieu's intellectual product. They reinforce a proselytising tendency. From the field of consumption, they are not much concerned to ask whether a different product might have performed a different or better task. This analysis of the critical response to Bourdieu's work must turn, finally, to those criticisms which question his conceptual schema at its point of origin from within the field of its production.

Almost as if in reaction to his encounters with American sociologists, Bourdieu himself began to emphasise in the late 1980s that his work belonged to a different intellectual tradition. In 'Thinking about limits' (1992) – the translation of a paper given in 1989 – Bourdieu gave the following description of this tradition:

> What I now very quickly want to address is the epistemological tradition in which I have begun to work. This was for me like the air that we breathe, which is to say that it went unnoticed. It is a very local tradition tied to a number of French names: Koyré, Bachelard, Canguilhem and, if we go back a little, to Duhem . . . This historical tradition of epistemology very strongly linked reflection on science with the history of science. Differently from the neo-positivist Anglo-Saxon tradition, it was from the history of science that it isolated the principles of knowledge of scientific thought.[36]

An antecedent of this tradition was Claude Bernard. Bourdieu quoted from Bernard's *Introduction à l'étude de la médécine expérimentale* (1865) in his brief notes on 'Statistics and sociology' contained within *Travail et travailleurs en Algérie*. In his classic text, Bernard had argued that

> When a scientist pursues investigation, taking for his starting-point any particular philosophic system, he loses himself in regions too far removed from reality, or else the system gives his mind a misleading assurance and inflexibility which goes ill with the freedom and adaptibility which an experimenter should always preserve in his researches.[37]

As an experimental physiologist, Bernard was determined that his scientific work should not be contaminated by philosophical presuppositions which were the legacy, for instance, of scholastic thinking about the mind and the body. In following this tradition of thought, Bachelard emphasised that knowledge could only be advanced if scientific discourses could be constructed which would be appropriate to the phenomena under examination. His emphasis was more on the need for an 'epistemological break' of any kind rather than on a rejection of philosophy. Indeed, Bachelard was himself sufficiently a historian and philosopher of science to want to understand the social and historical conditions that made for historically different constructions of scientific discourse.

This shift of emphasis is important, because Bourdieu has followed Bachelard more than Bernard. Bourdieu has argued that the practice of sociology involves making a break with commonsense social perceptions, and he has also argued that the social conditions of that break need to be reflexively understood. In arguing these two positions, however, Bourdieu has effectively taken the *intellectual* sources of his break out of the equation. He has avoided direct confrontation with the problems which arise from adapting the language of pre-existing discourses to furnish explanations of social phenomena. There have been three fundamental criticisms of Bourdieu in France – from critics who breathe the same air as him. The first is that Bourdieu has *imported* philosophical concepts into social science. The second is that Bourdieu's transference of concepts between discourses has been to the detriment of social science. Thirdly, there has been the suggestion, from within a postwar French intellectual tradition as dependent on philosophical phenomenology as on Bachelardian philosophy of science, that Bourdieu's work blurs the distinction that has to be made between the capacity of concepts to be logically transferable and the capacity of human agents actually socially to convert and reconvert themselves.

The first two criticisms are different versions of the same concern about the relationship between the process of social scientific inquiry and the language used in formulating hypotheses and in offering explanations. Héran's 'La seconde nature de l'habitus. Tradition philosophique et sens commun dans le langage sociologique',[38] published in the *Revue française de sociologie* in 1987, offers not so much a critique of Bourdieu as a recognition and articulation of the problems with which he has grappled. Following a disciple of Husserl – Eugen Fink – Héran distinguishes between 'thematic' and 'operational' concepts and he argues that the attempt to pin down the thematic meanings of concepts has to be renounced. He proceeds to examine Bourdieu's use of the concept of *habitus* as a case study from which to draw conclusions about the relations between philosophy and sociology. He asks whether sociology can enlist the aid of philosophical concepts for its own operational purposes '. . . without acquiring with the words themselves all of the difficulties which are deposited in them? Conversely, does sociology have the means to forge from new its own concepts by rejecting the categories already refined by the philosophical tradition?'[39] By analogy, Bernard's response to these questions would be that it would be essential for sociology to forge its own discourse. It is clear, however, that Héran conducts his analysis within the philosophical tradition which generated Bourdieu's practice. In making the comment that 'Like many French philosophers trained at this time [in the late 1950s and early 1960s], Bourdieu has a kind of familiarity with phenomenology which sometimes does not need to be stated in detail'[40] Héran implies that Bourdieu's use of the concept was itself a manifestation of its almost unconscious activity or influence: a concept of *habitus* was part of Bourdieu's *habitus*. It follows that Héran concludes that it is never possible to retrieve philosophical concepts from their various discourse uses, that '. . . to retrieve consciously the integrity of intellectual endeavours which have become assimilated is unthinkable'.[41]

Héran raises the question of the exchangeability of intellectual discourses in a manner which would have been congenial to Bourdieu and, indeed, Bourdieu's 'The genesis of the concepts of *habitus* and field' (1985) explores his own practice within the same philosophical assumptions. Other French critics, however, considered the problem with particular reference to Bourdieu's sociological deployment of economic terms. Caillé's 'La sociologie de l'intérêt est-elle intéressante'[42] first raised this issue in 1981 in the journal, *Sociologie du Travail*, where it was subsequently sustained in Adair's 'La sociologie phagocytée par l'économique: remarques critiques à propos de "ce que parler veut dire" de P. Bourdieu'[43] (1984).

Whereas Honneth was, at about the same time, arguing that Bourdieu was wrongly overemphasising the economic determination of the social and aesthetic actions of agents, the French critics were more concerned about Bourdieu's strategic confusion of the languages of different disciplines. Adair observed that '. . . the paradoxical virtue offered by recourse to economic concepts consists for the sociologist in enabling him to avoid falling into economism'.[44] For Adair, there were two consequences of Bourdieu's paradoxical use of economic language. Bourdieu had, by this ambiguous means, by his 'subtle game of recourse to/rejection of economics',[45] maximised his personal distinction and safeguarded the *institutional* survival of a discipline – sociology – that was finding itself threatened by 'the imperialism of economics'[46] but, at the same time, he had forfeited the *intellectual* autonomy of properly sociological explanation. Sociology had become intellectually absorbed into political economy. The institutional and personal victory was Pyrrhic.

In the terms outlined by Héran, it should be retorted that no recourse is possible to 'pure' sociology or 'pure' economics. Bourdieu would surely argue that recent developments towards the establishment of 'socio-economics' or 'sociological economics' indicate that 'economics' is in the process of being sociologised as much as, in the 1980s, it appeared that sociology was being economised. As Zelizer argued in a paper given to the first annual seminar of the Center for Economy and Society in California in 1988, 'The market is no longer a safe place to theorize. Its longstanding neutrality is being increasingly violated by scholars from various disciplines who refuse to treat the market as a purely economic institution'.[47] Bourdieu could be thought to be prominent amongst those scholars determined to violate the neutrality of economics. What is at issue, therefore, for some French critics, is not so much the direction of conceptual transfer as the fluctuating and unpredictable nature of the exchange. This, finally, raises the question of the relationship between conceptual and actual change.

In a revealing footnote to an article on Bourdieu and Passeron's 'theory of symbolic violence', Lakomski digressed to make the following comment on Giddens' position in the structure/agency debate:

> Thus I do not think that one of Anthony Giddens's most central arguments regarding agency, namely that the agent 'could have acted otherwise' is tenable if he thinks that 'could' denotes a real psychological possibility. If, on the other hand, 'could' merely indicates a *logical* possibility, then no harm is done.[48]

Whether or not Giddens would want to take the defence that is proffered here, Bourdieu certainly could not. His philosophical position requires that he is not able to distinguish between logical and actual possibilities. Consistent with his socio-logical position, Bourdieu argues that the capacity of descriptions to become prescriptive depends on the power that can be mobilised in support of them. There is no fixed equation that can cover the transference of logic into practice. The relative autonomy of the two spheres is a function of the power situation when they encounter each other. In an early French review of *Esquisse d'une théorie de la pratique*, Liénard and Servais recognized that it had been Bourdieu's intention to break the divide between anthropology and sociology, or, better, to effect a transfer of concepts from traditionally anthropological objects to socio- logical ones: 'The radical challenge represented by the theory of practice would not have been possible without the intent to abolish in practice the break between these disciplines. Each of these disciplines governs a par- ticular theoretical tradition having specific epistemological pitfalls.'[49] Within the French tradition, they accept that disciplines are socially con- structed discourses which, to some extent, self-fulfillingly reproduce the perspectives which they adopt. They praise Bourdieu's attempt to break down these closed explanatory systems, but they assume that the Bachelar- dian 'epistemological break' must be absolute rather than itself historically contingent. For Bourdieu, however, 'breaks' must always be contingent in two respects. Bourdieu applies to his own theorising his thinking about the validity of Marxist explanation in 'Condition de classe et position de classe' or of structuralist explanation in 'The three forms of theoretical know- ledge'. The linguistic frameworks available to analysts are functions of their social positions just as are the conditions which are accessible to their observation. Logical description is a function of the actual and perceived world of the observer, but it only acquires prescriptive validity when its power to impose explanation is endorsed by those who receive it within that perceived world. Bourdieu does not set himself up to be a liberal intellectual version of an Olympian god. He has not wantonly shifted be- tween philosophical, anthropological, sociological or cultural discourses. Instead, he has attempted to move conceptually with the flow of events, constructing his logical shifts contingently by reference to circumstances within which he has been a participant. *Sociologie de l'Algérie* was a politi- cal intervention in that it sought to objectify indigenous Algerian cultures and bring them to the consciousnesses of citizens of metropolitan France, whereas *Travail et travailleurs en Algérie* and *Le Déracinement* were at- tempts to influence the course of Algerian independence from within. The transference from a structuralist anthropological logic to a sociological one was effected by advocating intellectual reflexivity (in *Le Métier de so- ciologue*), by preaching and practising a deconstruction of his own struc- turalism (in *Esquisse d'une théorie de la pratique*), but, also, crucially, by sounding out the validity of the transference by reference to a region – the Béarn – where the actual conditions within mainland France bore com- parison with those in Algeria. The endorsement of the process of logical transferability was provided interpersonally by Bourdieu's familial situa- tion within the Béarn and this experiential corroboration persisted, for Bourdieu, in his adoption of the language of anthropology in *Les Héritiers* to describe the situation of students whose social and intellectual trajecto- ries mirrored his own.

The culmination of this point, of course, is reached in considering our current reception of Bourdieu's works in this light. We are the respondents to his texts. Bourdieu has mobilised his authority to speak to us, but we have the capacity to judge, not whether his concepts have abstract value but whether they are useful to us, apt to our situations. This chapter began by arguing that judgements of Bourdieu's work are of an indeterminate nature. It has tried to show that criticisms that might have been thought to relate intrinsically to Bourdieu's work emanate in part from the attempts of different intellectual traditions to assimilate it – either positively or negatively. It has shown, finally, that criticisms advanced within the distinctively French intellectual tradition have served to clarify that Bourdieu amalgamated the legacies of phenomenology and Bachelardian history and philosophy of science to construct an unique version of philosophical pragmatism or, more correctly, instrumentalism. As pragmatic respondents in our cultures, how are we to reach a conclusion about the analyses which Bourdieu pragmatically offers us from his?

Notes

1. P. Bourdieu (1993) 'Concluding remarks: For a sociogenetic understanding of intellectual works', in C. Calhoun *et al.*, eds. *Bourdieu: Critical Perspectives*, Oxford, Polity Press, 263–4.
2. *Ibid.*, 264.
3. A. MacIntyre (1985) *After Virtue. A Study in Moral Theory* (2nd edn), London, Duckworth, 6.
4. *Ibid.*, 8.
5. B.M. Berger (1986) 'Review essay: "Taste and domination"', *American Journal of Sociology*, 91, 6, 1447.
6. *The Culture of the Poor: A Study of the Life-Style of the Popular Classes in England.*
7. R. Hoggart (1973) 'Growing up', in *Speaking to Each Other*, Harmondsworth, Penguin Books, 11.
8. See S. Hall (1978) 'The hinterland of science: ideology and the "sociology of knowledge"', in *On Ideology*, London, CCCS/Hutchinson, 31, footnote 43; for the English translation of Bourdieu's paper, 'Symbolic power', cf. (1977) *Two Bourdieu Texts* (trans. R. Nice), Birmingham, CCCS Stencilled Papers no.46.
9. D.E. Foley (1989) 'Does the working class have a culture in the anthropological sense?', *Cultural Anthropology*, 4, 137.
10. *Ibid.*
11. See: R. Williams (1977) 'Plaisantes perspectives. Invention du paysage et abolition du paysan', *Actes de la recherche en sciences sociales*, 17–18, 29–36. E.P. Thompson (1976) 'Modes de domination et révolutions en Angleterre', *Actes de la recherche en sciences sociales*, 2–3, 133–151. F. Klingender (1978) 'Joseph Wright de Derby, peintre de la révolution industrielle', *Actes de la recherche en sciences sociales*, 23, 23–36. P. Willis (1978) 'L'école des ouvriers', *Actes de la recherche en sciences sociales*, 24, 50–61.
12. N. Garnham and R. Williams (1980) 'Pierre Bourdieu and the sociology of culture', *Media, Culture and Society*, 2, 222.
13. J. Habermas (1987) *The Philosophical Discourse of Modernity*, Oxford, Polity Press, 75.
14. *Ibid.*
15. *Ibid.*, 75–6.
16. *Ibid.*, 76.

17. *Ibid.*
18. A. Honneth, H. Kocyba and B. Schwibs (1986) 'The struggle for symbolic order. An interview with Pierre Bourdieu', *Theory, Culture and Society*, 3, 3, 35. (The introductory statement does not appear in the French publication of the interview – entitled 'Fieldwork in philosophy' – in P. Bourdieu (1987) *Choses dites*, Paris, Éditions de Minuit, nor in the English translation in P. Bourdieu (1990) *In Other Words*, Oxford, Polity Press.)
19. A. Honneth (1986) 'The fragmented world of symbolic forms: reflections on Pierre Bourdieu's sociology of culture', *Theory, Culture and Society*, 3, 3, 55.
20. *Ibid.*, 56.
21. *Ibid.*, 65.
22. *Ibid.*
23. See C. Joppke (1986) 'The cultural dimensions of class formation and class struggle: on the social theory of Pierre Bourdieu', *Berkeley Journal of Sociology*, 31, 78, footnote 25. See also H.-P. Müller (1986) 'Kultur, Geschmack und Distinktion. Grundzüge der Kultursoziologie Pierre Bourdieus', Kölner Zeitschrift für Soziologie und Sozialforschung, supplement, 63: 'Dabei wird die These verfolgt, dass *Bourdieu* die *Webersche* Problematik von *Klasse* und *Stand* weiterentwickelt . . .'
24. R. Brubaker (1984) *The Limits of Rationality: An Essay on the Social and Moral Thought of Max Weber*, London, Allen & Unwin, 87.
25. *Ibid.*, 98.
26. R. Brubaker (1985) 'Rethinking classical theory. The sociological vision of Pierre Bourdieu', *Theory and Society*, 14, 746.
27. *Ibid.*, 760.
28. C. Camic (1986) 'The matter of habit', *American Journal of Sociology*, 91, 5, 1039.
29. J.M. Ostrow (1981) 'Culture as a fundamental dimension of experience: a discussion of Pierre Bourdieu's theory of human habitus', *Human Studies*, 4, 281, fn. 4. The secondary text to which Ostrow refers is: V. Kestenbaum (1977) *The Phenomenological Sense of John Dewey; Habit and Meaning*, Atlantic Highlands, NJ, Humanities Press.
30. J.D. Baldwin (1988) 'Habit, emotion, and self-conscious action', *Sociological Perspectives*, 31, 1, 35.
31. L.J.D. Wacquant (1987) 'Symbolic violence and the making of the French agriculturalist: an enquiry into Pierre Bourdieu's sociology', *Australian and New Zealand Journal of Sociology*, 23, 1, 65.
32. P. Bourdieu (1992) 'Preface' to P. Bourdieu and L.J.D. Wacquant, *An Invitation to Reflexive Sociology*, Chicago, IL, University of Chicago Press and Oxford, Polity Press, vii.
33. J.S. Coleman (1991) 'Prologue: constructed social organization', in P. Bourdieu and J.S. Coleman, eds. *Social Theory for a Changing Society*, Boulder, CO, San Francisco, CA, and Oxford, Westview Press, and New York, Sage Foundation, 8.
34. Wacquant, 'Symbolic violence', 82.
35. See M. Schiltz (1982) 'Habitus and peasantization in Nigeria: a Yoruba case study', *Man* (NS), 17, 728–46; G.C. Bentley (1987) 'Ethnicity and practice', *Society for Comparative Study of Society and History*, 29, 24–55; W.F. Hanks (1987) 'Discourse genres in a theory of practice', *American Ethnologist*, 14, 4, 668–92; H.-G. Sack (1988) 'The relationship between sport involvement and life-style in youth cultures', *International Review for the Sociology of Sport*, 23, 3, 213–32; J. Gerhards and H.K. Anheier (1989) 'The literary field: an empirical investigation of Bourdieu's sociology of art', *International Sociology*, 4, 2, 131–46; J.C.L. Rupp and R. de Lange (1989) 'Social order, cultural capital and citizenship. An essay concerning educational status and educational power versus comprehensiveness of elementary schools', *The Sociological Review*,

37, 4, 668–75; F. Ringer (1990) 'The intellectual field, intellectual history, and the sociology of knowledge', *Theory and Society*, 19, 269–94.
36. P. Bourdieu (1992) 'Thinking about limits', *Theory, Culture and Society*, 9, 37–49.
37. C. Bernard (1865) *Introduction à l'étude de la médécine expérimentale.*
38. 'The second nature of *habitus*. Philosophical tradition and common sense in sociological language.'
39. F. Héran (1987) 'La seconde nature de l'habitus. Tradition philosophique et sens commun dans le langage sociologique', *Revue française de sociologie*, 28, 387.
40. *Ibid.*, 413.
41. *Ibid.*
42. 'Is the sociology of interest interesting?'
43. 'Sociology absorbed by economics. Critical remarks on Bourdieu's *Ce que parler veut dire.*'
44. P. Adair (1984) 'La sociologie phagocytée par l'économique: remarques critiques à propos de "ce que parler veut dire" de P. Bourdieu,' *Sociologie du Travail*, 26, 1, 112.
45. *Ibid.*, 113.
46. *Ibid.*
47. V.A. Zelizer (1988) 'Beyond the polemics on the market: establishing a theoretical and empirical agenda', *Sociological Forum*, 3, 614.
48. G. Lakomski (1984) 'On agency and structure: Pierre Bourdieu and Jean-Claude Passeron's theory of symbolic violence', *Curriculum Inquiry*, 14, 2, 161, footnote 7.
49. G. Liénard and E. Servais (1979) 'Practical sense: on Bourdieu', *Critique of Anthropology*, 13, 209. (This was a review article of *Outline*. All references are to the original French. This review originally appeared in *Revue française de sociologie* (1974), 15, 413–21.)

9 Conclusion: commending the Bourdieu paradigm: the sociologist as conceptual artist

In an article which sought to evaluate Bourdieu's contribution to political science, Caro contended that he encountered in acute form a difficulty which is well known in the epistemology of the social sciences – that

> ... scientific criticism of a legitimate scientific theory, that is to say one conforming to the dominant rules of scientificity, in particular to the rule of non-contradiction of the facts that it provides, is often not pertinent when it tries to take up an external point of view, that is to say to set one theory against another.[1]

In this situation, Caro believed that there were only two possible options for the critic – either to deny the scientificity of the 'whole edifice'[2] or to be resigned to being satisfied with subjecting 'external' theories to the limited, 'internal' scrutiny of particular disciplines. For Caro, the denial of scientificity was no option and he reluctantly sought to expose contradictions and inadequacies in what he took to be Bourdieu's contribution to political science in the terms set by that science and without reference to the superstructure of relational meaning that Bourdieu's concepts acquire across many scientific disciplines. Caro set himself a limited task but he recognised that the potency of Bourdieu's concepts in any one discipline derives, in part, from the potency acquired as a result of their efficacy in others. He supposed, however, that this network of meta-disciplinary conceptual power might be exposed, that the further development of Bourdieu's paradigm might lead 'some day to the appearance of problems which are insoluble in its own terms' but that such a 'search for incoherence'[3] would take a long time.

As we have seen, many critics of Bourdieu would echo Caro's sentiments. They have made criticisms from their own subject specialisms and, in doing so, have confined Bourdieu's work within the boundaries of those specialisms. Some have innocently ignored the wider scope of Bourdieu's work. Others have been guilty of deliberate disregard. Others, like Caro, have sought to make a virtue out of a constrained perspective but, again like Caro, have shown deference to the existence of a total system, external to all disciplines, which seems to be beyond the scope of any criteria of assessment.

Such critical deference might be appropriate in evaluating the systems of thought of Parsons, or Weber, or Durkheim, but it is not, however, appropriate in considering the work of Bourdieu. It has been Bourdieu's consistent contention that he has not wanted to construct a systematic social theory. He has consistently argued that individuals do not possess intrinsic identities and that there can never be any reference to authorial 'selves' expressing their 'intentions' in their texts. There is not an unitary 'Bourdieu' bestowing coherent meaning on all his texts, nor is there any a priori, logical unity to be discovered – no ultimate key to the interlocking concepts which seem to make up a closed system. Bourdieu has consistently argued that his thinking is as polysemic as that of the Algerian people which he described in *Outline of a Theory of Practice*. These, of course, are Bourdieu's claims. In his own terms, he cannot deny that he is the product of a French tradition which esteems 'intellectuals' and that he shares with Sartre a *habitus* which must incline him to elevate the social function of the 'totalising' intellectual. He has studiously dissociated himself from Sartre's self-perception, but the overt rejection of Sartre's inherent Cartesianism sometimes seems to conceal an assimilation of it within a rival, Leibnizian, rational framework. Bourdieu celebrates the randomness of plurality, the multiplicity of possible worlds. In doing so, he legitimately inserts his totalising tendency as just one random activity within that world, but that pre-emptive relativisation of his own position can seem to be a Sartrean appropriation of the views of others within the plurality.

This book has attempted to accept Bourdieu's claim to be non-systematic at face value. It has not deferred to any notion that there might be a complete meaning of Bourdieu that might be ascertained from the scrutiny of his completed work. It accepts Bourdieu's view that a *corpus* of work is a corpse. At the same time, cultural analysis does not constitute a defined discipline in terms of which a limited articulation of the strengths and weaknesses of Bourdieu's particular contribution might be evaluated. In these circumstances, the book has sought to promote a pragmatic reading of Bourdieu's work, but there are two significantly different pragmatic responses, one of which still defers to a totalising tendency and the other of which sustains an open plurality. The book has been a heuristic device to maintain an emphasis on openness.

The first section offered an account of the man and his social trajectory. By distinguishing three phases of Bourdieu's career, the raw materials were given for correlating the development of Bourdieu's conceptualisation with the changes in his practice and his social position. The second section gave an outline of the genesis and modification of some of Bourdieu's key concepts, suggesting all the time that there was a reciprocal relationship between concepts and empirical inquiry whilst, equally, that they were advanced and refined in the context of meanings which were already sedimented. The third section sought to see how Bourdieu applied his concepts in three case studies. These could be thought to be tests of the use of Bourdieu's work in three limited disciplines – the sociology of literature or literary criticism, the sociology of fashion, and the sociology of art or art history and criticism. It is clear that these case studies expose the inadequacies of Bourdieu's analyses in terms of the norms and expectations of these disciplines. It is not the case that Bourdieu's concepts have been preformulated by him as working hypotheses. Bourdieu's concepts have not enabled him to make major contributions towards the literary critical appreciation of Flaubert or the art appreciation of Manet. Instead, by working on Flaubert, Courrèges and Manet, Bourdieu was able to refine his thinking about the ways in which social observation was transformed within the conventions of the novel in the second half of the nineteenth century in France; the ways in which all cultural fashions are produced by analogy with the production of Parisian fashion houses and in which fashion labels acquire meaning independent of their creators; and, finally, the ways in which the contemporary display of the paintings of Manet is the locus for a cultural struggle which reproduces the competitive conditions within which Manet first produced them. These are all insights which are tangential to the disciplines within which they might be constrained but, cumulatively, they illuminate Bourdieu's developing self-understanding and, more importantly, his developing understanding of the limited function of these limited disciplines in the context of the emergence of mass cultures and of the commodification of cultures.

The final section turned to the criticisms that have been made of Bourdieu's work and suggested that the solution to the indeterminacy of critical judgement might be to understand the various criticisms as functions of the conditions of cultural consumption in different countries and intellectual traditions, and also to see Bourdieu's work in the context of some debates within his own country and tradition.

In his 'Concluding remarks: for a sociogenetic understanding of intellectual works', Bourdieu writes: 'The *sociogenetic point of view* that, in my opinion, one must adopt towards any "creation of the mind" (whether it be Flaubert, Manet, or Heidegger), I am obviously inclined to expect of those who deal with my work – without ignoring the risks that it implies, particularly that of relativization.'[4] This injunction exemplifies the totalising tendency in Bourdieu's approach that he himself overtly tries to disown. He asks to be analysed in the way in which he has analysed others and, in doing so, he invites analysis which has already been critically disarmed. Bourdieu asks for analysis of his work which appreciates the reciprocal relationship between his thinking and his social trajectory. The unspoken assumption is that this mode of analysis will lead to a proper appreciation of the content of his work and to a proper understanding of how his concepts might pragmatically be deployed. Analysts are invited to use his work – on the understanding that it has been properly contexted – but to use his work, nevertheless. However, the analogy between Bourdieu's creativity and that of Flaubert, Manet or Heidegger is imprecise. Bourdieu's sociogenetic analyses of their work involved, as we have seen, primarily an attention to the social conditions of production. Attention to content was relatively slight. If we are now invited to analyse Bourdieu in the same way and if his content is primarily a prescriptive analytical procedure, then our sociogenetic understanding of Bourdieu logically obliterates the generalisable validity of the process we are supposed to be adopting. We are forced, therefore, into a more fundamental pragmatism which Bourdieu should condone. We should endeavour to understand the reciprocity between his life and his work so as to generate our own, perhaps different, perhaps similar, strategies rather than to assimilate or imitate his.

Bourdieu's analyses of his culture have become parts of our structured perceptions of our own. I have tried to outline the genesis and structure of Bourdieu's critical engagement with his culture. The importance of his contribution to cultural analysis, however, does not lie in the conceptual structure itself but in the invitation which he extends to follow him in a continuous process of conceptual generation and regeneration, establishing frameworks of thought which modify what we receive from him in accordance with the conditions in which we find ourselves.

Notes

1. J.-Y. Caro (1980) 'La sociologie de Pierre Bourdieu. Éléments pour une théorie du champ politique', *Revue française de science politique*, 6, 1194.
2. *Ibid.*
3. *Ibid.*
4. P. Bourdieu (1993) 'Concluding remarks: for a sociogenetic understanding of intellectual works', in C. Calhoun *et al.* eds., *Bourdieu: Critical Perspectives*, Oxford, Polity Press, 264.

Bibliography

Accardo, A. (1983) *Initiation à la sociologie de l'illusionisme social. Lire Bourdieu.* Bordeaux: Éditions Le Mascaret.

Ackerman, J.S. (1973) 'Toward a new social theory of art', *New Literary History*, 4, 315–30.

Adair, P. (1984) 'La sociologie phagocytée par l'économique: remarques critiques à propos de "ce que parler veut dire" de P. Bourdieu', *Sociologie du Travail*, 26, 1, 105–14.

Alquié, F. (1933) *Notes sur la première partie des principes de la philosophie de Descartes.* Carcassonne: Éditions Chantiers.

Althusser, L. (1959) *Montesquieu. La politique et l'histoire.* Paris: Quadrage/Presses Universitaires Françaises.

Althusser, L. (1965) Préface: 'Du "Capital" à la philosophie de Marx', in Althusser, L. *et al. Lire le Capital* (Vol. 1.) Paris: Maspéro.

Althusser, L. (1965) *Pour Marx.* Paris: Maspéro.

Althusser, L. (1992) *L'avenir dure longtemps* suivi de *Les faits.* Paris: Éditions STOCK/IMEC.

Archer, M.S. (1983) 'Process without system', *Archives européennes de sociologie*, 24, 4, 713–19.

Arnold, M. (1964) 'The function of criticism at the present time', in Arnold, M. *Essays in Criticism.* London: Everyman's Library, Dent.

Arnold, M. (1964) *Essays in Criticism.* London: Everyman's Library, Dent.

Ayers, M. (1978) 'Analytical philosophy and the history of philosophy', in Rée, J. *et al.* eds. *Philosophy and its Past.* Hassocks: Harvester Press.

Bachelard, G. (1970) *Études* (présentation de Canguilhem, G.). Paris: J. Vrin.

Bachelard, G. (1984) Trans. Goldhammer, A. *The New Scientific Spirit.* Boston, MA: Beacon Press.

Baldwin, J.B. (1988) 'Habit, emotion, and self-conscious action', *Sociological Perspectives*, 31, 1, 35–58.

Balibar, R. (1974) *Les Français fictifs. Le rapport des styles littéraires au français national* (présentation de Balibar, É. et Macherey, P.) Paris: Hachette Littérature.

Barral, M.R. (1965) *Merleau-Ponty. The Role of the Body-Subject in Interpersonal Relations.* Pittsburgh, PA: Duquesne University Press.

Barthes, R. (1957) *Mythologies.* Paris: Éditions du Seuil.

Barthes, R. (1967) *Système de la Mode.* Paris: Éditions du Seuil.

Barthes, R. (1985) *The Fashion System.* London: Jonathan Cape.

Barthes, R. (1993) Trans. and selected by Lavers, A. *Mythologies.* London: Vintage Books.

Baudrillard, J. (1988) ed. Poster, M. *Selected Writings.* Stanford, CA: Stanford University Press.

Baudrillard, J. (1993) *Symbolic Exchange and Death.* London, Thousand Oaks, CA, and New Delhi: Sage.

Baxandall, L. and Morawski, S. (1973) *Marx and Engels on Literature and Art. A Selection of Writings.* St. Louis, MO, and Milwaukee: Telos Press.

Becker, G.S. (1964) *Human Capital. A Theoretical and Empirical Analysis, with Special Reference to Education.* New York: National Bureau of Economic Research.

Bell, D. (1990) *Husserl*. London: Routledge.

Bendix, R. (1962) *Max Weber. An Intellectual Portrait*. London: Methuen.

Benjamin, W. (1973) *Understanding Brecht*. London: New Left Books.

Benjamin, W. (1992) *Illuminations*. London: Fontana Press.

Bentley, G.C. (1987) 'Ethnicity and practice', *Society for Comparative Study of Society and History*, 29, 1, 24–55.

Berger, B.M. (1986) 'Review essay: "Taste and Domination"', *American Journal of Sociology*, 91, 6, 1445–53.

Bergson, H. (1970) *Matter and Memory*, authorised translation by Paul, N.M. and Palmer, W.S. London: George Allen & Unwin Ltd/New York: Humanities Press (first published 1911. Trans. of 5th edn of *Matière et mémoire* of 1908).

Bernard, C (1865) *Introduction à l'étude de la médécine expérimentale*.

Billaz, A. (1981) 'La problématique de la "réception" dans les deux Allemagnes', *Revue d'histoire de la littérature française*, 81, 1, 109–20.

Bourdieu, P. (1958) *Sociologie de l'Algérie*. Paris: Presses Universitaires de France.

Bourdieu, P. (1961) *Sociologie de l'Algérie* (2nd edn). Paris: Presses Universitaires de France.

Bourdieu, P. (1962) trans. Ross, A.C.M. *The Algerians*. Boston, MA: Beacon Press.

Bourdieu, P. (1962) 'Célibat et condition paysanne', *Études rurales*, 5–6, 32–136.

Bourdieu, P. *et al.* (1963) *Travail et travailleurs en Algérie*. Paris and The Hague: Mouton.

Bourdieu, P. (with Passeron, J.-C.) (1964) *Les Étudiants et leurs études*. Paris and The Hague: Mouton, Cahiers du Centre de Sociologie Européenne, 1.

Bourdieu, P. (with Passeron, J.-C.) (1964) *Les Héritiers. Les Étudiants et la culture*. Paris: Éditions de Minuit.

Bourdieu, P., Passeron, J.-C. and de Saint Martin, M. eds. (1965) *Rapport pédagogique et communication*. Paris and The Hague: Mouton, Cahiers du Centre de Sociologie Européenne, 2.

Bourdieu, P. (with Boltanski, L., Castel, R. and Chamboredon, J.C.) (1965) *Un art moyen. Essai sur les usages sociaux de la photographie*. Paris: Éditions de Minuit.

Bourdieu, P. (with Reynaud, J.D.) (1966) 'Une sociologie de l'action est-elle possible?', *Revue française de sociologie*, VII, 4, 508–17.

Bourdieu, P. (1966) 'Condition de classe et position de classe', *Archives européennes de sociologie*, VII, 2, 201–23.

Bourdieu, P. (1966) 'Champ intellectuel et projet créateur', *Les Temps modernes*, 246, 865–906.

Bourdieu, P. (with Darbel, A. and Schnapper, D.) (1966) *L'Amour de l'art. Les Musées d'art et leur public*. Paris: Éditions de Minuit.

Bourdieu, P. (1967) Postface to Panofsky, E. *Architecture gothique et pensée scolastique*. Paris: Éditions de Minuit.

Bourdieu, P. (with Passeron, J.-C.) (1967) 'Sociology and philosophy in France since 1945: death and resurrection of a philosophy without subject', *Social Research*, 34, 1, 162–212.

Bourdieu, P. (1968) 'Structuralism and theory of sociological knowledge', trans. Zanotti-Karp, A., *Social Research*, 35, 4, 681–706.

Bourdieu, P. (with Chamboredon, J.C. and Passeron, J.-C.) (1968) *Le Métier de sociologue*. Paris: Mouton-Bordas.

Bourdieu, P. (1968) 'Outline of a sociological theory of art perception', *International Social Science Journal*, XX, 4, 589–612.

Bourdieu, P. (with Passeron, J.-C.) (1970) *La Reproduction. Éléments pour une théorie du système d'enseignement*. Paris: Éditions de Minuit.

Bourdieu, P. (1971) 'Champ du pouvoir, champ intellectuel et habitus de classe', *Scolies* (cahiers de recherches de l'école normale supérieure) 1, 7–26.

Bourdieu, P. (1971) 'Une interprétation de la théorie de la religion selon Max Weber', *Archives européennes de sociologie*, XII, 1, 3–21.

Bourdieu, P. (1971) 'Genèse et structure du champ religieux', *Revue française de sociologie*, XII, 3, 295–334.

Bourdieu, P. (1971) 'Intellectual field and creative project', in Young, M.F.D. ed. *Knowledge and Control. New Directions for the Sociology of Education*. London: Collier-Macmillan.

Bourdieu, P. (1971) 'Systems of education and systems of thought', in Young, M.F.D. ed. *Knowledge and Control. New Directions for the Sociology of Education*. London: Collier-Macmillan.

Bourdieu, P. (1972) *Esquisse d'une théorie de la pratique, précédé de trois études d'ethnologie kabyle*. Geneva: Droz.

Bourdieu, P. (1973) 'Cultural reproduction and social reproduction', in Brown, R. ed. *Knowledge, Education and Cultural Change*. London: Tavistock.

Bourdieu, P. (with Reynaud, J.D.) (1974) 'Is a sociology of action possible?', in Giddens, A. ed. *Positivism and Sociology*. London: Heinemann Educational Books.

Bourdieu, P. (1975) 'Méthode scientifique et hiérarchie sociale des objets', *Actes de la recherche en sciences sociales*, 1, 4–6.

Bourdieu. P. (with Delsaut, Y.) (1975) 'Le couturier et sa griffe. Contribution à une théorie de la magie', *Actes de la recherche en sciences sociales*, 1, 7–36.

Bourdieu, P. (1975) 'L'invention de la vie d'artiste', *Actes de la recherche en sciences sociales*, 2, 67–94.

Bourdieu, P. (1975) 'L'ontologie politique de Martin Heidegger', *Actes de la recherche en sciences sociales*, 5–6, 109–56.

Bourdieu, P. (1976) 'La lecture de Marx, ou quelques remarques critiques à propos de "quelques critiques à propos de *Lire le Capital*"', *Actes de la recherche en sciences sociales*, 5–6, 65–79.

Bourdieu, P. (with de Saint Martin, M.) (1976) 'Anatomie du goût', *Actes de la recherche en sciences sociales*, 5, 2–112.

Bourdieu, P. (1977) 'Sur le pouvoir symbolique', *Annales*, 3, 405–11.

Bourdieu, P. (1977) 'La production de la croyance: contribution à une économie des biens symboliques', *Actes de la recherche en sciences sociales*, 13, 3–43.

Bourdieu, P. (with Passeron, J.-C.) (1977) Trans Nice, R. *Reproduction in Education, Society and Culture*. London and Beverly Hills, CA: Sage.

Bourdieu, P. (1977) Trans. Nice, R. *Outline of a Theory of Practice*. Cambridge: Cambridge University Press.

Bourdieu, P. (with Passeron, J.-C.) (1979) Trans Nice, R. *The Inheritors, French Students and their Relation to Culture*. Chicago, IL, and London: University of Chicago Press.

Bourdieu, P. (1979) *La Distinction. Critique sociale du jugement*. Paris: Éditions de Minuit.

Bourdieu, P. (1979) 'On symbolic power', *Critique of Anthropology*, 4, 77–85.

Bourdieu, P. (1979) 'Les trois états du capital culturel', *Actes de la recherche en sciences sociales*, 30, 3–6.

Bourdieu, P. (1980) Trans. Nice, R. 'Sartre', *London Review of Books*, 2.

Bourdieu, P. (1980) 'Le capital social. Notes provisoires', *Actes de la recherche en sciences sociales*, 31, 2–3.

Bourdieu, P. (1980) 'The aristocracy of culture', *Media, Culture and Society*, 2, 225–54.

Bourdieu, P. (1980) 'A diagram of social position and life-style', *Media, Culture and Society*, 2, 255–9.

Bourdieu, P. (1980) 'The production of belief: contribution to an economy of symbolic goods', *Media, Culture and Society*, 2, 261–93.

Bourdieu, P. (1980) *Le Sens pratique*. Paris: Éditions de Minuit.

Bourdieu, P. (1980) *Questions de sociologie*. Paris: Éditions de Minuit.

Bourdieu, P. (1980) 'Le mort saisit le vif. Les relations entre l'histoire réifiée et l'histoire incorporée', *Actes de la recherche en sciences sociales*, 32–3, 3–14.

Bourdieu, P. (1981) 'La représentation politique. Eléments pour une théorie du champ politique', *Actes de la recherche en sciences sociales*, 36–7, 3–24.

Bourdieu, P. (1981) 'Décrire et prescrire. Note sur les conditions de possibilité et les limites de l'efficacité politique', *Actes de la recherche en sciences sociales*, 38, 69–73.

Bourdieu, P. (1982) *Ce que parler veut dire. L'Économie des échanges linguistiques*. Paris: Fayard.

Bourdieu, P. (1982) *Leçon sur la leçon*. Paris: Éditions de Minuit.

Bourdieu, P. (1982) 'Les rites d'institution', *Actes de la recherche en sciences sociales*, 43, 58–63.

Bourdieu, P. and de Saint Martin, M. (1982) 'La sainte famille. L'épiscopat français et le champ du pouvoir', *Actes de la recherche en sciences sociales*, 44–5, 2–53.

Bourdieu, P. (1984) 'Le champ littéraire. Préalables critiques et principes de méthode', *Lendemains*, IX, 36, 5–20.

Bourdieu, P. (1984) *Distinction, A Social Critique of the Judgement of Taste*. London: Routledge & Kegan Paul.

Bourdieu, P. (1984) *Homo Academicus*. Paris: Éditions de Minuit.

Bourdieu, P. (1985) 'The genesis of the concepts of *habitus* and *field*', trans. Newman, C., *Sociocriticism*, 2, 11–24.

Bourdieu, P. (1985) 'Existe-t-il une littérature belge: limites d'un champ et frontières politiques', *Études de lettres* (Lausanne), 4, 3–6.

Bourdieu, P. (1986) 'D'abord défendre les intellectuels', *Le Nouvel Observateur*, 82.

Bourdieu, P. (1986) 'An antimony in the notion of collective protest', in Foxley, A. *et al.* eds. *Development, Democracy, and the Art of Trespassing: Essays in Honor of Albert O. Hirschman*. Notre Dame, IN: University of Notre Dame Press.

Bourdieu, P. (with Honneth, A. *et al.*) (1986) 'Der Kampf um die symbolische Ordnung', *Ästhetik und Kommunikation*, 16, 142–165.

Bourdieu, P. (1986) 'La force du droit. Éléments pour une sociologie du champ juridique', *Actes de la recherche en sciences sociales*, 64, 5–19.

Bourdieu, P. (1987) *Choses dites*. Paris: Éditions de Minuit.

Bourdieu, P. (1987) 'The force of law: toward a sociology of the juridical field', *Hastings Law Journal*, 38, 5, 814–53.

Bourdieu, P. (1987) 'La révolution impressionniste', *Noroit*, 303, 3–18.

Bourdieu, P. (1988) *L'Ontologie politique de Martin Heidegger*. Paris: Éditions de Minuit.

Bourdieu, P. (1988) *Homo Academicus*. Oxford: Polity Press.

Bourdieu, P. (1989) 'For a socio-analysis of intellectuals; on *Homo Academicus*', *Berkeley Journal of Sociology*, xxxiv, 1–29.

Bourdieu, P. (1989) *La Noblesse d'état. Grandes Écoles et esprit de corps*. Paris: Éditions de Minuit.

Bourdieu, P. (with Darbel, A. and Schnapper, D.) (1990) *The Love of Art, European Art Museums and Their Public*. Oxford: Polity Press.

Bourdieu, P. (with Boltanski, L., Castel, R. and Chamboredon, J.C.) (1990) *Photography, a Middle-Brow Art*. Oxford: Polity Press.

Bourdieu, P. (1990) Trans Nice, R. *The Logic of Practice*. Oxford: Polity Press.

Bourdieu, P. (1990) Trans. Adamson, M. *In Other Words. Essays Towards a Reflexive Sociology*. Oxford: Polity Press.

Bourdieu, P. (1991) *The Political Ontology of Martin Heidegger*. Oxford: Polity Press.

Bourdieu, P. (1991) Ed. and int. by Thompson, J.B. *Language and Symbolic Power*. Oxford: Polity Press.

Bourdieu, P. (with Chamboredon, J.C. and Passeron, J.-C.) (1991) *The Craft of Sociology*. Berlin and New York: de Gruyter.

Bourdieu, P. and Coleman, J.S. eds. (1991) *Social Theory for a Changing Society*. Boulder, CO, San Francisco, CA, and Oxford: Westview Press.

Bourdieu, P. (1992) *Les Règles de l'art. Genèse et structure du champ littéraire*. Paris: Éditions du Seuil.

Bourdieu, P. (1992) 'Thinking about limits', *Theory, Culture and Society*, 9, 37–49.

Bourdieu, P. (1992) 'Tout est social!', *Magazine littéraire*, 303, 104–11.

Bourdieu, P. (with Wacquant, L.J.D.) (1992) *Réponses. Pour une anthropologie réflexive*. Paris: Éditions du Seuil.

Bourdieu, P. (with Wacquant, L.J.D.) (1992) *An Invitation to Reflexive Sociology*. Oxford: Polity Press.

Bourdieu, P. *et al.* (1993) *La Misère du monde*. Paris: Éditions du Seuil.

Bourdieu, P. (1993) Ed. and intro. by Johnson, R. *The Field of Cultural Production. Essays on Art and Literature*. Oxford: Polity Press.

Bourdieu, P. (1993) 'Concluding remarks: for a sociogenetic understanding of intellectual works', in Calhoun, C. *et al.* eds. *Bourdieu: Critical Perspectives*. Oxford; Polity Press.

Bourdieu, P. (1993) Trans. Nice, R. *Sociology in Question*. London, Thousand Oaks, CA, and New Delhi: Sage.

Bourdieu, P. and Haacke, H. (1994) *Libre-Échange*. Paris: Éditions du Seuil.

Bourdieu, P., Passeron, J.-C. and de Saint Martin, M. (1994) *Academic Discourse. Linguistic Misunderstanding and Professorial Power*. Oxford: Polity Press.

Bourdieu, P. (1994) *Raisons pratiques. Sur la théorie de l'action*. Paris: Éditions du Seuil.

Bourdieu, P. (1994) 'Statistics and sociology', extract from *Travail et travailleurs en Algérie* trans. and int. by Robbins, D.M., Group for Research into Access and Student Programmes, *Working Paper* 10. London: University of East London.

Bourdieu, P. and Haacke, H. (1995) *Free Exchange*. Oxford: Polity Press.

Bourdieu, P. (1996) *The Rules of Art. Genesis and Structure of the Literary Field*. Oxford: Polity Press.

Bourdieu, P. (1996) *Sur la télévision, suivi de l'emprise du journalisme*. Paris: LIBER Éditions.

Bourdieu, P. (1997) *Méditations pascaliennes*. Paris: Éditions du Seuil.

Bourdieu, P. (1998) *On Television*. Oxford: Polity Press.

Bourdieu, P. (1998) *Contre-feux*. Paris: LIBER Raisons d'Agir.

Bourdieu, P. (1998) *Acts of Resistance*. Oxford: Polity Press.

Bourdieu, P. (1998) *La Domination masculine*. Paris: Éditions du Seuil.

Bourdieu, P. (with Wacquant, L.) (1998) 'Sur les ruses de la raison impérialiste', *Actes de la recherche en sciences sociales*, 121–22, 109–18.

Bredo, E. and Feinberg, W. (1979) 'Meaning, power and pedagogy: Pierre Bourdieu and Jean-Claude Passeron, "Reproduction in education, society and culture"', *Journal of Curriculum Studies*, 11, 4, 315–32.

Brière, G. (1924) *Musée National du Louvre. Catalogue des peintures exposées dans les galeries. I. École française*. Paris: Musées Nationaux.

Brière, G. (1930) *Histoire des collections de peinture au Musée du Louvre. I. L'École française*. Paris: Musée National du Louvre.

Broad, C.D. (1975) (edited by) Lewy, C. *Leibniz. An Introduction*. Cambridge: Cambridge University Press.

Brown, R. ed. (1973) *Knowledge, Education and Cultural Change*. London: Tavistock.

Brubaker, R. (1984) *The Limits of Rationality: An Essay on the Social and Moral Thought of Max Weber*. London: Allen & Unwin.

Brubaker, R. (1989) 'Review of *Choses dites*', *Contemporary Sociology*, 18, 5, 783–4.

Burckhardt, J. (1990) *The Civilization of the Renaissance in Italy* (Intr. by Burke, P.). Harmondsworth: Penguin Classics.

Cachin, F. (1994) *Manet 'J'ai fait ce que j'ai vu'*. Paris: Découvertes Gallimard, Réunion des Musées Nationaux, Peinture.

Calhoun, C., LiPuma, E. and Postone, M. (1993) *Bourdieu: Critical Perspectives*. Oxford: Polity Press.

Camic, C. (1986) 'The matter of habit', *American Journal of Sociology*, 91, 5, 1039–87.

Camus, A. (1975) *The Myth of Sisyphus*. Harmondsworth: Penguin Modern Classics.

Canguilhem, G. (1978) Trans. by Fawcett, C.R. and int. by Foucault, M. *On the Normal and the Pathological*.

Canguilhem, G. (1984) 'Puissance et limites de la rationalité en médécine', in *Médécine, science, et technique. Recueil d'études redigées à l'occasion du centenaire de la mort de Claude Bernard (1813–1878)*. Paris: Éditions CNRS.

Caro, J.-Y. (1980) 'La sociologie de Pierre Bourdieu. Éléments pour une théorie du champ politique', *Revue française de science politique*, 6, 1171–97.

Cassagne, A. (1906) *La Théorie de l'art pour l'art en France chez les derniers romantiques et les premiers réalistes*. Paris: Hachette.

Cassirer, E. (1923) Trans. Swabey, W. and Swabey, M. *Substance and Function* and *Einstein's Theory of Relativity*. Chicago, IL, and London: The Open Court Publishing Co.

Castel, R. and Passeron, J.-C. eds. (1967) *Éducation, développement et démocratie*. Paris and The Hague: Mouton, Cahiers du Centre de Sociologie Européenne, 4.

Centre Culturel International de Cérisy-la-Salle (1965) *Entretiens sur les notions de genèse et de structure* (EPHE-Sorbonne – 6th Section. Congrès et Colloque IX, 1959) Paris: Mouton.

Clark, T.N. (1973) *Prophets and Patrons. The French University and the Emergence of the Social Sciences*. Cambridge, MA: Harvard University Press.

Cogniat, R. (1983) *Édouard Manet*. (trans Brenton, J.). London: Methuen.

Conquest, R. (1972) *Lenin*. London: Fontana/Collins.

Courthion, P. (1988) *Édouard Manet*. London: Thames & Hudson.

Cranston, M. (1970) *Sartre*. Edinburgh: Oliver & Boyd. (first published 1962).

Culler, J. (1974) *Flaubert. The Uses of Uncertainty*. London: Paul Elek.

Culler, J. (1975) *Structuralist Poetics. Structuralism, Linguistics and the Study of Literature*. London: Routledge & Kegan Paul.

Culler, J. (1985) *Saussure* (2nd edn). London: Fontana Press.

Culler, J. (1990) *Barthes*. London: Fontana Press.

Cunningham, G.W. (1933) *The Idealistic Argument in Recent British and American Philosophy*. New York and London: The Century.

Davis, K. and Moore, W.E. (1945) 'Some principles of stratification', *American Sociological Review*, X, 2, 242–9.

diMaggio, P. (1979) 'Review of P. Bourdieu, *Reproduction in Education, Society and Culture* and *Outline of a Theory of Practice*', *American Journal of Sociology*, 84, 6, 1460–74.

Dufay, F. and Dufort, P.-B. (1993) *Les Normaliens. De Charles Péguy à Bernard-Henri Lévy. Un siècle d'histoire*. Paris: Éditions J.-C Lattès.

Durkheim, E. (1976) 'The role of universities in the social education of the country'. Introduced by G.Weisz, *Minerva*, 14, 377–88.

Eagleton, T. (1976) *Marxism and Literary Criticism*. London: Routledge.

Eagleton, T. (1980) *Criticism and Ideology. A Study in Marxist Literary Theory*. London: Verso.

Faguet, E. (1899) *Flaubert*.

Faguet, E. (1914) *Flaubert* (trans. Devonshire, R.L.) London: Constable.

Farber, M. (1968) *The Foundation of Phenomenology. Edmund Husserl and the Quest for a Rigorous Science of Philosophy* (3rd edn). Albany, NY: State University of New York Press.

Fischer, E. (1963) *The Necessity of Art. A Marxist Approach*. Harmondsworth: Penguin.

Focillon, H. (1928) *La Peinture aux XIXe et XXe siècles. Du réalisme à nos jours*. Paris: Librairie Renouard.

Focillon, H. (1932) 'L'Art du dix-neuvième siècle', in Aubert, M. ed. *Nouvelle Histoire universelle de l'art*. Vol. II Paris: Firmin-Didot.

Focillon, H. (1934) *La Vie des formes*.

Focillon, H. (1989) *The Life of Forms in Art*. New York: Zone Books.

Foley, D.E. (1989) 'Does the working class have a culture in the anthropological sense?', *Cultural Anthropology*, 4, 2, 137–62.

Foucault, M. (1968) 'Réponse au cercle d'épistémologie', *Cahiers pour l'Analyse*, 9, 9–40.

Fowler, B. (1997) *Pierre Bourdieu and Cultural Theory. Critical Investigations*. London, Thousand Oaks, CA, and New Delhi: Sage.

Fowlie, W. (1968) *The French Critic, 1549–1967*. Carbondale, IL: Southern Illinois University Press.

Garnham, N. and Williams, R. (1980) 'Pierre Bourdieu and the sociology of culture', *Media, Culture and Society*, 2, 209–23.

Garnham, N. and Williams, R. (1980) 'Class and culture, the work of Bourdieu', *Media, Culture and Society*, 2, 245–6.

Garnham, N. (1986) 'Extended review: "Bourdieu's *Distinction*"', *The Sociological Review*, 34, 2, 423–33.

Gawronsky, D. (1949) 'Ernst Cassirer: his life and work', in Schilpp, P.A. ed. *The Philosophy of Ernst Cassirer*. Evanston, IL: The Library of Living Philosophers, Vol. VI.

Gerhards, J. and Anheier, H.K. (1989) 'The literary field: an empirical investigation of Bourdieu's sociology of art', *International Sociology*, 4, 2, 131–46.

Giddens, A. (1969) 'Simmel,' in Raison,T. ed. *The Founding Fathers of Social Science*. Harmondsworth: Penguin Books.

Giddens, A. ed. (1974) *Positivism and Sociology*. London: Heinemann Educational Books.

Glauser, A. (1952) *Albert Thibaudet et la critique créatrice*. Paris: Éditions contemporains, Boivin & Cie.

Goldmann, L. (1948) *La Communauté humaine et l'univers chez Kant*. Paris.

Goldmann, L. (1959) *Recherches dialectiques*. Paris: Gallimard.

Gorder, K.L. (1980) 'Understanding school knowledge: a critical appraisal of Basil Bernstein and Pierre Bourdieu', *Educational Theory*, 30, 4, 335–46.

Granovetter, M. (1985), 'Economic Action and Social Structure: The Problem of Embeddedness', *American Journal of Sociology*, Vol. 91, No. 3, 481–510.

Grenfell, M. and James, D. (1998) *Bourdieu and Education. Acts of Practical Theory*. London: Falmer Press.

Grodecki, L. (1963) *Bibliographie Henri Focillon*. New Haven and London: Yale U. Press.

Grogin, R.C. (1978) 'Rationalists and anti-rationalists in pre-World War I France: the Bergson–Benda Affair'. *Historical Reflections*, 5, 223–31.

Habermas, J. (1987) *The Philosophical Discourse of Modernity*. Oxford: Polity Press.

Hall, S. (1978) 'The Hinterland of Science: Ideology and the "Sociology of Knowledge"', in *On Ideology*, London: CCCS/Hutchinson.

Hanks, W.F. (1987) 'Discourse genres in a theory of practice', *American Ethnologist*, 14, 4, 668–92.

Harker, R., Mahar, C. and Wilkes, C. (1990) *An Introduction to the Work of Pierre Bourdieu. The Practice of Theory*. London: Macmillan.

Hegel, G.W.F. (1977) *Phenomenology of Spirit* (trans. Miller, A.V. with analysis of the text and Foreword by Findlay, J.N.). Oxford: Oxford University Press.

Hegel, G.W.F. (1993) *Introductory Lectures on Aesthetics* (Introduction by Inwood, M). Harmondsworth: Penguin Classics.

Heidegger, M. (1978) *Basic Writings, from Being and Time (1927) to The Task of Thinking (1964)* (ed. with general introduction and introductions to each selection, Krell, D.F.). London and Henley: Routledge & Kegan Paul.

Heidegger, M. (1993) *Being and Time* (trans Macquarrie, J. and Robinson, E.). Oxford: Blackwell.

Héran, F. (1987) 'La seconde nature de l'habitus. Tradition philosophique et sens commun dans le langage sociologique', *Revue française de sociologie*, 28, 3, 385–416.

Herskovits, M.J. (1938) *Acculturation*. New York.

Hippolyte, J. (1966) *Hegel. Préface de la phénoménologie de l'esprit*, trans., int. and notes.

Hirst, P.Q. (1975) *Durkheim, Bernard and Epistemology*. London: Routledge & Kegan Paul.

Hobsbawm, E. (1978) 'Sexe, symboles, vêtements et socialisme', *Actes de la recherche en sciences sociales*, 23, 2–18.

Hodges, H.A. (1944) *Wilhelm Dilthey. An Introduction*. London: Kegan Paul, Trench, Trubner & Co.

Hoggart, R. (1957) *The Uses of Literacy*. Harmondsworth: Penguin Books.

Hoggart, R. (1970) *La Culture du pauvre* (présentation de Passeron, J.-C.). Paris: Éditions de Minuit.

Hoggart, R. (1973) *Speaking to Each Other*. Harmondsworth: Penguin Books.

Hohendahl, P.U. (1982) *The Institution of Criticism*. Ithaca, NY, and London: Cornell University Press.

Holborn, H. (1950) 'Dilthey and the critique of historical reason', *Journal of the History of Ideas*, xi, 1, 93–118.

Holly, M.A. (1984) *Panofsky and the Foundations of Art History*. Ithaca, NY, and London: Cornell University Press.

Honneth, A. (1986) 'The fragmented world of symbolic forms: reflections on Pierre Bourdieu's Sociology of Culture', *Theory, Culture and Society*, 3, 3, 55–66.

Honneth, A., Kocyba, H. and Schwibs, B. (1986) 'The struggle for symbolic order. An interview with Pierre Bourdieu', *Theory, Culture and Society*, 3, 3, 35–51.

Hoog, M. (1983) *The Themes and Motifs of Manet* (trans. Brenton, J.). London: Methuen.

Husserl, E. (1985) *The Paris Lectures* (trans. and introductory essay by Koestenbaum, P.). The Hague: Martinus Nijhoff.

Inglis, F. (1995) *Raymond Williams*. London: Routledge.

Iser, W. (1978) *The Act of Reading. A Theory of Aesthetic Response*. Baltimore, MD, and London: Johns Hopkins University Press.

Iser, W. (1974) *The Implied Reader: Patterns of Communications in Prose Fiction from Bunyan to Beckett*. Baltimore and London: Johns Hopkins University Press.

Iser, W. (1985) *L'Acte de lecture. Théorie de l'effet esthétique*. Brussels: Mardaga.

Iser, W. (1989) *Prospecting. From Reader Response to Literary Anthropology*. Baltimore, MD, and London: Johns Hopkins University Press.

Jauss, H.R. (1978) 'L'histoire de la littérature: un défi à la théorie littéraire', in Jauss, H.R. *Pour une esthétique de la réception* (trans. from the German by Maillard, C.). Paris: Gallimard.

Jauss, H.R. (1978) *Pour une esthétique de la réception* (trans. from the German by Maillard, C.). Paris: Gallimard.

Jay, M. (1973) *The Dialectical Imagination. A History of the Frankfurt School and the Institute of Social Research 1923–1950*. London: Heinemann Educational.

Jenkins, R. (1986) 'Review of P. Bourdieu, *Distinction*', *Sociology*, 20, 1, 103–5.

Jenkins, R. (1992) *Pierre Bourdieu*. London: Routledge.

Joll, J. (1980) *Europe since 1870. An international history*. Harmondsworth: Penguin.

Jones, M.M. (1991) *Gaston Bachelard, Submissive Humanist. Texts and Readings*. Madison, WI: University of Wisconsin Press.

Joppke, C. (1986) 'The cultural dimensions of class formation and class struggle: on the social theory of Pierre Bourdieu', *Berkeley Journal of Sociology*, 31, 53–78.

Jurt, J. (1989) 'De l'analyse immanente à l'histoire sociale de la littérature. À propos des recherches littéraires en Allemagne depuis 1945', *Actes de la recherche en sciences sociales*, 78, 94–101.

Jurt, J. (1992) 'Autonomie ou hétéronomie. Le champ littéraire en France et en Allemagne', *Regards sociologiques*, 4, 3–16.

Kant, I. (1934) *Critique of Pure Reason* (trans. Meiklejohn, J.M.D., introduction by Lindsay, A.D.). London: Dent & Sons.

Kant, I. (1951) *Critique of Judgement* (trans. with an introduction by Bernard, J.H.). London: Collier-Macmillan, The Hafner Library of Classics.

Keesing, F.M. (1953) *Culture Change. An Analysis and Bibliography of Anthropological Sources to 1952.* Stanford, CA: Stanford University Press.

Klingender, F. (1978) 'Joseph Wright de Derby, peintre de la Révolution industrielle', *Actes de la recherche en sciences sociales*, 23, 23–36.

LaCapra, D. (1979) *A Preface to Sartre. A Critical Introduction to Sartre's Literary and Philosophical Writings.* London: Methuen.

Lakomski, G. (1984) 'On agency and structure: Pierre Bourdieu and Jean-Claude Passeron's theory of symbolic violence', *Curriculum Inquiry*, 14, 2, 151–63.

Lamont, M., & Lareau, A. (1988) 'Cultural capital: allusions, gaps and glissandos in recent theoretical developments', *Sociological Theory*, 6, 2, 153–68.

Lamont, M. (1989) 'Slipping the world back in: Bourdieu on Heidegger', *Contemporary Sociology*, 18, 5, 781–83.

Lanson, G. (1896) *Histoire de la littérature française* (4th edn.). Paris.

Lanson, G. (1965) *Essais de méthode, de critique et d'histoire littéraire* (rassemblés et présentés par Peyre, H.). Paris: Librairie Hachette.

Lecourt, D. (1975) *Marxism and Epistemology. Bachelard, Canguilhem and Foucault* (trans. Brewster, B.). London: New Left Books.

Leibniz, G.W. von (1965) *Monadology and Other Philosophical Essays* (trans. Schrecker, P. and A.M., with an introduction and notes by Schrecker, P.). New York: The Library of Liberal Arts, Bobbs-Merrill Co.

Lemert, C. (1981) 'Literary politics and the *champ* of French sociology', *Theory and Society*, 10, 5, 645–69.

Lewin, K. (1949) 'Cassirer's philosophy of science and the social sciences', in Schilpp, P.A. ed. *The Philosophy of Ernst Cassirer.* Evanston, IL: Library of Living Philosophers.

Lewin, K. (1952) ed. Cartwright, D. *Field Theory in Social Science. Selected Theoretical Papers.* London: Tavistock Publications.

Lichtheim, G. (1970) *Lukacs.* London: Fontana/Collins.

Liénard, G. and Servais, E. (1979) 'Practical sense: on Bourdieu', *Critique of Anthropology*, 13, 14, 209–19.

Luc, J.-N. and Barbé, A. (1982) *Des Normaliens. Histoire de l'École Normale Supérieure de Saint-Cloud.* Paris: Presses de la Fondation Nationale des Sciences Politiques.

Lukacs, G. (1963) *La Théorie du roman* (avec une introduction aux premiers écrits de Georges Lukacs par Lucien Goldmann). Paris: Éditions Gouthier.

Lukács, G. (1971) *History and Class Consciousness. Studies in Marxist Dialectics* (trans. Livingstone, R.). London: Merlin Press.

Lukes, S. (1973) *Émile Durkheim. His Life and Work: A Historical and Critical Study.* Harmondsworth: Penguin Books.

Macherey, P. (1964) 'La philosophie de la science de Georges Canguilhem. Épistémologie et histoire des sciences' (présentation par Althusser, L.), *La Pensée*, 113, 50–74.

Macherey, P. (1965) 'Àpropos du processus d'exposition du "Capital"', in Althusser, L. ed. *Lire le Capital.* Vol. I, Paris: François Maspéro.

Macherey, P. (1966) 'L'analyse littéraire, tombeau des structures', *Les Temps modernes*, 246, 907–28.

Macherey, P. (1974) *Pour une théorie de la production littéraire.* Paris: Maspéro.

Macherey, P. (1978) *A Theory of Literary Production.* London: Routledge & Kegan Paul.

Macherey, P. (1979) *Hegel ou Spinoza.* Paris: Maspéro.

MacIntyre, A. (1985) *After Virtue. A Study in Moral Theory* (2nd edn). London: Duckworth.

MacRae, D.G. (1974) *Weber.* London: Fontana/Collins.

Mauss, M. (1979) Trans. Brewster, B. *Sociology and Psychology. Essays.* London: Routledge & Kegan Paul.

McLellan, D. (1977) *Karl Marx. Selected Writings*. Oxford: Oxford University Press.

Mead, M. (1955) *Cultural Patterns and Technical Change*. New York: UNESCO (Mentor Book).

Merleau-Ponty, M. (1962) Trans. Smith, C. *Phenomenology of Perception*. London: Routledge.

Merleau-Ponty, M. (1965) Trans. Fisher, A. *The Structure of Behaviour*. London: Methuen.

Miller, D. (1987) *Material Culture and Mass Consumption*. Oxford: Blackwell.

Müller, H.-P. (1986) 'Kultur, Geschmack und Distinktion. Grundzüge der Kultursoziologie Pierre Bourdieus', Kölner Zeitschrift für Soziologie und Sozialforschung. Supplement, 162–70.

O'Brien, C.C. (1970) *Camus*. London: Fontana.

Olmstead, J.M.D. (1939) *Claude Bernard, Physiologist*. London: Cassell.

Ostrow, J.M. (1981) 'Culture as a fundamental dimension of experience: a discussion of Pierre Bourdieu's Theory of Human Habitus', *Human Studies*, 4, 3, 279–97.

Parkin, F. (1992) *Durkheim*. Oxford and New York: Oxford University Press.

Passeron, J.-C. (1986) 'Theories of socio-cultural reproduction', *International Social Science Journal*, 38, 4, 619–29.

Passmore, J.A. (1965) 'The idea of a history of philosophy', in *History and Theory. Studies in the Philosophy of History*, special number on 'The Historiography of the History of Philosophy'. 's – Gravenhage: Mouton & Co.

Passmore, J.A. (1970) *A Hundred Years of Philosophy*. Harmondsworth: Pelican.

Pevsner, N. (1989) Rev. by Cherry, B. *The Buildings of England. London. I. The Cities of London and Westminster*. London: Penguin Books.

Peyrefitte, A. (1977) *Rue d'Ulm. Chroniques de la vie normalienne*. Paris: Flammarion.

Poster, M. (1975) *Existential Marxism in Postwar France. From Sartre to Althusser*. Princeton, NJ: Princeton University Press.

Raphael, M. (1933) *Proudhon–Marx–Picasso. Trois études sur la sociologie de l'art*. Paris: Éditions Excelsior.

Raphael, M. (1980) Trans. Marcuse, I. *Proudhon, Marx, Picasso. Three Studies in the Sociology of Art*. London:

Rée, J. (1978) 'Philosophy and the history of philosophy', in Rée, J. *et al. Philosophy and its Past*. Hassocks: Harvester Press.

Ringer, F.K. (1969) *The Decline of the German Mandarins. The German Academic Community, 1890–1933*. Cambridge, MA: Harvard University Press.

Ringer, F.K. (1990) 'The intellectual field, intellectual history, and the sociology of knowledge', *Theory and Society*, 19, 269–94.

Ringer, F.K. (1992) *Fields of Knowledge. French Academic Culture in Comparative Perspective, 1890–1920*. Cambridge: Cambridge University Press.

Robbins, D.M. (1976) 'Culture and criticism: Willey, Richards and the present', in Foulkes, A.P. ed. *The Uses of Criticism*. Frankfurt: Peter Lang, and Bern: Herbert Lang.

Robbins, D. M. (1991) *The Work of Pierre Bourdieu: Recognizing Society*. Milton Keynes: Open University Press.

Robbins, D.M. (1996) The international transmission of ideas: Pierre Bourdieu in theory and practice, *Journal of the Institute of Romance Studies*, 4, 297–306.

Robbins, D.M. (1997) 'Ways of knowing cultures; Williams and Bourdieu', in Wallace, J. *et al.* eds. *Raymond Williams Now. Knowledge, Limits and the Future*. London: Macmillan.

Robinson, R.V. and Garnier, M.A. (1985) 'Class reproduction among men and women in France: reproduction theory on its home ground, *American Journal of Sociology*, 91, 2, 250–80.

Rupp, J.C.L. and de Lange, R. (1989) 'Social order, cultural capital and citizenship. An essay concerning educational status and educational power versus comprehensiveness of elementary schools', *The Sociological Review*, 37, 4, 668–75.

Russell, B. (1900) *A Critical Exposition of the Philosophy of Leibniz*. Cambridge:
Ryle, G. (1949) *The Concept of Mind*.
Sack, H.-G. (1988) 'The relationship between sport involvement and life-style in youth cultures', *International Review for the Sociology of Sport*, 23, 3, 213–32.
Saint Martin, M. de (1980) 'Une grande famille', *Actes de la recherche en sciences sociales*, 31, 4–21.
Saint Martin, M. de (1993) *L'Espace de la noblesse*. Paris: Éditions Métailié.
Sartre, J.-P. (1936) *L'Imagination*. Paris: Presses Universitaires de France.
Sartre, J.-P. (1948) *Qu'est-ce que la littérature*. Paris: Gallimard.
Sartre, J.-P. (1960) *Questions de méthode*. Paris: Gallimard.
Sartre, J.-P. (1962) *Sketch for a Theory of the Emotions* (trans. Mairet, P. with a Preface by Warnock, M.). London: Methuen.
Sartre, J.-P. (1966) 'La conscience de classe chez Flaubert (I)', *Les Temps modernes*, May, 240, 1921–51.
Sartre, J.-P. (1966) 'La conscience de classe chez Flaubert (II)' *Les Temps modernes*, June, 241, 2113–53.
Sartre, J.-P. (1967) *What is Literature?* (trans. Frechtman, B.). London: Methuen.
Sartre, J.-P. (1969) *L'Imagination*. Paris: Presses Universitaires Françaises.
Sartre, J.-P. (1972) *Being and Nothingness. An Essay on Phenomenological Ontology*. (trans. Barnes, H.E. with an Introduction by Warnock, M.). London: Routledge.
Sartre, J.-P. (1972) *The Psychology of Imagination* (Introduction by Warnock, M.). London: Methuen.
Saussure, F. de (1983) *Course in General Linguistics* (trans. Harris, R.). London: Duckworth.
Schatzki, T.R. (1987) 'Overdue analysis of Bourdieu's theory of practice', *Inquiry*, 30, 1–2, 113–36.
Schilpp, P.A. (ed) (1949) *The Philosophy of Ernst Cassirer*. Evanston, IL: Library of Living Philosophers.
Schiltz, M. (1982) 'Habitus and peasantization in Nigeria: a Yoruba case study', *Man* (NS), 17, 4, 728–46.
Schucking, L.L. (1966) *The Sociology of Literary Taste* (trans. Battershaw, B.). London: Routledge.
Scruton, R. (1982) *Kant*. Oxford and New York: Oxford University Press.
Siegel, B.J. (1955) *Acculturation*. Stanford, CA: Stanford University Press.
Simpson, G.E. (1973) *Melville J. Herskovits*. New York and London: Columbia University Press.
Singer, P. (1983) *Hegel*. Oxford: Oxford University Press (Past Masters).
Smith, C. (1964) *Contemporary French Philosophy. A Study in Norms and Values*. London: Methuen.
Spicer, E.H. (1955) *Human Problems in Technological Change*.
Starkie, E. (1967) *Flaubert. The Making of the Master*. London: Weidenfeld & Nicolson.
Steiner, G. (1978) *Heidegger*. London: Fontana Modern Masters.
Stern, J.P. (1985) *Nietzsche*. London: Fontana Press.
Swartz, D. (1977) 'Pierre Bourdieu: the cultural transmission of social inequality', *Harvard Educational Review*, 47, 4, 545–54.
Swartz, D. (1981) 'Classes, educational systems and labor markets. A critical evaluation of the contributions by Raymond Boudon and Pierre Bourdieu to the sociology of education', *Archives of European Sociology*, XXII, 2, 325–53.
Swartz, D. (1997) *Culture and Power. The Sociology of Pierre Bourdieu*. Chicago, IL, and London: University of Chicago Press.
Szondi, P. (1974) *Poésie et poétique de l'idéalisme allemand*. Paris: Éditions de Minuit.
Tapper, B. (1925) 'Dilthey's methodology of the Geisteswissenschaften', *Philosophical Review*, XXXIV, 332–49.

Taylor, C. (1975) *Hegel*. Cambridge: Cambridge University Press.

Thibaudet, A. (1922) *Gustave Flaubert 1821–1880. Sa vie – ses romans – son style*. Paris: Librairie Plon.

Thompson, E.P. (1976) 'Modes de domination et révolutions en Angleterre', *Actes de la recherche en sciences sociales*, 2–3, 133–51.

Thuillier, J. (1983) 'L'artiste et l'institution; l'École des Beaux-Arts et le Prix de Rome', in *Le Grand Prix de Peinture. Les concours des Prix de Rome de 1797 à 1863*. Paris: École des Beaux-Arts.

Touraine, A. (1965) *Sociologie de l'action*. Paris: Éditions du Seuil.

Tumin, M.M. (1967) *Social Stratification. The Forms and Functions of Inequality*. Englewood Cliffs, NJ: Prentice-Hall.

Tuttle, H.N. (1969) *Wilhelm Dilthey's Philosophy of Historical Understanding: A Critical Analysis*. Leiden: E.J. Brill.

Verdès-Leroux, J. (1998) *Le Savant et la politique. Essai sur le terrorisme sociologique de Pierre Bourdieu*. Paris: Grasset.

Voltaire (1965) *Lettres philosophiques* (ed. Taylor, F.A.). Oxford: Blackwell.

Wacquant, L.J.D. (1987) 'Symbolic violence and the making of the French agriculturalist: an enquiry into Pierre Bourdieu's sociology', *Australian and New Zealand Journal of Sociology*, 23, 1, 65–88.

Weber, M. (1948) *From Max Weber. Essays in Sociology* (ed. with introduction by Gerth, H.H. and Mills, C.W.). London: Routledge & Kegan Paul.

Wellek, R. (1931) *Immanuel Kant in England, 1793–1838*. Princeton, NJ: Princeton University Press.

Westoby, A. (1978) 'Hegel's "History of Philosophy"'. In Rée, J. *et al.* eds. *Philosophy and its Past*. Hassocks: Harvester Press.

Williams, R. (1958) *Culture and Society, 1780–1950*. Harmondsworth: Penguin Books.

Williams, R. (1971) 'Literature and sociology: in memory of Lucien Goldmann', *New Left Review*, 67, 3–18.

Williams, R. (1976) *Keywords: A Vocabulary of Culture and Society*. London: Collins.

Williams, R. (1977) *Marxism and Literature*. Oxford: Oxford University Press.

Williams, R. (1977) 'Plaisantes perspectives. Invention du paysage et abolition du paysan', *Actes de la recherche en sciences sociales*, 17–18, 29–36.

Wilson, W.J. (1987) *The truly disadvantaged: the inner city, the underclass, and public policy*, Chicago, London: The University of Chicago Press.

Wilson-Bareau, J. (1992) *Manet: The Execution of Maximilian. Painting, Politics and Censorship*. London: National Gallery Publications.

Wind, E. (1925) 'Contemporary German philosophy', *Journal of Philosophy*, 22, 477–93 and 516–30.

Young, M.F.D. (ed.) (1971) *Knowledge and Control. New Directions for the Sociology of Education*. London: Collier-Macmillan.

Zelizer, V.A. (1988) 'Beyond the polemics on the market: establishing a theoretical and empirical agenda', *Sociological Forum*, 3, 4, 614–34.

Index